DYNAMICS IN CROSS-SECTION
AND PANEL DATA MODELS

The book is no. 69 of the Tinbergen Institute Research Series. This series is established through cooperation between Thesis Publishers and the Tinbergen Institute. A list of books which already appeared in the series can be found in the back.

Dynamics in Cross-Section and Panel Data Models

ACADEMISCH PROEFSCHRIFT

ter verkrijging van de graad van doctor
aan de Universiteit van Amsterdam,
op gezag van de Rector Magnificus
Prof.dr P.W.M. de Meijer
ten overstaan van een door het college van dekanen ingestelde commissie
in het openbaar te verdedigen in de Aula der Universiteit

op vrijdag 20 mei 1994 te 15.00 uur

door

Inge Truus van den Doel

geboren te Amsterdam

Promotoren: Prof.dr J.S. Cramer
Prof.dr J.F. Kiviet

Overige leden: Professor R.W. Blundell
Prof.dr J. Hartog
Prof.dr B.M.S. van Praag
Prof.dr T.J. Wansbeek

Faculteit der Economische Wetenschappen en Econometrie

This research was sponsored by the Economics Research Foundation, which is part of the Netherlands Organisation for Scientific Research (NWO).

Acknowledgements

This study would never have been written without the support of a number of people. I would like to thank all those who have helped me, especially the following:

- my parents, Truus and Hans, who first aroused my interest in mathematics and economics, respectively,

- Mars Cramer and Jan Kiviet, my thesis supervisors, who taught me how to write a proper doctoral thesis,

- Christine Crouwel-Bradshaw, who taught me how to write proper English,

- Badi Baltagi, Richard Blundell, Steve Bond, Cheng Hsiao, Ruud Koning, Theo Nijman and Tom Wansbeek, whose comments on earlier versions of parts of this book were most valuable,

- the members of the PhD committee, for their willingness to read and assess my thesis,

- colleagues from the Department of Actuarial Science and Econometrics, for joining me at tea-time and soothing my troubled brow,

- colleagues from the Department of Economics at Utrecht University and the Dutch central bank, for putting up with the stresses and strains of the home stretch,

- family and friends, for their moral support and sincere interest in how I was getting on,

- Walther, finally and foremost, for his love and understanding.

Amsterdam, March 1994   Inge van den Doel

V

Contents

List of Tables

List of Figures

Chapter 1

Introduction

1.1 Statement of the problem

For a long time, the two major branches of econometrics were the analysis of macroeconomic relationships on the basis of time series of aggregate data on the one hand, and the modelling of microeconomic phenomena on the basis of cross-section samples of individuals, households or firms on the other. To put it crudely, these separate schools coexisted without their practitioners understanding each other's problems and achievements. The first to state that the results from cross-section and time-series studies are incomparable, was Haavelmo (1947). Later, several attempts were made to explain the possible differences between pure cross-section and time-series estimates. In many studies, cross-section and time-series data were pooled to form a panel data set.

In aggregate time-series econometrics, special attention has been paid to the specification of dynamic processes, the misspecification analysis of such processes and the consequences of non-stationarities for the modelling of dynamic relationships. If dynamic processes are as important in microeconomics as they are in macroeconomics, then part of the established empirical knowledge derived from cross-section analyses could be misleading. Therefore, it seems interesting to examine whether the pure cross-section analysis of classical relationships, like Engel curves and age-earnings profiles, yields biased inference as a result of the neglect of processes in time. Or, to put it differently, does anything go wrong — and, if so, what — when dynamic processes are apparent in a microeconomic relationship, yet are nevertheless neglected when this relationship is estimated? Moreover, it would be interesting to know how certain characteristics of the relationship, such as non-stationarities, affect the answer to this question. If it is found that something does go wrong, then the next question would be how dynamic processes are to be modelled in the relationship and what techniques are available for its estimation. Finally, one would wish to know how possible dynamics in the relationship can be detected. And, of course, an empirical illustration of the above issues would be valuable as well.

This thesis tries to answer the questions posed above, by studying several static and dynamic specifications for cross-section and panel data. Consider the specification

$$y_{it} = \alpha_0 + \sum_{l=0}^{L} \beta_l x_{i,t-l} + \gamma y_{i,t-1} + \alpha_i + \epsilon_{it} \qquad (1.1)$$

for individuals $i = 1, \ldots, N$ and time periods $t = 1, \ldots, T$. This model accommodates a lagged dependent regressor $y_{i,t-1}$ and $K = 1 + L$ other regressors, which are current and lagged values of x. For notational simplicity and without losing generality, only one such a variable x occurs in this introduction. In a slightly different formulation, model (1.1) is known as the Balestra and Nerlove (1966) model. Usually, the individual effects α_i are treated as either fixed constants or random variables with mean zero and finite variance. With respect to the regressors, different assumptions about exogeneity can be made. For a more lengthy discussion of this model, see Section 3.1.

The dynamic relationships considered in this thesis are (1.1) and some of its special cases. In Hendry, Pagan and Sargan (1984), a typology for aggregate time-series relationships with a dynamic structure such as (1.1) is given. According to this typology, nine particular cases can be distinguished. Special cases of interest here are the *static model*

$$y_{it} = \alpha_0 + \beta_0 x_{it} + \alpha_i + \epsilon_{it} \qquad (1.2)$$

the *finite distributed lag model*

$$y_{it} = \alpha_0 + \sum_{l=0}^{L} \beta_l x_{i,t-l} + \alpha_i + \epsilon_{it} \qquad (1.3)$$

the *partial adjustment model* (see (2.3) and (2.4) for an interpretation of the coefficients)

$$y_{it} = \alpha_0 + \beta_0 x_{it} + \gamma y_{i,t-1} + \alpha_i + \epsilon_{it} \qquad (1.4)$$

the *common factor model*

$$y_{it} = \alpha_0 + \beta_0 (x_{it} - \gamma x_{i,t-1}) + \gamma y_{i,t-1} + \alpha_i + \epsilon_{it} \qquad (1.5)$$

the *'static' differenced data model*

$$\Delta y_{it} = \alpha_0 + \beta_0 \Delta x_{it} + \alpha_i + \epsilon_{it} \qquad (1.6)$$

and, finally, the model

$$y_{it} = \alpha_0 + \beta_0 x_{it} + \beta_1 x_{i,t-1} + \gamma y_{i,t-1} + \alpha_i + \epsilon_{it} \qquad (1.7)$$

when x is included with only one lag.

The thesis proceeds along two lines: both a theoretical and an empirical approach are followed. Beginning with theory, the behaviour of standard estimators for static cross-section as well as panel data models is studied, when in reality a dynamic adjustment mechanism such as (1.7) is present. The asymptotic properties are assessed analytically, while Monte Carlo simulations add to the insight into the small sample biases due to the neglect of dynamic processes. In other words, it is investigated what theory has to say to answer the first question above. After studying the theoretical consequences of neglected dynamics, the thesis considers the questions of how possible dynamics can be modelled and detected. In order to be able to detect any dynamics, panel data must be available; a single cross section is not sufficient. Existing tests for the presence of a lagged dependent variable among the regressors of a panel data model are valid only asymptotically, either for an infinite number of time periods or for an infinite number of individuals. It is studied whether time-series econometrics test statistics that are exact and similar for finite T and N can be adapted for use with panel data, and it is found that they can. Since panel data sets usually contain only a small number of time periods, an examination of the small sample properties of these tests, in comparison to the asymptotic tests, is carried out.

Next, an empirical illustration is given of the above issues. A panel data set on family expenditure, income and household characteristics is available from the Continuous Budget Surveys 1985, 1986 and 1987 of the Dutch Central Bureau of Statistics. These data are used to estimate several static and dynamic Engel curves for food, based on either a cross section or a panel. The general view is that the neglect of dynamics in Engel curves for everyday commodities is justified. A thorough misspecification analysis shows whether this is indeed the case.

1.2 Outline of the thesis

The first chapters of the thesis deal with theory, whereas Chapters 4 onwards concentrate on the empirical analysis.

Section 2.1 contains a survey of the (in)consistency of standard estimators for static cross-section as well as panel data models, when in reality a dynamic adjustment mechanism such as (1.7) is present. Two separate data generating cases are distinguished, i.e. stationary and non-stationary regressors x. The estimators studied are the standard cross-section OLS estimator and the static pooled OLS, Fixed Effects and Random Effects estimators for panel data. If the exogenous variables follow a stationary process, then the static estimators are found to underestimate the long-run effect. If the exogenous variables are non-stationary, then the estimators are found to be consistent (for $N \to \infty$) for the long-run effect. What sign and magnitude the biases may have in finite samples is examined in a Monte Carlo study in Section 2.2. In the Monte Carlo design, the exogenous variables are covariance stationary around a deterministic trend. It is concluded that the Fixed Effects or 'within' estimator is particularly sensitive to dynamic misspecification.

Some literature on dynamic panel data models is reviewed in Section 3.1: the questions of how standard panel data estimators behave in a dynamic context and how dynamic panel data models can be estimated consistently are briefly answered. In Section 3.2, two tests for the presence of dynamics in the form of a lagged dependent variable in panel data models are developed, which are exact and similar — that is, independent of nuisance parameters — for finite T and N. The small sample properties of these tests, in comparison to the asymptotic tests, are assessed in Section 3.3. The Monte Carlo results suggest a satisfactory power performance of the tests.

In Chapter 4, the panel data set consisting of the three waves 1985 to 1987 of the Continuous Budget Survey of the Dutch Central Bureau of Statistics is presented. Some features of the data are discussed. In subsequent chapters, this panel data set is used for the estimation of Engel curves for total food expenditure.

Chapter 5 discusses functional forms of static Engel curves, considering both the existing literature and the features of the data set. Two general functional forms are chosen that include the most commonly used specifications as special cases. Apart from (several transformations of) household income, variables for household size, age, socio-economic background and residential area are included in these general forms, as well as two variables accounting for possible non-random measurement errors in the dependent variable (recording month and holiday length).

Through statistical test procedures in Chapter 6, the data are left to decide which of these general forms and which of its special cases is going to be the preferred specification. In this chapter, static cross-section Engel curves for food are estimated, followed by static Engel curves for the full three-wave-panel described in Chapter 4. In the preferred cross-section specification, significant household characteristics include: number of adults and number of children in the household, age of the head of the household, education of the head of the household and of the partner and recording month. Of the variables included in the general forms, those measuring profession, geographical region, degree of urbanisation and holiday length are found to play an insignificant role in the determination of food expenditure.

The general view is that the neglect of dynamics in Engel curves for everyday commodities such as food is justified. In Chapter 7, a thorough misspecification analysis is carried out, to show whether this is indeed the case. Since only three consecutive waves of the panel data set are available, this analysis is unavoidably limited. The standard Generalised Method of Moments estimator for dynamic panel data models, which basically consists of writing the model in first differences and employing instruments in levels, yields disappointingly large standard errors and unsatisfactory results that may have to do with the fact that only three waves are available. Therefore, an alternative procedure is carried out, in which the model is specified in levels whereas instruments are employed in differenced form. Addition of lagged exogenous and lagged dependent variables in the preferred cross-section specification of Chapter 6, leads to the conclusion that both types of lagged variables are significant, especially the lagged expenditure variable. Both exact test statistics developed in Chapter 3, however, cannot conclude that the lagged dependent variable is significant.

Parts of the thesis have appeared before in research memoranda or journals. Forerunners of Section 2.1 are Doel (1991) and Doel and Kiviet (1991a), which developed into Doel and Kiviet (1994). Parts of Sections 2.2, 3.2 and 3.3, together with a highly simplified version of Section 7.3, can be found in Doel and Kiviet (1993), which was preluded by Doel and Kiviet (1991b).

1.3   Notation

In the remainder of this thesis, a matrix P_A is generally defined as the matrix that projects *on* the space spanned by the columns of A and a matrix M_A as the matrix that projects *off* this space. Also, the vectors ι_N, ι_T and ι_{NT} are defined respectively as $N \times 1$, $T \times 1$ and $NT \times 1$ vectors of 1's. Furthermore, I_s denotes an identity matrix of order s and

$$J = \iota_T \otimes I_N$$

Of special significance are the $NT \times NT$ matrices

$$P_J = P_{\iota_T} \otimes I_N \text{ and } M_J = M_{\iota_T} \otimes I_N = I_{NT} - P_J \tag{1.8}$$

Note that the matrix M_{ι_s} transforms a $s \times 1$ vector into deviations from the mean of its s elements. The matrices P_J and M_J are orthogonal projection matrices, on J and its orthogonal complement, respectively.

Chapter 2

Consequences of neglected dynamics

2.1 Asymptotic consequences

2.1.1 Introduction

The estimation methods for dynamic panel data models are considerably more complex than those for static ones. Although many regression packages allow estimation of static panel data models, the researcher who wants to estimate a dynamic panel data model must either draw on his or her own resources or rely on the DPD estimation programme by Arellano and Bond (1988), which requires an installed version of the GAUSS matrix programming language. Because of the complexities of estimating such models, in practice a static model may often be estimated where the model should have been dynamic. Usually only cross-section data are available and it is impossible to take intertemporal effects into account. This raises the question: What are the consequences of incorrectly estimating static models?

The first economist to state that the results from cross-section and time-series studies are incomparable was Haavelmo (1947). Nonetheless, this did not stop Stone (1954) from using cross-section data to obtain estimates for income elasticities (because in a cross section everyone is facing the same price), and then plug in these estimates in time-series regressions to obtain price elasticities.[1] Other early attempts to explain the possible differences between pure cross-section and time-series estimates are Grunfeld (1961) and Simon and Aigner (1970). Baltagi and Griffin (1984) show that, in general, biased estimates are obtained when pooled data (panels) are used and the estimated model is an underspecification of the true dynamic relationship. They focus

---

[1] For a review of Richard Stone's book: see Harberger (1955).

7

on variance components models and consider only the case of finite distributed lags. In Ridder and Wansbeek (1990, Section 2) much the same type of analysis is performed for the partial adjustment model, which is a particular infinite distributed lag model with exponentially decreasing lag coefficients. The studies mentioned above concentrate on the estimation bias induced by dynamic misspecification, and they present expressions for this bias obtained by loosely replacing sample moments by assumed time-invariant population characteristics.

In this section, the consequences of neglected dynamics in panel data models are again analysed, and separate attention is paid to the variance components model (random effects), the fixed effects model and the pooled regression model (no individual-specific effects). The analysis will be more formal than in the above-mentioned studies and its asymptotic nature will be recognised explicitly. In this respect, the number of observations in the time dimension (the number of waves) is supposed finite, whereas the number of individuals in the sample may increase asymptotically. Unlike the earlier studies, the analysis is not restricted to cases where the regressors are covariance stationary. Also non-stationary explanatory variables, which are most relevant in economic applications, are considered. At the same time, the scope of the study is extended by proceeding from a dynamic relationship which has a finite distributed lag model and the partial adjustment model as special cases. The analysis of the consequences of neglected dynamics in finite samples follows in Section 2.2.

The asymptotic results are found to be in agreement with the various particular earlier findings, but the investigation of the non-stationary regressor case shows that the asymptotic consequences of neglected dynamics may be less severe, as far as long-run multipliers are concerned, than might be concluded from the previous studies.[2]

This section is organised as follows. In Section 2.1.2, a comparatively general dynamic data generating process is presented and some special cases are discussed. In Section 2.1.3, the probability limit of the OLS estimator in a static model based on cross-section data is derived, when in reality the data are generated by the process given in Section 2.1.2. In Section 2.1.4, the probability limits of various estimators in static panel data models are assessed, when data on only a few time periods are available, while asymptotically the number of individuals goes to infinity. Section 2.1.5 concludes.

---

[2]Here 'asymptotic consequences' refers to the behaviour of sample statistics when the number of individuals goes to infinity, while 'long-run multiplier' refers to a population characteristic measured over an infinitely long time period.

2.1.2 The data generating process

Consider the dynamic relationship

$$y_{it} = \gamma y_{i,t-1} + \beta_0 x_{it} + \beta_1 x_{i,t-1} + \alpha_i + \epsilon_{it} \qquad (2.1)$$

with y_{it} the dependent variable, x_{it} an exogenous variable, α_i an individual-specific effect and ϵ_{it} a white noise error term, for individuals $i = 1, \ldots, N$ and time periods $t = 1, \ldots, T$. This relationship is virtually equivalent to (1.7). For $|\gamma| < 1$, the long-run stationary equilibrium ($x_{it} = \breve{x}_i$) implied by this dynamic process is

$$\breve{y}_i = \frac{\beta_0 + \beta_1}{1 - \gamma} \breve{x}_i + \frac{1}{1 - \gamma} \alpha_i$$

and, when assuming a steady-state where $x_{it} = \breve{x}_{it} = \breve{x}_{i,t-1} + \xi_i$, the long-run equilibrium is given by (see Appendix A.1 for the derivation and Currie (1981) for further background):

$$\breve{y}_{it} = \frac{\beta_0 + \beta_1}{1 - \gamma} \breve{x}_{it} + \frac{1}{1 - \gamma} \left(\alpha_i - \frac{\gamma \beta_0 + \beta_1}{1 - \gamma} \xi_i \right) \qquad (2.2)$$

Hence, irrespective of the values of ξ_i, the so-called total or long-run multiplier of the exogenous regressor is $(\beta_0 + \beta_1)/(1 - \gamma)$.

According to Hendry, Pagan and Sargan (1984), at least nine particular cases of (2.1) can be distinguished. Here, only three of them will be mentioned. Firstly, if $\gamma = 0$ the dynamics in (2.1) is characterised by a finite distributed lag: the process is then equivalent to (1.3) with $L = 1$. Secondly, if $0 < \gamma < 1$ and $\beta_1 = 0$, then (2.1) is equivalent to the partial adjustment mechanism

$$y_{it} - y_{i,t-1} = (1 - \gamma)(y_{it}^* - y_{i,t-1}) + \epsilon_{it} \qquad (2.3)$$

where y_{it}^* denotes the equilibrium or desired value of the dependent variable, given by

$$y_{it}^* = \beta^* x_{it} + \alpha_i^* \qquad (2.4)$$

with $\beta^* = \beta_0/(1 - \gamma)$ and $\alpha_i^* = \alpha_i/(1 - \gamma)$. The process is now equivalent to (1.4). Third, under the restriction $\beta_1 = 1 - \gamma - \beta_0$, (2.1) becomes

$$\triangle y_{it} = \beta_0 \triangle x_{it} - (1 - \gamma)(y_{i,t-1} - x_{i,t-1}) + \alpha_i + \epsilon_{it}$$

i.e. an error correction model with long-run elasticity equal to 1 (if y and x are measured in logarithms), which seems relevant for many economic relationships.

A possible application of model (2.1) would be an Engel curve for a certain category of consumer goods. In such a case, y_{it} denotes (the logarithm of) expenditure and x_{it} (the logarithm of) income of household i in period t. The effects of changes in x_{it} on y_{it} may occur with some delay. There is an immediate effect (the impact multiplier) equal to β_0 and a long-run effect $(\beta_0 + \beta_1)/(1 - \gamma)$. There is no a priori reason why one would suppose $\gamma = 0$ and/or $\beta_1 = 0$. So, especially estimation based on pure cross-section data is unsatisfactory. Also, it is reasonable to suppose that household income will be non-stationary. All individual-specific effects are supposed to be captured by α_i, but of course more regressors could be included in (2.1).

In the derivations below, it will be convenient to eliminate $y_{i,t-1}$ from (2.1). Continued substitution yields

$$y_{it} = \beta_0 \sum_{s=0}^{\infty} \gamma^s x_{i,t-s} + \beta_1 \sum_{s=0}^{\infty} \gamma^s x_{i,t-1-s} + \frac{1}{1-\gamma}\alpha_i + \sum_{s=0}^{\infty} \gamma^s \epsilon_{i,t-s} \qquad (2.5)$$

This representation of the data generating process will be used in the case of a stationary exogenous variable. If the exogenous variable is non-stationary, continued substitution until $-\infty$ is not convenient. Suppose that x_{it} follows a random walk with an individual-specific drift

$$x_{it} = x_{i,t-1} + \xi_i + \omega_{it} \text{ for } t = \ldots, 1, 2, \ldots$$

then it follows that

$$x_{it} = x_{i0} + t\xi_i + \sum_{s=1}^{t} \omega_{is} \text{ for } t = 1, 2, \ldots \qquad (2.6)$$

At $t = 0$ the process is supposed to be at its long-run equilibrium (2.2), hence

$$y_{i0} = \frac{\beta_0 + \beta_1}{1 - \gamma} x_{i0} + \frac{1}{1-\gamma}\left(\alpha_i - \frac{\gamma\beta_0 + \beta_1}{1-\gamma}\xi_i\right) \qquad (2.7)$$

Further assumptions concerning ξ_i and ω_{it} will be made in a later stage. Making use of (2.6) and (2.7), after straightforward but tedious manipulations, the data generating process (2.1) can be written as (see Appendix A.2):

$$y_{it} = \frac{\beta_0 + \beta_1}{1 - \gamma} x_{i0} + \frac{1}{1-\gamma}\alpha_i + \frac{\beta_0 + \beta_1}{1-\gamma} t\xi_i - \frac{\gamma\beta_0 + \beta_1}{(1-\gamma)^2}\xi_i$$

$$+ \frac{\beta_0 + \beta_1}{1-\gamma}\sum_{s=1}^{t}\omega_{is} - \frac{\gamma\beta_0 + \beta_1}{1-\gamma}\sum_{s=1}^{t}\gamma^{t-s}\omega_{is} + \sum_{s=1}^{t}\gamma^{t-s}\epsilon_{is} \qquad (2.8)$$

This expression for the data generating process will be used in subsequent analysis of the non-stationary case.

2.1.3 Estimation based on cross-section data

Suppose that, instead of the data generating process (2.1), the estimated model is

$$y_{it} = \delta + \beta x_{it} + \eta_{it} \tag{2.9}$$

for a cross section at period t. Note that (2.9) differs from (2.1) with respect to the parametrisation of both the dynamics and the individual effect. Model (2.9) presupposes $\gamma = 0$, $\beta_1 = 0$ (and $\beta_0 = \beta$) and $\eta_{it} = \epsilon_{it} + \alpha_i - \delta$. Define the scalars $\bar{y}_t = \frac{1}{N} \sum_{i=1}^{N} y_{it}$, $\tilde{y}_{it} = y_{it} - \bar{y}_t$ and analogously for all other variables. Also, define the $N \times 1$ vectors

$$
\tilde{y}_t = \begin{bmatrix} \tilde{y}_{1t} \\ \vdots \\ \tilde{y}_{Nt} \end{bmatrix} \quad
\tilde{x}_t = \begin{bmatrix} \tilde{x}_{1t} \\ \vdots \\ \tilde{x}_{Nt} \end{bmatrix} \quad
\tilde{\epsilon}_t = \begin{bmatrix} \tilde{\epsilon}_{1t} \\ \vdots \\ \tilde{\epsilon}_{Nt} \end{bmatrix} \quad
\tilde{\alpha} = \begin{bmatrix} \tilde{\alpha}_1 \\ \vdots \\ \tilde{\alpha}_N \end{bmatrix} \tag{2.10}
$$

Using these definitions, the cross-section OLS estimator of β in (2.9) for period t is

$$\hat{\beta}_t = \frac{\tilde{x}_t' \tilde{y}_t}{\tilde{x}_t' \tilde{x}_t} \tag{2.11}$$

Results for a stationary exogenous variable

The data generating process (2.5) can be written in vector form as

$$\tilde{y}_t = \beta_0 \sum_{s=0}^{\infty} \gamma^s \tilde{x}_{t-s} + \beta_1 \sum_{s=0}^{\infty} \gamma^s \tilde{x}_{t-1-s} + \frac{1}{1-\gamma} \tilde{\alpha} + \sum_{s=0}^{\infty} \gamma^s \tilde{\epsilon}_{t-s} \tag{2.12}$$

In order to derive the probability limit of (2.11), some assumptions must be made. First, consider the case that the exogenous variable is covariance stationary, such that

$$\operatorname*{plim}_{N \to \infty} \frac{1}{N} \tilde{x}_t' \tilde{x}_{t-s} = \sigma_x^2 \tilde{r}_s \quad \text{with } \tilde{r}_0 = 1 \tag{2.13}$$

and assume that the exogenous variable is independent of individual effects and error terms, in the sense that:

$$\operatorname*{plim}_{N \to \infty} \frac{1}{N} \tilde{x}_t' \tilde{\alpha} = 0 \tag{2.14}$$

$$\operatorname*{plim}_{N \to \infty} \frac{1}{N} \tilde{x}_t' \tilde{\epsilon}_{t-s} = 0 \quad \text{for every } s \tag{2.15}$$

Due to assumption (2.14), the omission of dynamics is the only serious misspecification. If α_i is the same for every individual, (2.14) holds automatically.

Of course, (2.14) is usually seen as a stronger assumption than (2.15), but the primary concern here is dynamic misspecification rather than the nature of unobserved heterogeneity. The probability limit of (2.11) is now easily derived. Making use of (2.12), (2.13), (2.14) and (2.15), the plim of the numerator can be established:

$$\operatorname*{plim}_{N\to\infty}\frac{1}{N}\tilde{x}_t'\tilde{y}_t =$$

$$\operatorname*{plim}_{N\to\infty}\frac{1}{N}\left(\beta_0\sum_{s=0}^{\infty}\gamma^s\tilde{x}_t'\tilde{x}_{t-s} + \beta_1\sum_{s=0}^{\infty}\gamma^s\tilde{x}_t'\tilde{x}_{t-1-s} + \frac{1}{1-\gamma}\tilde{x}_t'\tilde{\alpha} + \sum_{s=0}^{\infty}\gamma^s\tilde{x}_t'\tilde{\epsilon}_{t-s}\right)$$

$$= \beta_0\sum_{s=0}^{\infty}\gamma^s\sigma_x^2\tilde{r}_s + \beta_1\sum_{s=0}^{\infty}\gamma^s\sigma_x^2\tilde{r}_{s+1}$$

Since the plim of the denominator is

$$\operatorname*{plim}_{N\to\infty}\frac{1}{N}\tilde{x}_t'\tilde{x}_t = \sigma_x^2\tilde{r}_0 = \sigma_x^2$$

the final result is:

$$\operatorname*{plim}_{N\to\infty}\hat{\beta}_t = \frac{\operatorname*{plim}_{N\to\infty}\frac{1}{N}\tilde{x}_t'\tilde{y}_t}{\operatorname*{plim}_{N\to\infty}\frac{1}{N}\tilde{x}_t'\tilde{x}_t} = \sum_{s=0}^{\infty}\gamma^s\left(\beta_0\tilde{r}_s + \beta_1\tilde{r}_{s+1}\right) \qquad (2.16)$$

The implications of this result are interesting. The probability limit of the cross-section OLS estimator depends on the autocorrelation process of the exogenous variable. This was also found by Baltagi and Griffin (1984) and Ridder and Wansbeek (1990) in a more specific context. If the exogenous variable is serially uncorrelated, in the sense that $\tilde{r}_s = 0$ for $s \geq 1$, then plim $\hat{\beta}_t = \beta_0$, which is the immediate effect of a one-unit-change in x on y, known as the impact multiplier. If, on the other hand, $\tilde{r}_s = 1$ for $s \geq 0$, which means $x_t = x_{t-s}$ (an individual-specific regressor like sex or race), then $\hat{\beta}_t$ is consistent for the long-run effect $(\beta_0 + \beta_1)/(1 - \gamma)$. Generally speaking, the inconsistency for the long-run effect is less severe the higher the autocorrelation of the exogenous variable. The intuition behind this is that high autocorrelation means that a large amount of past information is embodied in the current value of the exogenous variable, so that this current value suffices to explain the value of the dependent variable. In practice, it is usually the case that $0 < \tilde{r}_s < 1$ for $s \geq 1$, so that

$$0 < \sum_{s=0}^{\infty}\gamma^s\tilde{r}_s < \frac{1}{1-\gamma} \quad \text{and} \quad 0 < \sum_{s=0}^{\infty}\gamma^s\tilde{r}_{s+1} < \frac{1}{1-\gamma}$$

which means that $\hat{\beta}_t$ will usually underestimate the long-run effect. This underestimation result conforms to the conclusions of Simon and Aigner (1970, p. 344).

For a more specific interpretation, consider the three special cases discussed in Section 2.1.2. If $\gamma = 0$, then plim $\hat{\beta}_t = \beta_0 + \beta_1 \tilde{r}_1$. So, the cross-section OLS estimator can only be a consistent estimator of the long-run effect $\beta_0 + \beta_1$ if $\tilde{r}_1 = 1$ indeed. In the partial adjustment case, (2.16) reduces to

$$\underset{N\to\infty}{\text{plim}}\hat{\beta}_t = (1-\gamma)\beta^* \sum_{s=0}^{\infty} \gamma^s \tilde{r}_s$$

So, if $\tilde{r}_s = 0$ for $s \geq 1$, $\hat{\beta}_t$ is a consistent estimator of the impact multiplier $(1-\gamma)\beta^*$. If, on the other hand, $\tilde{r}_s = 1$ for $s \geq 0$, then $\hat{\beta}_t$ is consistent for the long-run effect β^*. The inconsistency for the long-run effect is less severe the higher the speed of adjustment $1-\gamma$. This is intuitively clear: if adjustment takes place fast, then the impact multiplier tends to the total multiplier. The results for the partial adjustment model conform to those found by Grunfeld (1961) and Ridder and Wansbeek (1990). Finally, in the error correction model with unit total multiplier the probability limit of the OLS estimator can be written as

$$\underset{N\to\infty}{\text{plim}}\hat{\beta}_t = \sum_{s=0}^{\infty} \gamma^s \{\beta_0(\tilde{r}_s - \tilde{r}_{s+1}) + (1-\gamma)\tilde{r}_{s+1}\}$$

So again, if the regressor is time-constant plim $\hat{\beta}_t$ will equal 1.

Results for a non-stationary exogenous variable

Using definitions (2.10) and $\tilde{\xi} = [\tilde{\xi}_1, \ldots, \tilde{\xi}_N]'$ and $\tilde{\omega}_t = [\tilde{\omega}_{1t}, \ldots, \tilde{\omega}_{Nt}]'$, expression (2.8) for the data generating process can be written as

$$\tilde{y}_t = \frac{\beta_0 + \beta_1}{1-\gamma}\tilde{x}_0 + \frac{1}{1-\gamma}\tilde{\alpha} + \frac{\beta_0 + \beta_1}{1-\gamma}t\tilde{\xi} - \frac{\gamma\beta_0 + \beta_1}{(1-\gamma)^2}\tilde{\xi}$$

$$+ \frac{\beta_0 + \beta_1}{1-\gamma}\sum_{s=1}^{t}\tilde{\omega}_s - \frac{\gamma\beta_0 + \beta_1}{1-\gamma}\sum_{s=1}^{t}\gamma^{t-s}\tilde{\omega}_s + \sum_{s=1}^{t}\gamma^{t-s}\tilde{\epsilon}_s \qquad (2.17)$$

Concerning x_{i0}, ξ_i and ω_{it}, it is assumed that:

$$\underset{N\to\infty}{\text{plim}}\tfrac{1}{N}\tilde{x}_0'\tilde{x}_0 = \sigma_{x_0}^2 \qquad \underset{N\to\infty}{\text{plim}}\tfrac{1}{N}\tilde{\xi}'\tilde{\xi} = \sigma_\xi^2 \qquad \underset{N\to\infty}{\text{plim}}\tfrac{1}{N}\tilde{\omega}_s'\tilde{\omega}_s = \sigma_\omega^2$$

$$\underset{N\to\infty}{\text{plim}}\tfrac{1}{N}\tilde{x}_0'\tilde{\xi} = \sigma_{x_0\xi} \qquad \underset{N\to\infty}{\text{plim}}\tfrac{1}{N}\tilde{\xi}'\tilde{\omega}_s = 0 \qquad \underset{N\to\infty}{\text{plim}}\tfrac{1}{N}\tilde{\omega}_s'\tilde{\omega}_r = 0 \qquad (2.18)$$

$$\underset{N\to\infty}{\text{plim}}\tfrac{1}{N}\tilde{x}_0'\tilde{\omega}_s = 0 \qquad \text{for } s,r = 1,2,\ldots \text{ and } r \neq s$$

Furthermore, the generating process of the exogenous variable is again supposed to be independent of α_i and ϵ_{it}. Using (2.6), (2.17) and (2.18), the probability limit of estimator (2.11) can be derived. First the numerator (see Appendix A.3):

$$\operatorname*{plim}_{N\to\infty}\frac{1}{N}\tilde{x}'_t\tilde{y}_t = \frac{\beta_0+\beta_1}{1-\gamma}\left(\sigma^2_{x_0} + 2t\sigma_{x_0\xi} + t^2\sigma^2_\xi + t\sigma^2_\omega\right)$$

$$-\frac{\gamma\beta_0+\beta_1}{(1-\gamma)^2}\left(\sigma_{x_0\xi} + t\sigma^2_\xi + (1-\gamma^t)\sigma^2_\omega\right) \qquad (2.19)$$

Since the plim of the denominator is

$$\operatorname*{plim}_{N\to\infty}\frac{1}{N}\tilde{x}'_t\tilde{x}_t = \operatorname*{plim}_{N\to\infty}\frac{1}{N}\left(\tilde{x}'_0 + t\tilde{\xi}' + \sum_{s=1}^{t}\tilde{\omega}'_s\right)\left(\tilde{x}_0 + t\tilde{\xi} + \sum_{s=1}^{t}\tilde{\omega}_s\right)$$

$$= \sigma^2_{x_0} + 2t\sigma_{x_0\xi} + t^2\sigma^2_\xi + t\sigma^2_\omega$$

the plim of the estimator turns out to be:

$$\operatorname*{plim}_{N\to\infty}\hat{\beta}_t =$$

$$\frac{\frac{\beta_0+\beta_1}{1-\gamma}\left(\sigma^2_{x_0} + 2t\sigma_{x_0\xi} + t^2\sigma^2_\xi + t\sigma^2_\omega\right) - \frac{\gamma\beta_0+\beta_1}{(1-\gamma)^2}\left(\sigma_{x_0\xi} + t\sigma^2_\xi + (1-\gamma^t)\sigma^2_\omega\right)}{\sigma^2_{x_0} + 2t\sigma_{x_0\xi} + t^2\sigma^2_\xi + t\sigma^2_\omega} \qquad (2.20)$$

Parameters of period 0 are evident in this result. If period 0 is very long ago, this may be envisaged by $t \to \infty$. So, the probability limit of the cross-section OLS estimator (2.20) can be evaluated for $t \to \infty$. Dividing numerator and denominator by t^2, it follows that:

$$\lim_{t\to\infty}\left(\operatorname*{plim}_{N\to\infty}\hat{\beta}_t\right) = \frac{\beta_0+\beta_1}{1-\gamma} \qquad (2.21)$$

So, if the exogenous variable follows a random walk with individual-specific drift, the cross-section OLS estimator is a consistent estimator of the long-run effect. In a random walk — if the value of the drift is known — the current value of the variable embodies all systematic information available about past values of the variable. This makes it intuitively clear that the current value of the exogenous variable can explain the current value of the dependent variable. This conforms with the case of a time-constant regressor, where $\tilde{r}_s = 1$ for $s \geq 0$. Result (2.21) is also found when the drift is equal for every individual ($\sigma^2_\xi = 0$) or when there is no drift at all ($\xi_i = 0$). Of course, the result holds for the three special cases as well.

2.1.4   Estimation based on panel data

The two major advantages of estimation based on panel data are that individual heterogeneity and dynamics can be taken into account. This section investigates the case when, instead of (2.9), the static model

$$y_{it} = \beta x_{it} + \delta_i + \eta_{it} \qquad (2.22)$$

is estimated, where the individual effect δ_i is supposed to capture unobserved heterogeneity. A common estimator for β in models like (2.22) is the LSDV (least squares dummy variables) or 'within' estimator, which is based on OLS after transformation of the variables into deviations from the mean 'within' each individual over time. This transformation obviously eliminates the individual effects. If (2.22) is correctly specified and δ_i is a fixed unknown constant for each i, then the LSDV estimator is the Best Linear Unbiased Estimator for β (see Hsiao (1986, p. 30-31)). On the other hand, if the individual effects δ_i in model (2.22) are assumed to be random — more specifically: if $\delta_i \sim \text{IID}(0, \sigma_\delta^2)$ and δ_i independent of η_{it} — then the Best Linear Unbiased Estimator of β in (2.22) is the GLS estimator that takes account of the variance of the composite disturbance $\delta_i + \eta_{it}$. Of course, these estimators are no longer BLU when neglected dynamics are in fact present in the data generating process.

In order to analyse the asymptotic behaviour of these estimators under dynamic misspecification, define the $NT \times 1$ vectors y, x and ϵ and the $N \times 1$ vector α as:

$$
y = \begin{bmatrix} y_{11} \\ \vdots \\ y_{N1} \\ \vdots \\ y_{1T} \\ \vdots \\ y_{NT} \end{bmatrix}
\quad
x = \begin{bmatrix} x_{11} \\ \vdots \\ x_{N1} \\ \vdots \\ x_{1T} \\ \vdots \\ x_{NT} \end{bmatrix}
\quad
\epsilon = \begin{bmatrix} \epsilon_{11} \\ \vdots \\ \epsilon_{N1} \\ \vdots \\ \epsilon_{1T} \\ \vdots \\ \epsilon_{NT} \end{bmatrix}
\quad
\alpha = \begin{bmatrix} \alpha_1 \\ \vdots \\ \alpha_N \end{bmatrix}
\qquad (2.23)
$$

Following Maddala (1971), a class of estimators for β can be defined as

$$\hat{\beta}_\mu = \frac{x'(M_J + \mu P_J)y}{x'(M_J + \mu P_J)x} \qquad (2.24)$$

where M_J and P_J are defined in (1.8). Equation (2.24) represents a different estimator for β for each given value of μ. If $\mu = 1$, then $M_J + \mu P_J = I$, so the resulting estimator is the pooled OLS estimator of model (2.9) without constant term $(\delta = 0)$:

$$\hat{\beta}_{OLS} = \frac{x'y}{x'x}$$

On the other hand, if $\mu = 0$, then $M_J + \mu P_J = M_J$, which leads to the LSDV or fixed effects estimator:

$$\hat{\beta}_{FE} = \frac{x'M_J y}{x'M_J x} \qquad (2.25)$$

where $M_J y$ and $M_J x$ are the $NT \times 1$ vectors y and x transformed into deviations from the mean 'within' each individual over time. Finally, the GLS or random effects estimator is defined as

$$\hat{\beta}_{RE} = \frac{x'\Omega^{-1}y}{x'\Omega^{-1}x}$$

where Ω is the variance matrix of the composite disturbance

$$\iota_T \otimes [\delta_1, \ldots, \delta_N]' + [\eta_{11}, \ldots, \eta_{N1}, \ldots, \eta_{1T}, \ldots, \eta_{NT}]'$$

which in the static model equals (see Hsiao (1986, p. 34-35)):

$$\Omega = \sigma_\eta^2 (M_J + \lambda^{-1} P_J)$$

with $\lambda = \sigma_\eta^2/(\sigma_\eta^2 + T\sigma_\delta^2)$. It is easily verified that

$$\Omega^{-1} = \sigma_\eta^{-2}(M_J + \lambda P_J)$$

so that the random effects estimator of (2.22) is equal to (2.24) with $\mu = \lambda$.

Since $0 < \lambda < 1$, the random effects estimator can be seen as a matrix weighted average of the pooled OLS estimator without constant term and the fixed effects estimator with a different constant term for each individual. In practice, it is usually the case that $T\sigma_\delta^2 \gg \sigma_\eta^2$, so that λ will be closer to 0 than to 1. So, roughly speaking, in practice the fixed effects estimator will be a better approximation to the BLUE for the random effects model than the pooled OLS estimator.

Results for a stationary exogenous variable

Using the definitions given in (2.23), expression (2.5) for the data generating process reads in vector notation:

$$y = \beta_0 \sum_{s=0}^{\infty} \gamma^s x_{-s} + \beta_1 \sum_{s=0}^{\infty} \gamma^s x_{-1-s} + \frac{1}{1-\gamma} \iota_T \otimes \alpha + \sum_{s=0}^{\infty} \gamma^s \epsilon_{-s} \qquad (2.26)$$

The probability limit of each estimator (2.24), when the data generating process is given by (2.26), can be derived as follows. Assuming for a given value of μ

$$\underset{N\to\infty}{\text{plim}}\frac{1}{NT}x'(M_J + \mu P_J)x_{-s} = \sigma_x^2 r_s(\mu) \qquad (2.27)$$

$$\underset{N\to\infty}{\text{plim}}\frac{1}{NT}x'(\iota_T \otimes \alpha) = 0$$

$$\underset{N\to\infty}{\text{plim}}\frac{1}{NT}x'(M_J + \mu P_J)\epsilon_{-s} = 0 \quad \text{for every } s$$

and using

$$(M_J + \mu P_J)(\iota_T \otimes \alpha) = (M_J + \mu P_J)J\alpha = \mu J\alpha = \mu(\iota_T \otimes \alpha)$$

the probability limit of the numerator of (2.24) is

$$\underset{N\to\infty}{\text{plim}}\frac{1}{NT}x'(M_J + \mu P_J)y = \beta_0 \sum_{s=0}^{\infty} \gamma^s \sigma_x^2 r_s(\mu) + \beta_1 \sum_{s=0}^{\infty} \gamma^s \sigma_x^2 r_{s+1}(\mu)$$

Since the probability limit of the denominator is

$$\underset{N\to\infty}{\text{plim}}\frac{1}{NT}x'(M_J + \mu P_J)x = \sigma_x^2 r_0(\mu)$$

the result is:

$$\underset{N\to\infty}{\text{plim}}\hat{\beta}_\mu = \frac{\underset{N\to\infty}{\text{plim}}\frac{1}{NT}x'(M_J + \mu P_J)y}{\underset{N\to\infty}{\text{plim}}\frac{1}{NT}x'(M_J + \mu P_J)x} = \sum_{s=0}^{\infty} \gamma^s \frac{\beta_0 r_s(\mu) + \beta_1 r_{s+1}(\mu)}{r_0(\mu)}$$

This is more or less similar to the cross-section result (2.16). The probability limit of estimator $\hat{\beta}_\mu$ depends on the scalars $r_s(\mu)$. From (2.27), it follows that

$$r_s(\mu) = (1 - \mu)r_s(0) + \mu r_s(1)$$

so the scalars $r_s(\mu)$ can be interpreted as a weighted average of the two autocorrelation functions. It seems reasonable to suppose that $r_s(\mu) < r_0(\mu)$ for $s \geq 1$, so that $\hat{\beta}_\mu$ will usually underestimate the long-run effect $(\beta_0 + \beta_1)/(1 - \gamma)$. As far as the fixed effects estimator (2.25) is concerned, the scalars $r_s(0)$ represent the autocorrelation of the exogenous variable within each individual over time. The higher this autocorrelation, the closer the probability limit of the fixed effects estimator will be to the long-run effect.

Results for a non-stationary exogenous variable

As in the case of estimation based on pure cross-section data with a non-stationary exogenous variable, an elegant result for the probability limit of the estimator $\hat{\beta}_\mu$ of (2.24) requires the assumption that the data generating process has been going on for a very long time. On the other hand, it is undesirable to assume that the available panel data set has many observations in the time dimension. Therefore, it is supposed that the data generating process has been going on for $t = 1, \ldots, T$ while the panel data set consists of only three waves $T - 2$, $T - 1$ and T. The final result for $T \to \infty$ is found to be independent of the finite number of waves in the panel data set (here 3). The data supposed to be available can be stacked in $3N \times 1$ vectors y and x, where $y = [y_{1,T-2}, \ldots, y_{N,T-2}, \ldots, y_{1T}, \ldots, y_{NT}]'$ and $x = [x_{1,T-2}, \ldots, x_{N,T-2}, \ldots, x_{1T}, \ldots, x_{NT}]'$, and P_J and M_J of (1.8) are $3N \times 3N$ matrices, with $J = \iota_3 \otimes I_N$. Furthermore, define ϵ and α as in (2.23) and define x_0, ξ, ω_s $(s = 1, \ldots, T)$ and ω as

$$
x_0 = \begin{bmatrix} x_{10} \\ \vdots \\ x_{N0} \end{bmatrix} \qquad \xi = \begin{bmatrix} \xi_1 \\ \vdots \\ \xi_N \end{bmatrix} \qquad \omega_s = \begin{bmatrix} \omega_{1s} \\ \vdots \\ \omega_{Ns} \end{bmatrix} \qquad \omega = \begin{bmatrix} \omega_1 \\ \vdots \\ \omega_T \end{bmatrix}
$$

Also, define the $3 \times T$ matrices Z and Γ as

$$
Z = \begin{bmatrix} 1 & \cdots & 1 & 0 & 0 \\ 1 & \cdots & 1 & 1 & 0 \\ 1 & \cdots & 1 & 1 & 1 \end{bmatrix} \qquad \Gamma = \begin{bmatrix} \gamma^{T-3} & \cdots & \gamma^0 & 0 & 0 \\ \gamma^{T-2} & \cdots & \gamma^1 & \gamma^0 & 0 \\ \gamma^{T-1} & \cdots & \gamma^2 & \gamma^1 & \gamma^0 \end{bmatrix}
$$

Using these definitions and (2.6), it follows that:

$$
x = (\iota_3 \otimes I_N)x_0 + (Z\iota_T \otimes I_N)\xi + (Z \otimes I_N)\omega \tag{2.28}
$$

and expression (2.8) for the data generating process becomes:

$$
y = \frac{\beta_0 + \beta_1}{1 - \gamma}(\iota_3 \otimes I_N)x_0 + \frac{1}{1 - \gamma}(\iota_3 \otimes I_N)\alpha
$$

$$
+ \frac{\beta_0 + \beta_1}{1 - \gamma}(Z\iota_T \otimes I_N)\xi - \frac{\gamma\beta_0 + \beta_1}{(1 - \gamma)^2}(\iota_3 \otimes I_N)\xi
$$

$$
+ \frac{\beta_0 + \beta_1}{1 - \gamma}(Z \otimes I_N)\omega - \frac{\gamma\beta_0 + \beta_1}{1 - \gamma}(\Gamma \otimes I_N)\omega + (\Gamma \otimes I_N)\epsilon \tag{2.29}
$$

With respect to the generating process of the exogenous variable, the following assumptions are made:

$$\plim_{N\to\infty}\tfrac{1}{N}x_0'x_0 = \sigma_{x_0}^2 \qquad \plim_{N\to\infty}\tfrac{1}{N}\xi'\xi = \sigma_\xi^2 \qquad \plim_{N\to\infty}\tfrac{1}{N}\omega_s'\omega_s = \sigma_\omega^2$$

$$\plim_{N\to\infty}\tfrac{1}{N}x_0'\xi = \sigma_{x_0\xi} \qquad \plim_{N\to\infty}\tfrac{1}{N}\xi'\omega_s = 0 \qquad \plim_{N\to\infty}\tfrac{1}{N}\omega_s'\omega_r = 0 \qquad (2.30)$$

$$\plim_{N\to\infty}\tfrac{1}{N}x_0'\omega_s = 0 \qquad \text{for } s, r = 1, 2, \ldots, T \text{ and } r \neq s$$

Note that these assumptions differ from (2.18), where centralised second moments were supposed zero or fixed. Furthermore, the probability limits of the cross products between x_0, ξ, ω_s on the one hand and α, ϵ_t on the other hand (for $s, t = 1, 2, \ldots, T$) are supposed to be zero. Using expressions (2.28) and (2.29) and assumptions (2.30), the probability limit of the estimator $\hat{\beta}_\mu$ of (2.24) can be derived. The evaluation of the numerator gives (see Appendix A.3):

$$\plim_{N\to\infty}\tfrac{1}{NT}x'(M_J + \mu P_J)y = \frac{\beta_0 + \beta_1}{1 - \gamma}\left(3\mu\sigma_{x_0}^2 + 6\mu(T-1)\sigma_{x_0\xi} + \{2 + 3\mu(T-1)^2\}\sigma_\xi^2\right.$$

$$+\{3\mu(T-2) + \tfrac{4}{3} + \tfrac{5}{3}\mu\}\sigma_\omega^2\bigg) - \frac{\gamma\beta_0 + \beta_1}{(1-\gamma)^2}\left(3\mu\sigma_{x_0\xi} + 3\mu(T-1)\sigma_\xi^2\right.$$

$$+\{\mu\gamma^{T-1} + 2\mu\gamma^{T-2} + 3\mu\gamma^{T-3} + \ldots + 3\mu\gamma^2 + (\tfrac{1}{3} + 2\tfrac{2}{3}\mu)\gamma + (1 + 2\mu)\}\sigma_\omega^2\bigg) \quad (2.31)$$

The probability limit of the denominator of $\hat{\beta}_\mu$ in (2.24) is:

$$\plim_{N\to\infty}\tfrac{1}{NT}x'(M_J + \mu P_J)x = 3\mu\sigma_{x_0}^2 + 6\mu(T-1)\sigma_{x_0\xi} + \{2 + 3\mu(T-1)^2\}\sigma_\xi^2$$

$$+ \{3\mu(T-2) + \tfrac{4}{3} + \tfrac{5}{3}\mu\}\sigma_\omega^2 \quad (2.32)$$

Now, the plim of the estimator $\hat{\beta}_\mu$ can be established as the right hand side of (2.31) divided by the right hand side of (2.32). If it is assumed that the data generating process has been going on for a very long time, the plim of $\hat{\beta}_\mu$ may be evaluated for $T \to \infty$. On dividing numerator and denominator by T^2, the dependence on the number of waves cancels and

$$\lim_{T\to\infty}\left(\plim_{N\to\infty}\hat{\beta}_\mu\right) = \frac{\beta_0 + \beta_1}{1 - \gamma}$$

As in the case of the cross-section OLS estimator, if the exogenous variable follows a random walk with individual-specific drift, then the class of estimators $\hat{\beta}_\mu$ yields consistent estimators of the long-run effect, irrespective of the values of μ and the drift ξ_i.

2.1.5   Conclusions

This section examined the asymptotic consequences of estimating static models based on cross-section or panel data, when in reality the data are generated by a dynamic relationship involving both lagged dependent and current and lagged exogenous variables. If the exogenous variable follows a stationary process, it is found that the static estimators usually underestimate the long-run effect. This inconsistency is less severe, the higher the autocorrelation of the exogenous variable. If the exogenous variable follows a random walk with or without individual-specific drift and the process has been going on long enough to render the effects of initial conditions negligible, then the estimators are consistent for the long-run effect. These conclusions will be unaffected if the data generating process includes more exogenous explanatory variables.

It is surprising that the main finding for stationary explanatory variables — that is, the asymptotic ($N \to \infty$) underestimation of the long-run effect in static models — is in line with the result on underspecified finite distributed lag models for $T \to \infty$ established by Greene (1990, p. 549) in a pure time-series context. In the same sense, the rather reassuring asymptotic ($N \to \infty$) results for non-stationary panel data conform to what is found for non-stationary time series. If x_t and y_t are cointegrated (hence both are non-stationary while the error term in their dynamic relationship is stationary) then the static regression produces a consistent ($T \to \infty$) estimator for the long-run multiplier; see Stock (1987).

Whether or not the above results hold in samples with a finite number of individuals is still a largely unanswered question. Some results obtained from a Monte Carlo study can be found in the following section.

2.2   Small sample consequences

This section reports the results of a Monte Carlo study on the small sample characteristics of various well-known estimators for static cross-section and panel data models, when the actual data are generated by a partial adjustment mechanism. These static estimators are examined for various values of the dynamic adjustment parameter in the data generating process. In the simulation design, many aspects of the data generating process are kept constant.

Hence, the results do not necessarily indicate invariant characteristics of these estimators in finite samples. However, the design is constructed such that it mimics a particular type of relationship, which has great relevance as such and is closely related to the empirical application considered in this thesis.

2.2.1   Simulation design

The data have been generated according to the equilibrium relationship

$$y_{it}^* = \beta^* x_{it} + \alpha_i \tag{2.33}$$

and the simple partial adjustment mechanism (2.3) for individuals $i = 1, ..., N$ and time periods $t = 1, ..., T$. Here y_{it}^* denotes the equilibrium or desired value of the dependent variable y_{it}, x_{it} the exogenous variable, α_i an individual effect and ϵ_{it} a white noise error term, which is independent of $y_{i,t-j}$ for $j \geq 1$. Of course, $0 \leq \gamma < 1$.

The individual effects have been generated as

$$\alpha_i = \bar{\alpha} + \tilde{\alpha}_i \text{ with } \bar{\alpha} \text{ fixed and } \tilde{\alpha}_i \sim \text{IIN}(0, \sigma_\alpha^2)$$

The observations x_{it} are designed such that they exhibit characteristics of the natural logarithms of annual real disposable household income. The cross-section income distribution is chosen to be lognormal, such that

$$x_{it} \sim \text{N}(\mu_t, \sigma_x^2) \text{ with } \mu_t = \mu_0 + gt \text{ and } \sigma_x^2 \text{ constant}$$

Hence, the income inequality parameter σ_x does not change over time, but the average annual growth in the level of income is $100g\%$. If $x_{it} - \mu_t$ was chosen to behave like a random walk, then the variance of x_{it} (and hence the income inequality) would be non-constant. Therefore, the regressor variables x_{it} have been generated as

$$x_{i0} = \mu_0 + \phi\tilde{\alpha}_i + (1 - \rho^2)^{-\frac{1}{2}}\xi_{i0} \tag{2.34}$$

and next

$$(x_{it} - \mu_t - \phi\tilde{\alpha}_i) = \rho(x_{i,t-1} - \mu_{t-1} - \phi\tilde{\alpha}_i) + \xi_{it}$$

with $\xi_{it} \sim \text{IIN}(0, \sigma_\xi^2)$ and $\tilde{\alpha}_i$ and ξ_{it} independent. Hence, the N series $(x_{it} - \mu_t - \phi\tilde{\alpha}_i)$ are mutually stochastically independent stationary AR(1) processes with equivalent parameters. The variance of x_{it}

$$\sigma_x^2 = \phi^2\sigma_\alpha^2 + (1 - \rho^2)^{-1}\sigma_\xi^2$$

is constant. With respect to the parameter ϕ, two different simulation experiments have been run: one with doubly exogenous regressor variables (x_{it}

independent of α_i and ϵ_{it}, hence $\phi = 0$) and one with singly exogenous regressor variables (x_{it} independent of ϵ_{it} but $\phi \neq 0$). The correlation of x_{it} and α_i is given by

$$\omega = \frac{\text{cov}(x_{it}, \alpha_i)}{\sigma_x \sigma_\alpha} = \phi \frac{\sigma_\alpha}{\sigma_x}$$

In the first experiment, $\omega = 0$ and in the second ω was chosen to be 0.5. The other parameters (σ_x, μ_0, g and σ_ξ) were equivalent in both experiments and chosen such, that the generated observations x_{it} resemble the natural logarithm of annual disposable household income, used in the estimation of Engel curves in Chapters 6 and 7. This means an income inequality of $\sigma_x = 0.425$ (see for comparison Cramer (1969, p. 73, Table 10)), $\mu_0 = 4$, $g = 0.02$ (an average annual growth in income of about 2%) and $\sigma_\xi = 0.03$ (an incidental annual change in income in the range of about plus or minus 6%). This yields

$$\rho = \sqrt{1 - \frac{\sigma_\xi^2}{\sigma_x^2(1 - \omega^2)}} = \begin{cases} 0.9975 \text{ if } \omega = 0 \\ 0.9967 \text{ if } \omega = 0.5 \end{cases} \tag{2.35}$$

Note that

$$x_{it} = \rho x_{i,t-1} + (1 - \rho)\mu_0 + \rho g + (1 - \rho)gt + (1 - \rho)\phi\tilde{\alpha}_i + \xi_{it} \tag{2.36}$$

For reasons to be clarified below, $\bar{\alpha} = -1.8$, $\sigma_\alpha = 0.4$ and $\beta^* = 1$. In each replication of the Monte Carlo study, starting values for x_{i0} were produced according to (2.34) and for the dependent variable according to

$$y_{i0} = \beta^* x_{i0} + \alpha_i + (1 - \gamma^2)^{-\frac{1}{2}} \epsilon_{i0} \tag{2.37}$$

Next, the regressors were generated according to (2.36) and also

$$y_{it} = \gamma y_{i,t-1} + (1 - \gamma)(\beta^* x_{it} + \alpha_i) + \epsilon_{it} \tag{2.38}$$

where $\epsilon_{it} \sim \text{IIN}(0, \sigma_\epsilon^2)$ with $\sigma_\epsilon = 0.3$. The computer generated 15000 replications of the individual effects α_i, the regressors x_{it} in (2.36) and the series y_{it} in (2.38) for $i = 1, ..., N$ and $t = 1, ..., T$ with $N = 100$ and $T = 3$. Especially this latter value is rather small, but is equal to the number of waves available in the data set described in Chapter 4.

If $y_{it}^* = \ln Y_{it}^*$ and $x_{it}^* = \ln X_{it}^*$, then the long-run relationship (2.33) is

$$Y_{it}^* = X_{it} \exp(\alpha_i) = 0.165 X_{it} \exp(\tilde{\alpha}_i)$$

since $\exp(-1.8) = 0.165$. The chosen values for σ_α and σ_ϵ imply that the standard deviation of the individual effect α_i is 40% of $X_{it} \exp(\bar{\alpha})$ and the standard error of the disturbance in the adjustment equation (2.3) is 30% of $Y_{it} = \exp(y_{it})$. This parametrisation is supposed to represent reasonably well the phenomena encountered in the case of for instance an Engel curve for a category of consumer goods with an average share of between 15% and 20%, such as food.

2.2.2 Estimation methods for static models

In the simulation design described above, the small sample characteristics of different estimators for static models are examined for four different values of the dynamic adjustment parameter γ in (2.3). The first estimator is the static cross-section OLS estimator

$$\hat{\beta}_t = \frac{x_t' M_{\iota_N} y_t}{x_t' M_{\iota_N} x_t} \tag{2.39}$$

for the cross section at period t, where x_t and y_t are $N \times 1$ vectors with elements x_{it} and y_{it}. This estimator is BLU, if there is only a single cross section available and the data generating process is such that $\omega = 0$ (no individual effects *or* doubly exogenous regressor variables) and $\gamma = 0$ (no lagged dependent regressor variable). For the examination of this cross-section estimator, the first wave of the panel has been used. The second is the static pooled OLS estimator

$$\hat{\beta}_P = \frac{x' M_{\iota_{NT}} y}{x' M_{\iota_{NT}} x} \tag{2.40}$$

where x and y are $NT \times 1$ vectors with elements x_{it} and y_{it} respectively. The pooled OLS estimator is BLU, if there are no individual effects ($\alpha_i = \bar{\alpha}$ or $\sigma_\alpha = 0$) and no lagged dependent variable ($\gamma = 0$) in the data generating process. The third estimator is the static 'within' or Fixed Effects estimator, which is here equivalent to (2.25) in Section 2.1.4. The FE estimator is BLU, if the individual effects are considered to be fixed (irrespective of the value of ω) and $\gamma = 0$ in the data generating process. Finally, the behaviour of the static two-step GLS or Random Effects estimator has been examined, which is defined as

$$\hat{\beta}_{RE} = \frac{\hat{\lambda} x' M_{\iota_{NT}} y + (1 - \hat{\lambda}) x' M_J y}{\hat{\lambda} x' M_{\iota_{NT}} x + (1 - \hat{\lambda}) x' M_J x} \quad \text{with } \hat{\lambda} = \frac{\hat{\sigma}_\epsilon^2}{\hat{\sigma}_\epsilon^2 + T \hat{\sigma}_\alpha^2} \tag{2.41}$$

If $\sigma_\alpha / \sigma_\epsilon$ is known, $\omega = 0$ and $\gamma = 0$, this estimator is BLU. If $\sigma_\alpha / \sigma_\epsilon$ is unknown, the variance ratio has to be estimated first: see, for instance, Hsiao (1986, p. 40) or Appendix B.

In the simulation results, the FE estimator has a much larger variance than the OLS and RE estimators. In order to understand this difference, the variance of the FE estimator and of the pooled OLS estimator in a model with fixed regressors are examined. Suppose the data generating process is given by

$$y = X\beta + (\iota_T \otimes I_N)\alpha + \epsilon \quad \text{with E}(\epsilon) = 0 \text{ and V}(\epsilon) = \sigma_\epsilon^2 I_{NT}$$

where

$$\alpha = \bar{\alpha} \iota_N + \tilde{\alpha} \quad \text{with E}(\tilde{\alpha}) = 0 \text{ and V}(\tilde{\alpha}) = \sigma_\alpha^2 I_N$$

For the pooled OLS estimator

$$\hat{\beta}_P = (\breve{X}'\breve{X})^{-1}\breve{X}'y = \beta + (\breve{X}'\breve{X})^{-1}\breve{X}'J\alpha + (\breve{X}'\breve{X})^{-1}\breve{X}'\epsilon$$
$$= \beta + (\breve{X}'\breve{X})^{-1}\breve{X}'J\tilde{\alpha} + (\breve{X}'\breve{X})^{-1}\breve{X}'\epsilon \qquad (2.42)$$

where $\breve{X} = M_{\iota_{NT}}X$. The expectation and variance of this estimator are β and

$$V(\hat{\beta}_P) = \sigma_\epsilon^2(\breve{X}'\breve{X})^{-1} + \sigma_\alpha^2(\breve{X}'\breve{X})^{-1}\breve{X}'JJ'\breve{X}(\breve{X}'\breve{X})^{-1} \qquad (2.43)$$

respectively. The FE estimator is

$$\hat{\beta}_{FE} = (X'M_JX)^{-1}X'M_Jy = \beta + (X'M_JX)^{-1}X'M_J\epsilon$$

The expectation and variance of $\hat{\beta}_{FE}$ are β and

$$V(\hat{\beta}_{FE}) = \sigma_\epsilon^2(X'M_JX)^{-1} \qquad (2.44)$$

respectively.

It can be shown that $M_JM_{\iota_{NT}} = M_J$ and

$$(X'M_JX)^{-1} = (\breve{X}'M_J\breve{X})^{-1} =$$
$$(\breve{X}'\breve{X})^{-1} + (\breve{X}'\breve{X})^{-1}\breve{X}'J(J'M_{\breve{X}}J)^{-1}J'\breve{X}(\breve{X}'\breve{X})^{-1}$$

with $M_{\breve{X}} = I_{NT} - \breve{X}(\breve{X}'\breve{X})^{-1}\breve{X}'$. If $\sigma_\alpha^2 = 0$, it follows that the variance matrix of the FE estimator is equal to the variance matrix of the pooled OLS estimator plus a positive definite matrix. For $\sigma_\alpha^2 > 0$, the difference in variance between the two estimators is not so easily established. Since

$$(J'M_{\breve{X}}J)^{-1} = (J'J)^{-1} + (J'J)^{-1}J'\breve{X}(\breve{X}'M_J\breve{X})^{-1}\breve{X}'J(J'J)^{-1}$$

and $(J'J)^{-1} = \frac{1}{T}I_N$, it follows that

$$V(\hat{\beta}_{FE}) = \sigma_\epsilon^2(\breve{X}'\breve{X})^{-1} + \frac{1}{T}\sigma_\epsilon^2(\breve{X}'\breve{X})^{-1}\breve{X}'JJ'\breve{X}(\breve{X}'\breve{X})^{-1}$$
$$+ \frac{1}{T^2}\sigma_\epsilon^2(\breve{X}'\breve{X})^{-1}\breve{X}'JJ'\breve{X}(\breve{X}'M_J\breve{X})^{-1}\breve{X}'JJ'\breve{X}(\breve{X}'\breve{X})^{-1}$$

So, the difference between the variances follows as

$$V(\hat{\beta}_{FE}) - V(\hat{\beta}_P) = (\frac{1}{T}\sigma_\epsilon^2 - \sigma_\alpha^2)(\breve{X}'\breve{X})^{-1}\breve{X}'JJ'\breve{X}(\breve{X}'\breve{X})^{-1}$$
$$+ \frac{1}{T^2}\sigma_\epsilon^2(\breve{X}'\breve{X})^{-1}\breve{X}'JJ'\breve{X}(\breve{X}'M_J\breve{X})^{-1}\breve{X}'JJ'\breve{X}(\breve{X}'\breve{X})^{-1}$$

For $\sigma_\alpha^2 > 0$, the difference between the variances of the FE and pooled OLS estimators depends on the values of σ_ϵ, σ_α and T and on the characteristics of $\breve{X}$.

2.2.3   Simulation results

Figures 2.1 to 2.4 show the cumulative distribution functions of the estimators (2.39) to (2.41) (obtained in static models) for a data generating process where $\gamma = 0$, $\gamma = 0.2$, $\gamma = 0.4$ and $\gamma = 0.6$ respectively, and where $\omega = 0$. Graphs of cumulative distributions are an elegant way to describe simulation results, because they contain more information than any table possibly can and because they do not need to be smoothed, as a density graph must. Figures 2.5 to 2.8 depict the singly exogenous regressor case where $\omega = 0.5$.[3]

In the case of $\gamma = 0$ and $\omega = 0$ (no dynamics and doubly exogenous regressor variables in the data generating process), all estimators are consistent for β^*; see Section 2.1. Figure 2.1 shows that in that case the median of all estimators is equal to $\beta^* = 1$, and the pooled OLS estimator is the most efficient, closely followed by cross-section OLS, RE and finally FE. However, this does not mean that the pooled OLS estimator leads to the most efficient and accurate inference on β. Only the cross-section OLS, FE and RE estimators will estimate their standard errors appropriately. The estimated standard error of the cross-section OLS and FE estimators are unbiased, and the standard error of the RE estimator is estimated consistently for $N \to \infty$. The standard formula for the variance of the pooled OLS estimator is inappropriate, because it does not take account of the heteroscedasticity in the disturbances $\alpha_i + \epsilon_{it}$.

From Figures 2.2 to 2.4, it is seen that all distribution functions, except for FE, are remarkably stable as γ increases. This is probably caused by the high autocorrelation (2.35) of the regressors x_{it} in the simulation design: according to the results in Section 2.1, high autocorrelation leads to a relatively minor underestimation of the long-run effect. The behaviour of the FE estimator's distribution, however, is severely affected. For $\gamma = 0.6$, the median of the FE estimator has fallen to 0.55, which indicates a downward bias of almost 50% of β^* and a positive bias in relation to the impact multiplier $\beta^*(1 - \gamma) = 0.4$.

From Figures 2.5 to 2.8, it is seen that the pictures change dramatically when ω is positive. If $\gamma = 0$, only the FE estimator remains unbiased. From Figure 2.5, it can be seen that the median of the FE estimator is equal to β^*, while Figures 2.6 to 2.8 show that it becomes smaller when γ increases. The other estimators are biased upwards almost 50%, irrespective of the value of γ. However, because of the large variance of the FE estimator, the mean squared error (MSE) of the FE estimator is still larger than that of the other estimators. For $\gamma = 0$, the average MSE over the replications of the FE estimator is 0.45, compared to 0.21 for RE and 0.23 for pooled OLS. (In the doubly exogenous regressor case, these figures were 0.45, 0.01 and 0.01 respectively.)

---

[3]The figures in this thesis have been designed with the software package Presenter for Acorn RISC computers, written by Walther Schoonenberg.

The simulation results described above suggest that the FE estimator is much more sensitive to neglected dynamics than both OLS and RE estimators, and that, in case of positive γ, the downward bias in the FE estimator can be substantial. This conforms to the results of Baltagi and Griffin (1984). In a different context, they find that the relative importance of the within-groups variation (variation in x_i over time) compared to the between-groups variation (variation between x_i and x_j) affects the relative performance of the FE and OLS estimators. If the within-groups variation is relatively small, then the OLS estimator will perform relatively well compared to the FE estimator. In the simulation design here, a relatively high autocorrelation parameter ρ induces a relatively small within-groups variation. In addition, the disappointing performance of the FE estimator may be partly caused by the shortness of the panel (only three time periods). The results also illustrate the sensitivity of the OLS and RE estimators to correlation between the regressors and individual effects, whereas the FE estimator is not affected by such correlation. Despite their bias, the relative efficiency of the simple OLS estimators, which involve misspecification with respect to both the dynamics and the individual effects, is most remarkable.

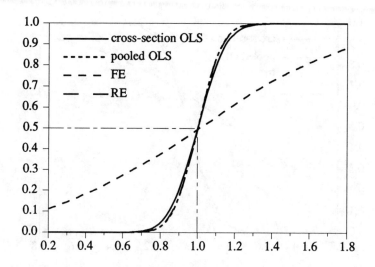

Figure 2.1: The cdf of static estimators for β if $\omega = 0$ and $\gamma = 0$

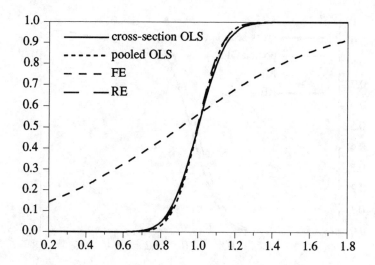

Figure 2.2: The cdf of static estimators for β if $\omega = 0$ and $\gamma = 0.2$

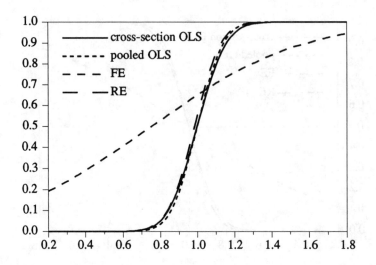

Figure 2.3: The cdf of static estimators for β if $\omega = 0$ and $\gamma = 0.4$

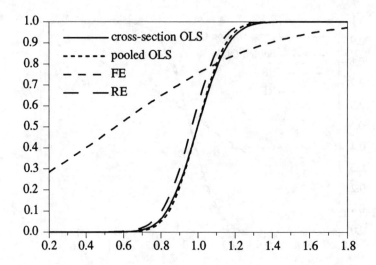

Figure 2.4: The cdf of static estimators for β if $\omega = 0$ and $\gamma = 0.6$

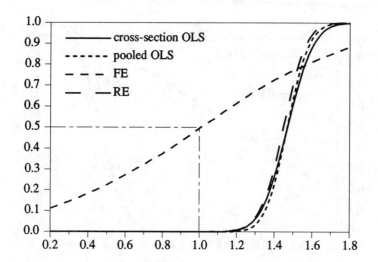

Figure 2.5: The cdf of static estimators for β if $\omega = 0.5$ and $\gamma = 0$

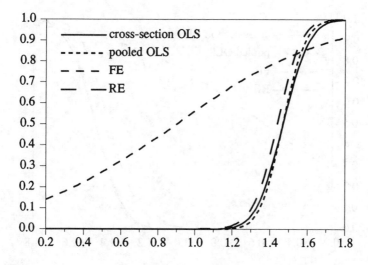

Figure 2.6: The cdf of static estimators for β if $\omega = 0.5$ and $\gamma = 0.2$

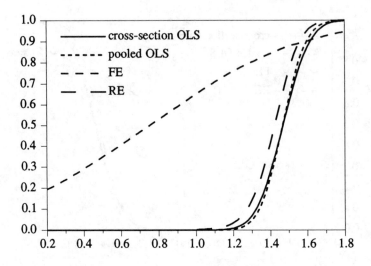

Figure 2.7: The cdf of static estimators for β if $\omega = 0.5$ and $\gamma = 0.4$

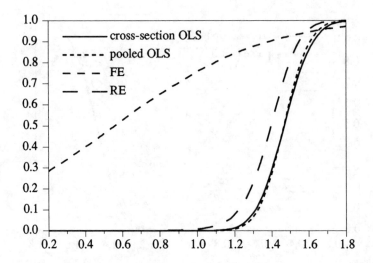

Figure 2.8: The cdf of static estimators for β if $\omega = 0.5$ and $\gamma = 0.6$

Chapter 3

Dynamic panel data modelling

3.1 Consistent estimation of dynamic panel data models

Consider the dynamic panel data model (1.1). If not just one but J different exogenous regressor variables are included, then the model can be written as

$$y_{it} = \alpha_0 + \sum_{j=1}^{J} \sum_{l=0}^{L(j)} \beta_{jl} x_{ji,t-l} + \gamma y_{i,t-1} + \alpha_i + \epsilon_{it} \qquad (3.1)$$

for individuals $i = 1, \ldots, N$ and time periods $t = 1, \ldots, T$. This model accommodates a lagged dependent regressor $y_{i,t-1}$ and $K = \sum_{j=1}^{J} \sum_{l=0}^{L(j)} = J + \sum_{j=1}^{J} L(j)$ other regressors, which may be current or lagged values of the J different variables x_j. In a slightly different formulation, model (3.1) is known as the Balestra and Nerlove (1966) model. Usually, as in static panel data models, the individual effects α_i are either treated as fixed constants (a necessary condition for identification of the N parameters α_i is then $\alpha_0 = 0$) or as random variables with mean zero and finite variance.

For the random individual effects model, following Cornwell, Schmidt and Wyhowski (1992), the thesis distinguishes endogenous, singly exogenous and doubly exogenous variables. Endogenous variables are correlated with both the individual effects α_i and the disturbances ϵ_{it}, singly exogenous variables are correlated with α_i but uncorrelated with ϵ_{it}, and doubly exogenous variables are uncorrelated both with α_i and ϵ_{it}. Another decomposition into strictly exogenous and predetermined variables is convenient: strict exogeneity means $\text{cov}(x_{it}, \epsilon_{is}) = 0$ for all s, t, whereas predeterminedness allows $\text{cov}(x_{it}, \epsilon_{i,t-s}) \neq 0$ for $s > 0$.[1] In theory, endogenous, singly predetermined, doubly predetermined, singly strictly exogenous and doubly strictly exogenous variables can

---

[1] In state-of-the-art time-series econometrics, the concepts strict exogeneity and prede-

31

be distinguished. It must be noted, however, that double predeterminedness is a somewhat strange concept: a variable that is correlated with $\epsilon_{i,t-s}$ for $s > 0$ may be expected to be correlated with α_i as well. Therefore, endogenous, (singly) predetermined, singly (strictly) exogenous and doubly (strictly) exogenous variables are classified.

If the individual effects are fixed, the distinction between singly and doubly exogenous variables is irrelevant. This is also the case when the individual effects have been substituted out, as in, for instance, a differenced equation. In (3.1), y_{it} is endogenous, if ϵ_{it} is serially uncorrelated $y_{i,t-1}$ is predetermined and $x_{ji,t-l}$ are for the moment assumed singly exogenous.

When no lagged exogenous variables are included in the model, then $L(j) = 0$ for all j, $K = J$ and (3.1) becomes

$$y_{it} = \alpha_0 + \sum_{j=1}^{J} \beta_{j0} x_{jit} + \gamma y_{i,t-1} + \alpha_i + \epsilon_{it}$$

If there is only one exogenous variable, so $J = 1$, and if this variable is included with one lag, so $L(1) = 1$, then the model reduces to

$$y_{it} = \alpha_0 + \beta_{10} x_{1it} + \beta_{11} x_{1i,t-1} + \gamma y_{i,t-1} + \alpha_i + \epsilon_{it}$$

which is virtually equivalent to (2.1).

The dynamic relationships considered in this thesis are (3.1) for $L(j) \leq 2$ and some of its special cases. According to the typology of Hendry, Pagan and Sargan (1984), at least nine particular cases can be distinguished. Special cases of interest here are the *static model*

$$\beta_{jl} = 0 \ (\forall j, \ \forall l > 0) \ \wedge \ \gamma = 0 \ \Rightarrow \ y_{it} = \alpha_0 + \sum_{j=1}^{J} \beta_{j0} x_{jit} + \alpha_i + \epsilon_{it} \qquad (3.2)$$

the *finite distributed lag model*

$$\gamma = 0 \ \Rightarrow \ y_{it} = \alpha_0 + \sum_{j=1}^{J} \sum_{l=0}^{L(j)} \beta_{jl} x_{ji,t-l} + \alpha_i + \epsilon_{it} \qquad (3.3)$$

the *partial adjustment model* (see (2.3) and (2.4) for an interpretation of the coefficients)

$$\beta_{jl} = 0 \ (\forall j, \ \forall l > 0) \ \wedge \ 0 < \gamma < 1 \ \Rightarrow$$

---

terminedness have been replaced by weak, strong and super exogeneity, as introduced by Engle, Hendry and Richard (1983). Since these concepts have not yet been worked out for panel data models, the thesis sticks to the old-fashioned terminology.

$$y_{it} = \alpha_0 + \sum_{j=1}^{J} \beta_{j0} x_{jit} + \gamma y_{i,t-1} + \alpha_i + \epsilon_{it} \qquad (3.4)$$

the *common factor model*

$$\beta_{jl} = 0 \ (\forall j, \ \forall l > 1) \ \wedge \ \beta_{j1} = -\gamma \beta_{j0} \ (\forall j) \ \wedge \ |\gamma| < 1 \ \Rightarrow$$

$$y_{it} = \alpha_0 + \sum_{j=1}^{J} \beta_{j0}(x_{jit} - \gamma x_{ji,t-1}) + \gamma y_{i,t-1} + \alpha_i + \epsilon_{it} \qquad (3.5)$$

and the *'static' differenced data model*

$$\beta_{jl} = 0 \ (\forall j, \ \forall l > 1) \ \wedge \ \beta_{j1} = -\beta_{j0} \ (\forall j) \ \wedge \ \gamma = 1 \ \Rightarrow$$

$$\triangle y_{it} = \alpha_0 + \sum_{j=1}^{J} \beta_{j0} \triangle x_{jit} + \alpha_i + \epsilon_{it} \qquad (3.6)$$

Standard estimators for static panel data models with fixed or random effects are biased in dynamic models such as (3.1) and — depending on the way in which N and T tend to infinity and on the assumptions made on the initial values y_{i0} — often inconsistent, due to the lagged dependent variable.

If the individual effects are treated as random, then the composite disturbance $\alpha_i + \epsilon_{it}$ is contemporaneously correlated with the regressor $y_{i,t-1}$. This leads to simultaneity bias in common estimators like OLS and GLS, generally upward for γ and toward zero for β_{jl}. These biases are more pronounced the greater the variance of the individual effects and do not necessarily disappear when N or T or both tend to infinity. Early Monte Carlo studies on these biases are Nerlove (1967) and Nerlove (1971). Detailed derivations of the asymptotic behaviour of estimators in random effects models with a lagged dependent variable are given in Trognon (1978), Anderson and Hsiao (1981), Anderson and Hsiao (1982) and Ridder and Wansbeek (1990, Section 3).

A common estimator for fixed individual effects is the Least Squares Dummy Variables or Fixed Effects or 'within' estimator, which starts by eliminating the individual effects by writing the model in deviations of the mean within each individual over time:

$$y_{it} - y_{i\cdot} = \sum_{j=1}^{J} \sum_{l=0}^{L(j)} \beta_{jl}(x_{ji,t-l} - x_{ji\cdot,-l}) + \gamma(y_{i,t-1} - y_{i\cdot,-1}) + (\epsilon_{it} - \epsilon_{i\cdot})$$

where a dot denotes averaging over the respective index. Contemporaneous correlation between regressors and disturbance crops up again: for instance, between $y_{i,t-1}$ and $\epsilon_{i\cdot}$. This correlation does not go to zero as N goes to infinity; however, it does disappear for an arbitrarily large T. In Nickell (1981) and

Hsiao (1986, Section 4.2), formulae for the inconsistency for large N and fixed T are derived. Beggs and Nerlove (1988) suggest an approach to approximate the bias in a model without exogenous regressors, when both N and T are finite. In Kiviet (1992), results of Monte Carlo simulations give some idea of the extent of the small sample bias in a model with exogenous regressors; in addition, an analytical approximation of the bias is given.

To summarise, models with a lagged dependent variable and fixed or random individual effects such as (3.1) suffer from contemporaneous correlation between regressors and disturbance and therefore standard estimation methods for static models lead to biased and often inconsistent estimators.

A widely used method to circumvent contemporaneous correlation problems is estimation with instrumental variables (see Sargan (1958)). In the usual regression model, if the regressor matrix $X = [X_1 : X_2]$ contains k_1 endogenous regressors X_1 and k_2 predetermined or exogenous regressors X_2, then $k_3 >= k_1$ instruments W_3, which are (asymptotically) uncorrelated with the disturbance term but correlated with the columns of X_1, may yield consistent estimates in the following way. Writing $W = [W_3 : X_2]$, the instrumental variable estimator for the model $y = X\beta + \epsilon$ is

$$\hat{\beta}_{IV} = [X'W(W'W)^{-1}W'X]^{-1}X'W(W'W)^{-1}W'y = [\hat{X}'\hat{X}]^{-1}\hat{X}'y \qquad (3.7)$$

and the asymptotic variance matrix of this estimator is given by

$$V(\hat{\beta}_{IV}) = \sigma^2[X'W(W'W)^{-1}W'X]^{-1} = \sigma^2[\hat{X}'\hat{X}]^{-1} \qquad (3.8)$$

where

$$\hat{X} = W(W'W)^{-1}W'X = [W(W'W)^{-1}W'X_1 : X_2]$$

If $k_3 = k_1$, (3.7) reduces to

$$\hat{\beta}_{IV} = (W'X)^{-1}W'y$$

Anderson and Hsiao (1981) and Anderson and Hsiao (1982) suggested writing model (3.1) in first differences as

$$y_{it} - y_{i,t-1} = \sum_{j=1}^{J}\sum_{l=0}^{L(j)} \beta_{jl}(x_{ji,t-l} - x_{ji,t-1-l}) + \gamma(y_{i,t-1} - y_{i,t-2}) + (\epsilon_{it} - \epsilon_{i,t-1}) \quad (3.9)$$

and then estimating this model by IV, using $y_{i,t-2}$ or $(y_{i,t-2} - y_{i,t-3})$ as instrument for $(y_{i,t-1} - y_{i,t-2})$. Arellano (1989) showed that the estimator which uses $y_{i,t-2}$ as instrument often has a smaller variance than the estimator which uses $(y_{i,t-2} - y_{i,t-3})$ as instrument. Both estimators proposed by Anderson and Hsiao use only one instrument for the endogenous explanatory variable.

When more instruments are available, efficiency may be increased. The question how to use the available instruments to obtain the most efficient estimators for β_{jl} and γ in (3.9) is a special case of problems analysed by White (1982), Hansen (1982) and Chamberlain (1987). Direct application of (3.7) does not lead to an asymptotically efficient estimator, because the disturbances $(\epsilon_{it}-\epsilon_{i,t-1})$ are not i.i.d. However, an optimal Generalised Method of Moments or two-stage instrumental variables estimator is readily available.

GMM estimators for the static panel data model, in which some explanatory variables may be singly exogenous, are developed in Hausman and Taylor (1981), Amemiya and MaCurdy (1986) and Breusch, Mizon and Schmidt (1989). These authors subsequently increase asymptotic efficiency by introducing more linear orthogonality conditions. Their estimators reduce to the Fixed Effects estimator if all of the explanatory variables are singly exogenous and to the Random Effects GLS estimator if they are all doubly exogenous. In Arellano and Bover (1990), it is shown that these estimators are invariant to certain transformations of the original equations. Cornwell and Rupert (1988) give a comparison of the performance of these estimators in small samples and find that efficiency gains are limited to the coefficients of time-invariant singly exogenous variables. Baltagi and Khanti-Akom (1990) (have tried to) replicate the Cornwell and Rupert (1988) study and obtain different results, notably smaller efficiency gains. Revankar (1992) shows that under certain assumptions these estimators are all numerically identical.

For panel data models with lagged dependent variables among the regressors, GMM has been worked out by Holtz-Eakin, Newey and Rosen (1988), Holtz-Eakin (1988) and Arellano and Bond (1991). The vector autoregression model in Holtz-Eakin, Newey and Rosen (1988) builds upon Chamberlain (1982) and Chamberlain (1984), who established minimum distance estimators for static and dynamic panel data models which are robust to residual autocorrelation. Holtz-Eakin (1988) and Arellano and Bond (1991) start from model (3.9) with the lagged dependent variable as the only regressor. Noting that not only $y_{i,t-2}$ but earlier levels of the dependent variable too are valid instruments for $(y_{i,t-1} - y_{i,t-2})$, they formulate the following $m = 1 + 2 + 3 + \cdots + (T - 2)$

orthogonality conditions:

$$
E \begin{bmatrix}
y_{i1}(\epsilon_{i3} - \epsilon_{i2}) \\
y_{i1}(\epsilon_{i4} - \epsilon_{i3}) \\
y_{i2}(\epsilon_{i4} - \epsilon_{i3}) \\
y_{i1}(\epsilon_{i5} - \epsilon_{i4}) \\
y_{i2}(\epsilon_{i5} - \epsilon_{i4}) \\
y_{i3}(\epsilon_{i5} - \epsilon_{i4}) \\
\vdots \\
y_{i1}(\epsilon_{iT} - \epsilon_{i,T-1}) \\
\vdots \\
y_{i,T-2}(\epsilon_{iT} - \epsilon_{i,T-1})
\end{bmatrix} = E(Z_i' \triangle \epsilon_i) = 0 \qquad (3.10)
$$

where Z_i is a $(T-2) \times m$ block diagonal matrix whose s-th block is given by $[y_{i1} \cdots y_{is}]$ and $\triangle \epsilon_i = [\epsilon_{i3} - \epsilon_{i2}, \epsilon_{i4} - \epsilon_{i3}, \epsilon_{i5} - \epsilon_{i4}, \ldots, \epsilon_{iT} - \epsilon_{i,T-1}]'$. In this formulation, there are $m = (T-1)(T-2)/2$ instruments available for $T-2$ equations, giving rise to $(T-2)(T-3)/2$ overidentifying restrictions.

Reintroducing other regressor variables x, the s-th block in the matrix of available instruments Z_i becomes $[y_{i1} \cdots y_{is} x_{i1} \cdots x_{i,s+1}]$ if these variables are predetermined and $[y_{i1} \cdots y_{is} x_{i1} \cdots x_{iT}]$ if they are strictly exogenous. In Blundell, Bond, Devereux and Schiantarelli (1992, footnote 8), the complete instrument set Z_i is given.

The GMM estimator is based on the sample moments $\frac{1}{N} \sum_{i=1}^{N} Z_i' \triangle \epsilon_i = \frac{1}{N} Z' \triangle \epsilon$ where $Z = [Z_1', \ldots, Z_N']'$ and $\triangle \epsilon = [\triangle \epsilon_1', \ldots, \triangle \epsilon_N']'$, and is obtained by minimising

$$
(\triangle \epsilon' Z) \left(\frac{1}{N} \sum_{i=1}^{N} Z_i' H_i Z_i \right)^{-1} (Z' \triangle \epsilon)
$$

If the ϵ_{it} are independent and homoskedastic both across units and over time, then the optimal choice for H_i is the $(T-2) \times (T-2)$ matrix H with main diagonal elements equal to 2, first subdiagonal elements equal to -1 and other elements 0. In this case, the estimator can be computed in one step. The two-step estimator is computed by choosing $H_i = \triangle e_i \triangle e_i'$, where $\triangle e_i$ are residuals from a preliminary consistent estimator. This estimator is to be preferred when the disturbances ϵ_{it} are heteroskedastic or mutually dependent, either across units or over time.

So far, only linear moment conditions have been taken into account. Ahn and Schmidt (1992a) and Ahn and Schmidt (1992b) give more efficient estimators by exploiting more orthogonality conditions, for instance quadratic moment conditions. This leads to iterative procedures.

Alternatively to estimating the differenced equation (3.9), model (3.1) in levels can be estimated. In this equation, instruments constructed out of values of the dependent variable should be in first-differenced form, to ensure independence of the individual effects. Instruments made of other regressors are similar to those developed for the static panel data model by Hausman and Taylor (1981) and others.

An alternative estimation method for panel data models with a lagged dependent variable and random individual effects is maximum likelihood. A disadvantage of maximum likelihood is that specific assumptions about the initial values of the dependent variable have to be made and that the consistency property depends upon these assumptions; see for instance Bhargava and Sargan (1983) and Ridder and Wansbeek (1990, Sections 4 and 5). For models with a large number of explanatory variables, such as the empirical models considered in Chapter 7 of this thesis, maximum likelihood is not a feasible method.

3.2 Small sample tests for a lagged dependent variable

In the previous section, several estimation and testing procedures for dynamic panel data were discussed. A distinguishing feature of these procedures is that they are valid only asymptotically, for large N. Here, tests for the detection of dynamics in individual effects models are developed, which are exact and similar for finite T and N.

Consider a dynamic model with K explanatory variables and individual effects, given by the adjustment mechanism (2.3) and the equilibrium relationship

$$y_{it}^* = x_{it}'\beta^* + \alpha_i \qquad (3.11)$$

where x_{it} and β^* now denote $K \times 1$ vectors. The individual effects may be fixed or random and the regressors x_{it} may be singly or doubly exogenous. Substitution yields

$$y_{it} = \gamma y_{i,t-1} + (1-\gamma)x_{it}'\beta^* + (1-\gamma)\alpha_i + \epsilon_{it} \qquad (3.12)$$

which is rewritten for convenience as

$$y_{it} = \gamma y_{i,t-1} + x_{it}'\beta + \delta_i + \epsilon_{it} \qquad (3.13)$$

where β is a $K \times 1$ vector, δ_i denotes the individual effect and $\epsilon_{it} \sim \text{IIN}(0, \sigma_\epsilon^2)$ is a white noise error term, for $i = 1, \ldots, N$ and $t = 1, \ldots, T$.

Because of the serious consequences of incorrectly (if $\gamma \neq 0$) estimating a static model and because of the inefficiency and complexity of estimating (3.13) when the relationship is in fact static ($\gamma = 0$), a technique for accurate and powerful inference on the actual value of γ would be invaluable. The usual tests of the significance of γ are based on estimates of (3.13) which are either consistent for $T \to \infty$ or for $N \to \infty$. The former can be obtained from straightforward application of least squares. The latter follow from estimation of (3.13) or its differenced form by instrumental variables or GMM, see for example Holtz-Eakin, Newey and Rosen (1988), Arellano and Bond (1991) or Ahn and Schmidt (1992a). Tests for $\gamma = 1$ (a unit root in a panel data model) have been investigated by Breitung and Meyer (1991) for $N \to \infty$ and Levin and Lin (1992) for both T and N arbitrarily large. In practical applications, where the sample size is finite and T is often extremely small, the accuracy of the resulting inference on γ could be rather poor, as it seems.

Here a procedure for exact inference on γ will be derived, which is based on an approach set out in Kiviet and Phillips (1990) and Kiviet and Phillips (1992) for the time-series case. Estimating γ by least squares in an augmented regression model leads to a statistic whose distribution (in finite samples) under the hypothesis $\gamma = \gamma_0$ can be assessed and which is independent of nuisance parameters. Hence, an exact similar test for $H_0 : \gamma = 0$ (static versus dynamic) or more generally $H_0 : \gamma = \gamma_0$ can be developed. In what follows, the derivation of this and a closely related test statistic will be shown.

3.2.1   Derivation of the test statistics for $H_0 : \gamma = 0$

Model (3.13) can be written in vector notation as

$$y_t = y_{t-1}\gamma + X_t\beta + \delta + \epsilon_t \qquad (3.14)$$

where y_t, ϵ_t, δ and y_0 are $N \times 1$ vectors and X_t is an $N \times K$ matrix, for $t = 1, \ldots, T$. In a straightforward manner, all data in the system can be collected:

$$y = y_{-1}\gamma + X\beta + \iota_T \otimes \delta + \epsilon \qquad (3.15)$$

where X is $NT \times K$ etc. Let $Z = [X : \iota_T \otimes I_N]$ and $\theta' = [\beta', \delta']$ then the model may be written as

$$y = y_{-1}\gamma + Z\theta + \epsilon \qquad (3.16)$$

Using standard results on partitioned regression, the least squares estimator of γ can be written as

$$\hat{\gamma} = \frac{y'_{-1}M_Z y}{y'_{-1}M_Z y_{-1}} = \gamma + \frac{y'_{-1}M_Z \epsilon}{y'_{-1}M_Z y_{-1}} \qquad (3.17)$$

where $M_Z = I_{NT} - Z(Z'Z)^{-1}Z'$. Note that this is in fact the fixed effects estimator of γ. Even when $\gamma = 0$, the finite sample distribution of $\hat{\gamma}$ is quite complicated and depends on θ, σ_ϵ^2 and y_0 (the latter is the $N \times 1$ vector of initial values of the dependent variable for each individual). To illustrate this dependence, the vector $M_Z y_{-1}$ can be explored, which is a prominent element of (3.17).

If $H_0 : \gamma = 0$ is true, then from (3.16) it follows that $y = Z\theta + \epsilon$, thus, upon introducing the $T \times 1$ vector

$$e_1 = [1, 0, \ldots, 0]' \tag{3.18}$$

and the $T \times T$ matrix

$$L = \begin{bmatrix} 0' & 0 \\ I_{T-1} & 0 \end{bmatrix} \tag{3.19}$$

it follows that

$$y_{-1} = (e_1 \otimes I_N)y_0 + (L \otimes I_N)Z\theta + (L \otimes I_N)\epsilon \quad \text{under } H_0 : \gamma = 0 \tag{3.20}$$

From (3.20), it becomes clear that $M_Z y_{-1}$ can be decomposed into three parts. The first is determined by y_0, the second is fixed and determined by θ and the third is stochastic and determined by σ_ϵ^2. It is the second component of $M_Z y_{-1}$ in particular which prevents $\hat{\gamma}$ from being suitable for producing operational inference on γ, because of its dependence on the unknown nuisance parameter θ.

However, this problem can be resolved by estimating γ not in model (3.16) but in the augmented model

$$y = y_{-1}\gamma + Z\theta + (L \otimes I_N)Z\theta^* + \epsilon = y_{-1}\gamma + W\bar{\theta} + \epsilon \tag{3.21}$$

with W a full column rank matrix that spans the same subspace as $Z^* = [Z : (L \otimes I_N)Z]$. The resulting least squares estimator of γ is

$$\hat{\gamma}_W = \gamma + \frac{y'_{-1} M_W \epsilon}{y'_{-1} M_W y_{-1}} \tag{3.22}$$

where $M_W = I_{NT} - W(W'W)^{-1}W'$. Note that $(L \otimes I_N)Z$ consists of Z transformed in such a way that each of its T blocks of N elements is replaced by the previous block (a one-period-lag), with the first block set at zero, and that

$$Z^* = [Z : (L \otimes I_N)Z] = [X : \iota_T \otimes I_N : (L \otimes I_N)X : L\iota_T \otimes I_N] \tag{3.23}$$

Now, since $L\iota_T$ is just the $T \times 1$ vector ι_T with the first element set at zero, it is the case that

$$e_1 \otimes I_N = (\iota_T \otimes I_N) - (L\iota_T \otimes I_N) \tag{3.24}$$

In other words, the columns of $[\iota_T \otimes I_N : L\iota_T \otimes I_N]$ span the same subspace as those of $[\iota_T \otimes I_N : e_1 \otimes I_N]$. It follows that

$$M_W(e_1 \otimes I_N) = 0 \qquad (3.25)$$

Moreover, from the definition of W it follows that

$$M_W(L \otimes I_N)Z = 0 \qquad (3.26)$$

and hence, using (3.20), $M_W y_{-1}$ simplifies to

$$M_W y_{-1} = M_W(L \otimes I_N)\epsilon \quad \text{under } H_0 : \gamma = 0 \qquad (3.27)$$

Substitution in (3.22) yields

$$\hat{\gamma}_W = \frac{\epsilon'(L \otimes I_N)' M_W \epsilon}{\epsilon'(L \otimes I_N)' M_W(L \otimes I_N)\epsilon} \quad \text{under } H_0 : \gamma = 0 \qquad (3.28)$$

which clearly is invariant with respect to y_0, δ, β and σ_ϵ^2. Hence, $\hat{\gamma}_W$ can be used as a test statistic and yields a so-called similar test procedure. As can be seen from (3.28), under $H_0 : \gamma = 0$ the test statistic is a ratio of two quadratic forms in normal variables; its distribution function can be assessed with great precision by numerical or simulation methods. The test statistic is obtained by estimating γ by least squares not in model (3.15) but in an augmented model, where the redundant regressors $(L \otimes I_N)X$ have been added to the specification and where the first observation of each individual has been discarded (adding the N regressors $e_1 \otimes I_N$ is equivalent to discarding the N first observations). Since the augmented regression involves at least $N + K + 1$ and probably $N + 2K + 1$ regressors, at least $2N$ observations are needed, so, due to the lags, a minimum number of three observations in the time dimension is required to calculate the test statistic.

Note that the regressor matrix W of (3.21) has to be composed such that one does not run into singularity problems. This could happen, if the original set of regressors X already includes particular variables in combination with their first-order lags. The latter variables are in the space spanned by $[e_1 \otimes I_N : (L \otimes I_N)X]$. Such problems can be dealt with in the following way. Consider formula (3.22) for $\hat{\gamma}_W$, with $Z^* = [Z : (L \otimes I_N)Z]$. Instead of calculating M_W directly as $I_{NT} - Z^*(Z^{*\prime}Z^*)^{-1}Z^{*\prime}$, where $Z^{*\prime}Z^*$ might be singular, first perform a singular value decomposition of the $NT \times 2(K + N)$ matrix Z^*, such that

$$Z^* = U\Lambda V \qquad (3.29)$$

where U is $NT \times 2(K + N)$ too, and Λ and V are $2(K + N) \times 2(K + N)$, such that $U'U = I_{2(K+N)}$ and $\Lambda = \text{diag}(\lambda_i)$, where the elements are ordered in such a way that $\lambda_i \neq 0$ for $i = 1, \ldots, m$ and $\lambda_i = 0$ for $i = m + 1, \ldots, 2(K + N)$. Partition U as $[U_1 : U_2]$, with U_1 the $NT \times m$ matrix consisting of the first m columns of U. In the calculation of statistic $\hat{\gamma}_W$ according to (3.22), the idempotent matrix M_W may now be established as

$$M_W = I_{NT} - U_1 U_1' \tag{3.30}$$

Note that

$$M_W Z^* = (I_{NT} - U_1 U_1')[U_1 : U_2]\Lambda V = ([U_1 : U_2] - U_1[I_m : 0])\Lambda V$$

$$= [U_1 : U_2]\Lambda V - [U_1 : 0]\Lambda V = 0 \tag{3.31}$$

as it should be. Also note that if certain exogenous regressor variables appear both current and lagged in the specification, then more than three observations on these variables in the time dimension are needed to estimate the augmented regression model.

It can easily be shown that, apart from $\hat{\gamma}_W$ itself, also the usual t-ratio of the estimator $\hat{\gamma}_W$ yields an exact similar test procedure. Unlike the null-distribution, the power of the proposed test statistics is *not* invariant with respect to θ and σ_ϵ^2; it will be assessed in Section 3.3 by running Monte Carlo simulations. The performance of the two similar tests will be compared with the asymptotic ($T \to \infty$) standard t-ratio for $\hat{\gamma}$ of (3.17) and an asymptotic ($N \to \infty$) GMM test procedure.

3.2.2   Derivation of the test statistics for $H_0 : \gamma = \gamma_0$

When testing $H_0 : \gamma = \gamma_0$, the derivation of exact similar tests is slightly more complicated. To investigate the finite sample distribution of $\hat{\gamma}$ of (3.17) in this case, the vector $M_Z y_{-1}$ is explored again. From (3.14), it follows that

$$
\begin{aligned}
y_1 &= y_0\gamma + X_1\beta + \epsilon_1 + \delta \\
y_2 &= y_1\gamma + X_2\beta + \epsilon_2 + \delta = y_0\gamma^2 + (X_1\beta + \epsilon_1)\gamma + (X_2\beta + \epsilon_2) + (1 + \gamma)\delta \\
y_3 &= \cdots
\end{aligned}
\tag{3.32}
$$

and, upon introducing

$$
\Gamma(\gamma) = \begin{bmatrix} 1 & 0 & \cdots & 0 \\ \gamma & 1 & \ddots & \vdots \\ \vdots & \ddots & \ddots & 0 \\ \gamma^{T-1} & \cdots & \gamma & 1 \end{bmatrix} \quad \text{and} \quad \Gamma_1(\gamma) = \begin{bmatrix} 1 \\ \gamma \\ \vdots \\ \gamma^{T-1} \end{bmatrix} \tag{3.33}
$$

it can straightforwardly be checked that

$$
\begin{aligned}
y &= \{\Gamma_1(\gamma) \otimes I_N\}\gamma y_0 + \{\Gamma(\gamma) \otimes I_N\}(X\beta + \epsilon) + \{\Gamma(\gamma) \otimes I_N\}(\iota_T \otimes \delta) \\
&= \{\Gamma_1(\gamma) \otimes I_N\}\gamma y_0 + \{\Gamma(\gamma) \otimes I_N\}Z\theta + \{\Gamma(\gamma) \otimes I_N\}\epsilon
\end{aligned} \quad (3.34)
$$

It follows that

$$
y_{-1} = \{\Gamma_1(\gamma) \otimes I_N\}y_0 + \{L\Gamma(\gamma) \otimes I_N\}Z\theta + \{L\Gamma(\gamma) \otimes I_N\}\epsilon \quad (3.35)
$$

with L as defined in (3.19). As in the case of testing $H_0 : \gamma = 0$, $M_Z y_{-1}$ can be decomposed into three parts. All three depend on γ; the first is also determined by y_0, the second is fixed and determined by θ and the third is stochastic and affected by σ_ϵ.

Again, $\hat{\gamma}$ of (3.17) is unsuitable for producing exact inference on γ and this problem can be resolved by estimating γ not in model (3.16) but in an augmented model

$$
y = y_{-1}\gamma + W\overline{\theta} + \epsilon \quad (3.36)
$$

with W such that it has full column rank and now spans the same subspace as

$$
Z^* = [Z : \{L\Gamma(\gamma_0) \otimes I_N\}Z] =
$$

$$
[X : \iota_T \otimes I_N : \{L\Gamma(\gamma_0) \otimes I_N\}X : L\Gamma(\gamma_0)\iota_T \otimes I_N] \quad (3.37)
$$

The resulting least squares estimator of γ is again given by (3.22), where $M_W = I_{NT} - W(W'W)^{-1}W'$ and W follows from (3.37). Using (3.35), $M_W y_{-1}$ simplifies to

$$
M_W y_{-1} = M_W \{L\Gamma(\gamma_0) \otimes I_N\}\epsilon \quad \text{under } H_0 : \gamma = \gamma_0 \quad (3.38)
$$

This can be seen as follows. It is obvious from the definition of W that $M_W\{L\Gamma(\gamma_0) \otimes I_N\}Z = 0$, and from $\Gamma_1(\gamma_0) = (\gamma_0 - 1)L\Gamma(\gamma_0)\iota_T + \iota_T$ it is found that $\Gamma_1(\gamma_0) \otimes I_N$ is in the column space spanned by Z^*. Substitution in (3.22) yields the test statistic

$$
\hat{\gamma}_W = \gamma_0 + \frac{\epsilon'\{L\Gamma(\gamma_0) \otimes I_N\}'M_W\epsilon}{\epsilon'\{L\Gamma(\gamma_0) \otimes I_N\}'M_W\{L\Gamma(\gamma_0) \otimes I_N\}\epsilon} \quad \text{under } H_0 : \gamma = \gamma_0 \quad (3.39)
$$

which is invariant with respect to y_0, δ, β and σ_ϵ^2. Clearly, the null-distribution of the test statistic is as straightforward as in the case of testing $H_0 : \gamma = 0$. It can be established numerically by the algorithm given in Davies (1980) or by simulation. The t-ratio of $\hat{\gamma}_W$ has the same invariance properties and its distribution can easily be simulated.

If $\gamma_0 = 0$, (3.39) boils down to the simple procedure described in the previous section, which can be performed when at least three observations in the time dimension are available for each individual. If $\gamma_0 \neq 0$, then the augmented regression includes at least $2N + K$ regressors and hence $T \geq 3$ is required. Since this regression also involves lags of the regressors and regressand, at least four waves should be available now. Note that $H_0 : \gamma = 1$ (a unit root in a panel data model) can straightforwardly be tested with this procedure and that it requires the redundant regressors $L\Gamma(1)\iota_T \otimes I_N$, where $\Gamma(1)\iota_T$ is a simple linear trend term. Moreover, the exact tests for $H_0 : \gamma = \gamma_0$ enable the construction of a confidence interval for γ with exact coverage probability.

3.3 The performance of the tests

To evaluate the performance of the above tests for the detection of dynamics in individual effects models, the simulation design described in Section 2.2.1 is used. The power of the test statistic $\hat{\gamma}_W$ given in (3.28) and its t-ratio are assessed for the case of testing $H_0 : \gamma = 0$ against $H_1 : \gamma > 0$. In order to evaluate the power performance, the t-ratio for $\hat{\gamma}$ of (3.17) and the t-ratio of the two-step GMM estimator are examined too. This is done for various values of the dynamic adjustment parameter γ. Whether the regressor variables are correlated with the individual effects is of no consequence, since all examined test statistics allow for fixed effects.

Figure 3.1 shows the cumulative distribution function of the t-ratio

$$t(\hat{\gamma}) = \hat{\gamma}/s(\hat{\gamma}) \qquad (3.40)$$

with $\hat{\gamma}$ the estimator in (3.17) and $s(\hat{\gamma})$ the estimated standard error of $\hat{\gamma}$; this test is asymptotically valid for $T \to \infty$. Figure 3.2 shows the cumulative distribution function of the t-ratio of the two-step GMM estimator for γ, which is asymptotically valid for $N \to \infty$. For the calculation of this estimator, model (3.13) is written in first differences and instruments in levels are employed; see, for instance, Arellano and Bond (1991). Finally, the cumulative distribution functions of the test statistics that are exact in finite samples, $\hat{\gamma}_W$ of (3.28) and its t-ratio, are shown in Figures 3.3 and 3.4 respectively. As mentioned before in Section 2.2.3, graphs of cumulative distributions are an elegant way to describe simulation results, because they contain more information than any table possibly can and because they do not need to be smoothed, as a density graph must.

From Figure 3.1, the actual exact 5% critical value of $t(\hat{\gamma})$ for testing $H_0 : \gamma = 0$ against $H_1 : \gamma > 0$ can be found as the argument for which the cumulative distribution function for $\gamma = 0$ equals 0.95. It is seen that this value is equal to $t(\hat{\gamma})^{0.95} \approx -3.5$. Of course, the actual critical value of a nonsimular test statistic can be established only in a simulation study, where all the parameters are known. Due to the downward bias of $\hat{\gamma}$, this actual critical value is far below the nominal value for $NT - (N+2) = 198$ degrees of freedom. This nominal value $t_{198}^{0.95} = 1.65$ is indicated in the figure too and this critical value at the nominal 5% level is seen to entail an actual significance level of virtually 0%. At the exact 5% critical value, the power of the t-ratio test is very high. For $\gamma = 0.2$, the probability of a type II error is 0.35, so the power is 0.65. For $\gamma = 0.4$ the power is equal to 0.98 and for $\gamma = 0.6$ it is 1. However, in practice the null-distribution of this t-ratio is unknown, so these power values are not operational. On the basis of the nominal 5% critical value, the type II error probability is 1 for $\gamma = 0.2$ up to 0.4; if $\gamma = 0.6$ the naive t-test still has only a 0.08 probability of concluding that $\gamma > 0$.

From Figure 3.2, the actual exact 5% critical value of the two-step GMM t-ratio for testing $H_0 : \gamma = 0$ against $H_1 : \gamma > 0$ can again be found as the argument for which the cumulative distribution function for $\gamma = 0$ equals 0.95. This value is seen to be $t(\hat{\gamma}_{GMM})^{0.95} \approx 1.2$. Since inference based on $\hat{\gamma}_{GMM}$ is only asymptotically accurate, the nominal critical value is simply $N^{0.95} = 1.65$. In the figure, this critical value at the nominal 5% level is seen to entail an actual significance level of roughly 1%. On the basis of the nominal 5% critical value, the type II error probability is 0.95 for $\gamma = 0.2$, 0.85 for $\gamma = 0.4$ and 0.7 for $\gamma = 0.6$. The (impracticable) procedure based on the exact $t(\hat{\gamma}_{GMM})^{0.95}$ critical value would entail power values of 0.2, 0.35 and 0.5 respectively.

The exact similar test statistic $\hat{\gamma}_W$ has the advantage that the null-distribution is known and independent of nuisance parameters and hence can be calculated in practical applications. So, in contrast to the 'exactified' $t(\hat{\gamma})$ and $t(\hat{\gamma}_{GMM})$ tests, this procedure is operational and its power can be materialised. From Figure 3.3, the exact 5% critical value for testing $H_0 : \gamma = 0$ against $H_1 : \gamma > 0$ is found. This critical value $\hat{\gamma}_W^{0.95}$ is approximately equal to -0.35. From Figure 3.3, it is also seen that the power is 0.3 for $\gamma = 0.2$ and 0.7 for $\gamma = 0.4$; for $\gamma = 0.6$, the power at the 5% level is equal to 0.94. So, although this procedure may have less power than the impracticable exact FE test, it performs much better than the 'exactified' GMM test. The FE and GMM t-ratios clearly fail when evaluated at their nominal critical values.

From Figure 3.4, it is seen that the exact similar t-ratio $t(\hat{\gamma}_W)$ performs even better than $\hat{\gamma}_W$. At the exact 5% critical value $t(\hat{\gamma}_W)^{0.95} \approx -3.9$, the power is 0.35 for $\gamma = 0.2$, 0.8 for $\gamma = 0.4$ and 0.95 for $\gamma = 0.6$. Therefore, from this simulation study, it can be concluded that the power performance of the exact test statistics developed in Section 3.2 is most encouraging.

Since the fixed effects estimator is inconsistent for finite T, both in regression model (3.16) and in the augmented model (3.21), it is quite remarkable that an exact test can be constructed from the latter. The inconsistency explains the rather odd location of the distribution functions in Figures 3.3 and 3.4.

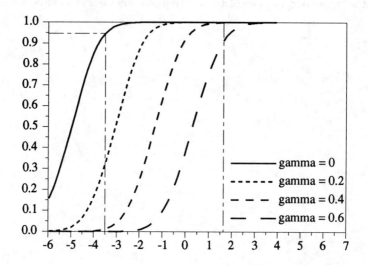

Figure 3.1: The cdf of the naive t-ratio $t(\hat{\gamma})$ for various values of γ

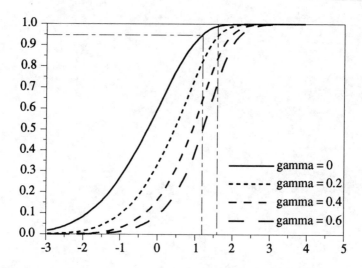

Figure 3.2: The cdf of the GMM t-ratio $t(\hat{\gamma}_{GMM})$ for various values of γ

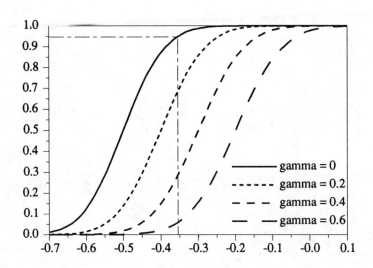

Figure 3.3: The cdf of the exact test statistic $\hat{\gamma}_W$ for various values of γ

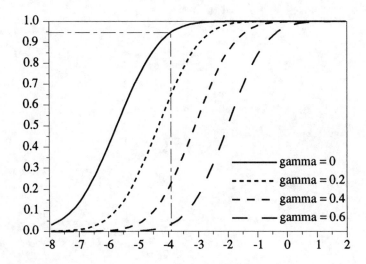

Figure 3.4: The cdf of the exact t-ratio $t(\hat{\gamma}_W)$ for various values of γ

Chapter 4

Description of the data

4.1 The Continuous Budget Survey

4.1.1 Introduction and sampling scheme

Since 1978, the Dutch Central Bureau of Statistics has held a budget survey each year, to obtain information on (changes in) spending habits of Dutch households. The variables measured by this Continuous Budget Survey (*Doorlopend Budgetonderzoek* or *DBO* in Dutch) include expenditure on all sorts of consumer goods, the level and composition of household income, the number and age of household members, and variables measuring socio-economic category, degree of urbanisation and geographical region. A household is defined as a group of two or more people living as a family and running a joint household, or a single person living on his or her own and running an independent household. The head of the household is defined as the person in the household who rents or owns the housing unit. If this is rented or owned by both members of a couple, the man is usually declared household head.

The sampling scheme consists of two stages. First a number of local authorities are selected, where the selection probability is proportional to the number of households within its jurisdiction, and then the actual households are selected. These are approached by census officials. Since completing the questionnaires and keeping a housekeeping book is somewhat time-consuming, roughly 70% of the households refuse to participate. Of the remaining households, about 50% are removed by the Central Bureau of Statistics in a pre-stratification, to compensate for the fact that ordinary families are usually more willing to join in than less common types of household. During the survey year, around 10% of the households fail to meet the obligations. So, in order to end up with a certain number of participating households, more than seven times as many have to be approached initially. Approximately three

49

thousand households participate each year. They are all asked to continue participation the next year, and over 50% are willing to do so. These households are again subjected to a pre-stratification, together with newly recruited households.

Households are not paid for their participation, though the census official brings a present generally three times a year, like a bunch of flowers, a towel or a frying-pan. If a household moves to another dwelling place, or if a household member leaves the household or dies during the survey period, the household remains in the sample. The income and expenditure of a person are included only over the period that he or she is a member of the household.

For the estimation and testing of dynamic panel data models, as is done in Chapter 7, a sample of households which have participated for at least three years is needed (see Chapter 3). Unfortunately, the Central Bureau of Statistics has changed the survey method several times. The years 1985 to 1987 form the only three-year-period with comparable survey characteristics. Of the 2570 households which participated in the 1987 Continuous Budget Survey, 1800 also participated in 1986, and of these 710 participated in 1985 as well. In order to facilitate comparison of static and dynamic Engel curves, the 710 households which participated from 1985 to 1987 were selected for estimation of both static and dynamic models. Of these, 11 were dropped because of inconsistent or absurd variable values. A sample of 699 'survivors' remains.

In the following chapters, the sample of survivors is assumed to be representative with respect to the estimated relationships and the behaviour of the disturbances. Possible selectivity or attrition biases are ignored; see Verbeek (1990), Verbeek (1991) and Verbeek and Nijman (1992).

4.1.2 Measurement of expenditures

Each participating household is allotted a specific month during which all expenses of the household, however small, are recorded in a housekeeping book and in pocket diaries. The adult(s) doing the bulk of the shopping keep the housekeeping book; other adults and older children keep pocket diaries, which may be sent directly to the census official. In the remaining eleven months, only expenditures above a certain threshold are reported. The household is also requested to give information on the length and type of holidays enjoyed. During holidays, expenditures are simply calculated as the difference between the amount of money taken from the bank and the amount of money brought back home, and this is categorised as holiday expenses.

The expenses during the recording month, the expenses above the threshold during the rest of the year and the length of holidays are inputs to a correction scheme, which has (estimated) annual expenditures on more than one hundred categories of consumer goods as outputs. Subsequently, these categories are aggregated on various levels. The highest level is total expenditure. On a lower level, six categories are distinguished: food; housing; clothing and shoes; hygiene and medical care; education, recreation (including holidays, television and stereo sets, toys and pets) and transport; other expenditures. On an even lower level, food, for example, is divided into bread and cereals, fruit and vegetables, drinks and sweets, oils and fats, meat and fish, dairy products, and other foodstuffs (including meals in restaurants, even when on some occasions family and friends are taken out to dinner).

In Table 4.1, the average annual expenditures on some categories of commodities are listed. For three consecutive years, this is done for two different samples, the first consisting of all participating households in each year, the second being the subsample of 699 survivors described in Section 4.1.1 above. The 699 households participating in all three years seem to spend a little less on almost all categories of consumer goods than the other households. This 'panel effect' is also found by Pol (1989), who mentions two possible explanations: keeping a diary for a long time may result in more conscious and careful spending, or households may become careless and forget to report some expenditures. No significant (self-)selection effect (i.e. survivors are different right from the start) is found by Pol (1989), but his analysis is based on the waves 1982 to 1984 of the Continuous Budget Survey. As will be seen in Section 4.1.3, the 699 survivors also have slightly lower incomes than the other households, in the same order of magnitude as their lower spending. Apparently, an explanation for the 'panel effect' can only be that poorer people are more willing to enrol for three years.

Returning to Table 4.1, it is seen that expenditure increases over the three years. For the subsample of 699 survivors, total expenditure in 1987 is 1.2% higher than in 1986, and in 1986 it is 2.5% higher than in 1985. This rising trend is hardly due to rising prices (see Section 4.2). Food constitutes approximately 18% of total expenditure. Of the six main categories, the largest share of total expenditure is devoted to housing: approximately 32%. Average expenditures in the country as a whole are calculated by weighting the sample of all participating households and are lower than in both samples considered here; for example, total average expenditure in 1987 is estimated as $f36432$ (see CBS (1990a)).

Table 4.1: Average expenditures over all households and over the sample of survivors

category of expenditures	1985		1986		1987	
	#	mean	#	mean	#	mean
bread and cereals	2852	1078	3003	1057	2570	1084
	699	1008	699	1032	699	1056
fruit and vegetables	2852	1069	3003	1052	2570	1075
	699	1035	699	1019	699	1043
drinks and sweets	2852	1577	3003	1595	2570	1525
	699	1524	699	1481	699	1432
oils and fats	2852	147	3003	108	2570	98
	699	132	699	110	699	103
meat and fish	2852	1617	3003	1527	2570	1515
	699	1498	699	1489	699	1458
dairy products	2852	1071	3003	1047	2570	1057
	699	1020	699	1033	699	1047
other foodstuffs	2852	1267	3003	1523	2570	1574
	699	1178	699	1217	699	1229
food	2852	7830	3003	7913	2570	7931
	699	7397	699	7385	699	7371
housing	2852	13261	3003	14022	2570	14030
	699	13125	699	13434	699	13240
clothing and shoes	2852	3019	3003	3296	2570	3383
	699	2845	699	3007	699	3151
hygiene and medical care	2852	5693	3003	5955	2570	6303
	699	5581	699	5750	699	6100
education, recreation and	2852	10756	3003	12017	2570	12038
transport	699	10559	699	10978	699	11145
other expenditures	2852	599	3003	600	2570	680
	699	502	699	462	699	512
total expenditure	2852	41162	3003	43805	2570	44367
	699	40011	699	41019	699	41521

Number of households and mean expenditure in guilders per annum

Table 4.2: Average annual gross and disposable income over all households
and over the sample of survivors

income variable	1985		1986		1987	
	#	mean	#	mean	#	mean
annual gross income	2852	57229	3003	62194	2570	63625
	699	55222	699	56810	699	58452
annual disposable income	2852	43972	3003	47467	2570	48460
	699	43012	699	44116	699	45329
Number of households and mean income in guilders per annum						

4.1.3 Measurement of income and household characteristics

The income questionnaire is completed during April of the following year, when
all necessary information has become available. The definition of household
income includes wages and other labour income, profit, income from property,
social security benefits, etc. Deduction of tax payments and social security
charges and aggregation over household members and months gives annual
disposable household income. In Table 4.2, average annual gross and disposable income are given for the years 1985 to 1987 for two different samples, the
first consisting of all participating households in each year, the second being
the subsample of 699 households participating in all three years. The 699
survivors have slightly lower incomes than the other households, which is consistent with the previous finding that they spend a little less. On average, gross
as well as disposable incomes have risen over the three years. Average gross
and disposable household incomes in the country as a whole are lower than in
both samples considered here; for example, the 1987 figures are calculated as
$f48600$ and $f37900$ respectively (see CBS (1990a)).

Several other household characteristics are measured by a number of categorical variables. Among them are:

household size: 1, 2, 3, 4, 5 or more persons

 # children younger than 16: 0, 1, 2, 3 or more

 # non-working unmarried children older than 16: 0, 1, 2 to 4, 5 or
more

age of head of household: younger than 30, from 30 to 35, from 35 to 40,
..., 65 and older

education of head of household: level 1, level 2.1, level 2.2, level 3.1, level 3.2

education of partner: no partner, level 1, level 2.1, level 2.2, level 3

profession of head of household: science and arts, politics and top management, administration, commerce, service, agriculture and fishing, manufacturing and transport, non-working

geographical region: NORTH (Groningen, Friesland, Drenthe), EAST (Overijssel, Gelderland, Flevoland), SOUTH (North-Brabant, Limburg), WEST (Utrecht, North-Holland, South-Holland, Zeeland, excluding the four major cities), MAJOR CITIES (Amsterdam, Rotterdam, the Hague, Utrecht)

degree of urbanisation: countryside, village, commuter town, small city, middle-sized city, big city

This information is collected at the beginning of each year. The education variables may require some additional explanation. Level 1 is just primary education, level 2.1 amounts to a few years secondary education, level 2.2 comprises full secondary education, level 3.1 includes bachelor's degrees and level 3.2 master's degrees. For more information on sampling scheme or method of measurement of any variable, see: CBS (1978), CBS (1988), CBS (1989) and CBS (1990a).

4.2 Data on prices

The Dutch Central Bureau of Statistics has been collecting data on consumer prices from 1937 onwards. These consumer price indices aim at reflecting changes in prices of goods and services consumed by households, value added taxes and subsidies being taken into account. Nowadays, these indices are constructed each month for three groups of people: the entire population, households of employees whose income is below the Dutch health insurance scheme threshold and households of employees whose income is above this threshold. For the purpose of this thesis, the series for the entire population of private households is relevant.

The consumer price indices are constructed in the following way. The price level of a particular commodity or category of commodities in the month under review is compared to the level in the base year, where the level in the base year is calculated as the mean over the twelve months of the weighted means

over all observed sales outlets in the country. The structure of a price index
in month t is

$$P(t) = \sum_{i=1}^{n} w_i \Pi_i(t) \quad \text{with} \quad \sum_{i=1}^{n} w_i = 1 \qquad (4.1)$$

Here, w_i is the share of good or category i in the value in the base year of
the total package of goods and services taken into account for this price index.
$\Pi_i(t)$ is the partial price index of good or category i in month t compared to
the base year. Since the weights are calculated as shares in the base year,
(4.1) can be seen as a Laspeyres price index. The weights for the series of
price indices for the entire population are directly calculated from the results
of the Continuous Budget Survey.

Generally, every five years a new base year is used. However, price indices
based on an earlier base year continue to be constructed for some time. In this
thesis, 1980 is used as the base year.

For the construction of partial price indices, three types of goods are distinguished:

'Ordinary' goods: Prices are observed once a month, namely on the Thursday of the week which contains the 15th of the month.

Goods with frequently changing prices: For potatoes, fresh vegetables,
fresh fruit, fish, flowers and plants, prices are observed once a week on
Thursday. Price indices are calculated as the mean of the observations
from the middle of the preceding month to the middle of the month under
review.

Goods with relatively constant prices: Prices are observed only once
every few months, always on the Thursday of the week which contains
the 15th of the month. Prices in not observed months are assumed to be
equal to the price in the latest observed month.

The number of observations for each commodity across the country varies from
one (goods with a uniform price or tariff) to about four hundred, depending on
the degree of price variation and on the relative importance of the particular
good or category of goods.

The price indices of potatoes, fresh vegetables, fresh fruit, flowers and
plants are corrected for seasonality. To achieve this, the price level in the
month under review is not compared to the level in the base year, but to the
level in the corresponding base month. Also, to mitigate the influence of random shocks, the indices in the month under review are averaged with those in
the two preceding months.

Unfortunately, the classification of goods for which partial price indices
are constructed is not identical to the classification of commodities in the

Table 4.3: Annual consumer price indices based on 1980=100

category of consumer goods	1985	1986	1987
bread and cereals	118.4	119.8	120.7
fruit and vegetables	117.3	110.3	110.3
meat and fish	114.1	114.1	113.0
dairy products	113.0	112.5	112.6
food	117.5	116.7	115.1
clothing and shoes	115.3	118.3	117.4
total expenditure	122.3	122.7	122.5

Continuous Budget Survey. Of the categories listed in Table 4.1, useful partial price indices are available only for bread and cereals, fruit and vegetables, meat and fish, dairy products, food, clothing and shoes and total expenditure. For these categories, annual price indices for 1985 to 1987 are listed in Table 4.3 and monthly price indices are shown in Figures 4.1 to 4.7; the figures are based on 1987=1.

As can be seen from the table and the figures, there is only little price variation over time for most categories of consumer goods. Only the prices of fruit and vegetables and clothing and shoes are rather volatile, and the latter fluctuation is mainly seasonal. Also, there seems to have been a considerable decrease in prices of fruit and vegetables between 1985 and 1986. In Figures 4.1 to 4.7 and also in Chapters 6 and 7, all prices are expressed on the basis 1987=1.

For more information on the consumer price indices constructed by the Central Bureau of Statistics, see CBS (1985), CBS (1990b) and Donkers (1981).

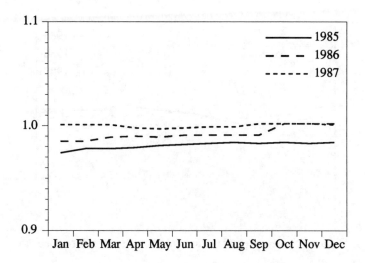

Figure 4.1: Monthly price indices of bread and cereals

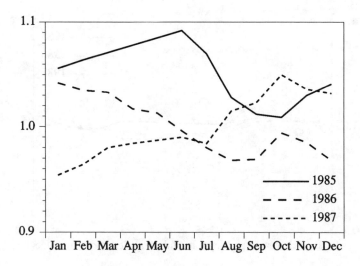

Figure 4.2: Monthly price indices of fruit and vegetables

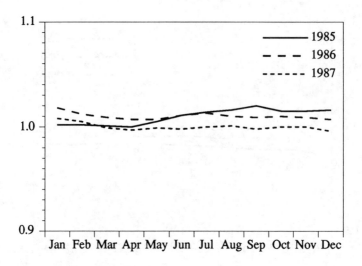

Figure 4.3: Monthly price indices of meat and fish

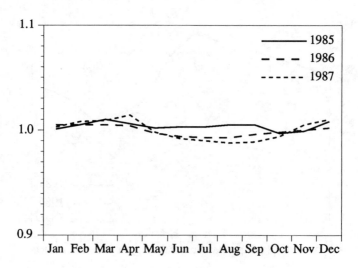

Figure 4.4: Monthly price indices of dairy products

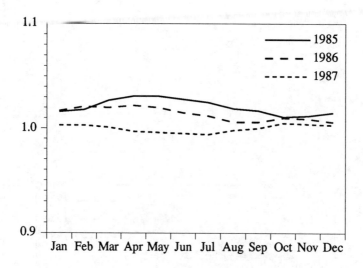

Figure 4.5: Monthly price indices of food

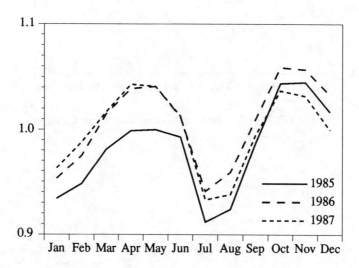

Figure 4.6: Monthly price indices of clothing and shoes

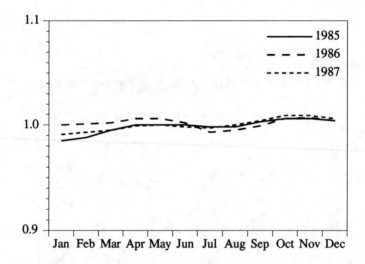

Figure 4.7: Monthly price indices of total expenditure

Chapter 5

Some theory on Engel curves

5.1   A short history of functional form

Naturally, any history of Engel curves should begin with the work of Engel himself. On Sunday 22 November 1857, his text 'Die Productions- und Consumtionsverhältnisse des Königreichs Sachsen' appeared as numbers 8 and 9 of the *Zeitschrift des Statistischen Büreaus des Königlich Sächsischen Ministeriums des Innern*, the journal of the institute of which he was the director. In this form, it is practically unavailable nowadays, but it was reprinted as 'Anlage I' to Engel (1895). His point of departure was one of the questions of the day, i.e. whether or not the Malthus postulate that a population would grow faster than its means of existence is true. Systematically arranging and studying detailed household budget data, collected by the statisticians Ducpetiaux and Le Play, he found that 'je ärmer eine Familie ist, einen desto grösseren Antheil von der Gesammtausgabe muss zur Beschaffung der Nahrung aufgewendet werden'[1] and concluded that 'einen je geringeren Procentsatz ... von sämmtlichen Ausgaben die Ausgaben für Nahrung ... in Anspruch nehmen ..., desto wohlhabender ist dies Volk und umgekehrt'.[2] Later, this was to become known as Engel's Law, and it was to be rephrased as 'food expenditure increases with income, but at a lesser rate, i.e. that food demand is inelastic with respect to income'.[3] Also later, 'the relation of any category of expenditure to income in a cross-section sample of households of varying income levels'[4] was to become known as an Engel curve.

In Engel (1895), the analysis is considerably more refined. Supposing that the nutritional value a person needs is a function of length and weight, and

---

[1]Engel (1895, Anlage I, p. 28).
[2]Engel (1895, Anlage I, p. 50).
[3]Cramer (1969, p. 107).
[4]Cramer (1969, p. 107).

using data on those variables for young people in Belgium collected by A.
Quetelet, he constructed a measure for food necessity he called *Quet* that
varies from 1 for newborn children to 3 for adult females and 3.5 for adult
males. Occupation, social class, geographical situation and the total number
of *Quets* in a household are supposed to influence food consumption, and tables of nutritional value and price of several types of bread, potatoes etc. help
to establish the money value of this consumption. Together with expenditure
on other categories of commodities (clothing, housing, heating and lighting,
physical and mental care, recreation and transport, and other expenses), the
so-called *Kostenwerth* of families is established. This is compared to the *Er-
tragswerth*, determined by the price of labour and characterised by sex, age,
occupation, race and geographical area.

The emphasis is on data from Belgium for the years 1853, 1886 and 1891,
because these were the best data available at the time. According to the pref-
ace, Engel had ambitious plans to analyse data for the United States, Germany,
France, Switzerland, England, the Netherlands, Scandinavia and Russia in the
future. However, these plans were never realised. Owing to his bad health, he
was incapacitated and — because of that — he lacked sufficient technical support (that is, computer assistants). In the eyes of a modern econometrician, it
is almost touching how he acknowledges his Thomas-Burckhardt and Billeter
adding machines, the last one especially designed for fast (!) processing of
less-than-five-digit-numbers.

For a long time, economists did not seem to be particularly interested in
the subject, until Allen and Bowley (1935) carried out a thorough analysis
of family budgets again. They estimated linear Engel curves, but were aware
that the linear form was only a first approximation.

The next major source in the literature is Working (1943), who uses the
mass of statistical data on family expenditures then available in the United
States and attempts to draw from this great body of data some significant gen-
eralisations, which may deserve to be regarded as laws of family expenditure.
He states that, 'as total expenditure per person increases, the proportion of
expenditure devoted to food decreases rapidly',[5] but no reference to Engel is
made. According to Working (1943), the relationship of food expenditure to
total expenditure is 'remarkable for the uniformity and closeness with which
it approximates the relation

$$\frac{F}{T} = a - b \log T$$

where F represents expenditure for food and T represents total expenditure'.[6]

---

[5]Working (1943, p. 45).
[6]Working (1943, p. 45).

Prais (1952) states that there is a saturation level of consumption for any particular commodity which is never exceeded, however high the consumer's income. He argues that it is advisable to choose a mathematical formula for Engel curves which possesses that asymptotic property. The desirability of an upper asymptote is most apparent in the case of necessities. Without paying any attention to Working (1943), Prais and Houthakker (1955) conclude that a semi-logarithmic form is suitable for necessities and that a (double) logarithmic form best describes demand for luxuries. A (double) logarithmic Engel curve gives a constant income elasticity, whereas a semi-logarithmic curve yields a decline of the elasticity, indicating the onset of saturation.

Aitchison and Brown (1954, p. 36) state that 'a form of Engel curve which possesses an upper asymptote and at the same time is capable of describing luxuries and necessities will be both elegant and useful'. Next, they say that a sigmoid Engel curve is compatible with an asymptotic saturation level of consumption and can describe demand for both necessities and luxuries: a sigmoid form implies that a typical commodity behaves as a luxury at low incomes and as a necessity at high incomes, where 'low' and 'high' are relative concepts, depending on the commodity in question. The cumulative distribution function of the lognormal distribution is sigmoid in shape, passes through the origin and approaches an asymptote of unity. Therefore, Aitchison and Brown (1954) conclude, it serves as a perfect basis for estimating Engel curves.

Investigating the properties of various forms of Engel functions, Leser (1963, p. 694) postulates that Engel functions for various commodity groups should 'have the same mathematical form and satisfy the additivity criterion'. He thinks that 'the errors, representing individual variations in tastes as differences between observed and habitual expenditure patterns, may be assumed to be proportional to total outlay on all goods and services'[7] and considers the following specifications:

$$w_i = \alpha_i + \beta_i M + \epsilon_i \tag{5.1}$$

$$v_i = \alpha_i + \beta_i M + \epsilon_i \tag{5.2}$$

$$w_i = \alpha_i + \beta_i / M + \epsilon_i \tag{5.3}$$

$$\ln w_i = \alpha_i + \beta_i \ln M - \ln \left(\sum_j \exp(\alpha_j + \beta_j \ln M) \right) + \epsilon_i \tag{5.4}$$

$$w_i = \alpha_i + \beta_i \ln M + \epsilon_i \tag{5.5}$$

where v_i is expenditure on commodity group i, M is income and $w_i = v_i/M$ represents expenditure proportions.[8] Given the error specification adopted

---

[7]Leser (1963, p. 695).

[8]Here, the notation of Leser (1963) and subsequent literature is followed. In Section 5.2 and the remainder of the thesis, income is denoted by x and expenditure by y.

by Leser (1963), (5.1) is linear, but otherwise he does not consider it very
attractive. Equation (5.2) is the linear form used by Allen and Bowley (1935),
and (5.3) is a version of it compatible with the error specification adopted
here. The (double) logarithmic function (5.4), adjusted for additivity, gives
constant elasticities and is incompatible with zero observations. Finally, (5.5)
is the form used by Working (1943). Using data on household expenditure
on 10 commodity groups in Ireland, of which 'it is realised that they contain
recording errors, particularly for alcoholic drinks',[9] he finds that the Working
specification (5.5) performs best, although the choice between (5.3) and (5.5)
is not always easy. He concludes that the fit could be further improved if a
combination of (5.3) and (5.5) was used, yielding

$$w_i = \alpha_i + \beta_i \ln M + \gamma_i / M + \epsilon_i \qquad (5.6)$$

However, this three-parameter Engel curve did not catch on in those days,
because — in the words of Cramer (1969, p. 143) — 'it is standard practice to
reduce the mass of data (on individual households) to manageable proportions
by taking group means over a much smaller number of distinct classes; published survey results almost invariably take the form of cell means for a given
classification of the sample households, and the individual household records
are seldom accessible. As a result most Engel curves are fitted to group means'.
With only four groups available, as in the case of the Irish data of Leser (1963),
one would hardly be inclined to increase the number of parameters beyond two.

The literature discussed above has produced a good deal of empirical evidence to support the proposition that for a wide range of commodities, income
elasticities are declining functions of income. As Brown and Deaton (1972, p.
1173) put it: 'Certainly we might extend Engel's law for food consumption,
namely that its income elasticity is less than unity, by the further proposition
that the income elasticity of food consumption ... declines as income increases.
... the evidence consists partly of the fact that ... Engel curves with declining
income elasticities fit budgetary data better than curves with constant elasticities, and partly that, over time or across countries, the results of a number of
budget studies display a negative association between average income and the
elasticity at average income'. A more recent illustration of this phenomenon is
given in Blundell (1988, p. 36, Table 3b). The hypothesis of declining income
elasticity is consistent with but weaker than the hypothesis of a saturation
level of demand.

In the 1970's and early 1980's, attention shifted from gathering empirical
evidence about functional form of Engel curves towards studying the theoretical implications of different functional forms. In the words of Deaton (1986,

---

[9]Leser (1963, p. 696).

p. 1799): 'More recent work on Engel curves has reflected the concern in the rest of the literature with the theoretical plausibility of the specification'. This brought about a renewed interest in Working's specification (5.5) because of its easy compliance with the requirements of a complete consumer demand system. If $\sum \alpha_i = 1$ and $\sum \beta_i = 0$ in (5.5), then the budget shares sum to unity. Therefore, as Deaton and Muellbauer (1980, p. 19) and Muellbauer (1980, p. 162) have made clear, this functional form is consistent with adding-up. Also, without the error term, the specification can be written as

$$v_i = \alpha_i M + \beta_i M \ln M$$

and the income elasticity follows as

$$\frac{M}{v_i} \frac{\partial v_i}{\partial M} = \frac{\alpha_i + \beta_i + \beta_i \ln M}{\alpha_i + \beta_i \ln M}$$

so that it allows luxuries ($\beta_i > 0$), necessities ($\beta_i < 0$) and even inferior goods: see Deaton and Muellbauer (1980, Figure 1.12). Gorman (1981) investigates polynomial Engel curves and finds that equations with more than three terms in income are degenerate in the sense that the matrix of coefficients linking each demand to each power of income cannot be of rank greater than 3. On the other hand, a functional form such as

$$w_i = \alpha_i + \beta_i \ln M + \gamma_i (\ln M)^2 \tag{5.7}$$

is allowed without restrictions on the coefficients. Of course, the Working form is a special case of it.

In recent years, highly sophisticated estimation techniques have become available. This has revived interest in the empirical estimation of Engel curves and more and more large samples of data on individual households are being analysed at the microeconomic level. Witte and Cramer (1986) are concerned with Engel curves for foodstuffs and assess the empirical performance of ten different functional forms, some of which are special cases of others, using the well-known Box-Cox transformation and maximum likelihood estimation. Assuming that the disturbance term is independently normally distributed and using the asymptotic likelihood ratio test, they conclude that the 'simple two-parameter Engel functions are all soundly rejected. ...The reason why the route to Working's function is blocked is that the transformation of the budget share is apparently essential. All acceptable functions ...have a Box-Cox transform of w_i as the dependent variable'.[10] They are aware that such transformations would not fit easily into the framework of a complete demand system.

---

[10]Witte and Cramer (1986, p. 912).

Using the same data set as Witte and Cramer (1986), i.e. the 1980 Budget Survey for the Netherlands, Bierens and Pott-Buter (1990) come to a rather different conclusion. Their model is derived directly from the data, without restricting its functional form. The nonparametric regression results are then translated to suitable parametric specifications, which are estimated by least squares. Various parameter restrictions are tested in order to simplify the models, which yields very simple final Engel curves, namely linear functions of income and the number of children in two age groups.

The nonparametric analysis of Banks, Blundell and Lewbel (1992) suggests that Engel curves with expenditure shares as the dependent variable should not be linear but quadratic in the logarithm of total expenditure, as in (5.7), although 'it is equally clear that for certain items, in particular food expenditures, linearity is unlikely to be rejected'.[11] Of course, this linearity is in fact the Working form.

If a conclusion is to be drawn from the literature reviewed above, then it should be that there is no clear-cut evidence supporting any particular functional form of Engel curve, although there seems to be more support for the Working form than there is for any other single specification. In addition, dynamic Engel curves are hardly considered in the literature. Even in the highly sophisticated analysis of Blundell, Pashardes and Weber (1993), based on a time series of repeated cross sections covering some 4000 households in each of 15 years, only static relationships are estimated.

5.2 Functional form of Engel curves in this thesis

5.2.1 Functional form of expenditure and income

As discussed in Section 5.1, commonly used functional forms of Engel curves for non-durable consumer goods are linear, logarithmic, semi-logarithmic and Working specifications. It is possible to construct two general functional form specifications of which these (and others) are a special case. These general specifications are given by

$$y = \alpha + \beta x + \gamma \ln x + \delta x \ln x + \epsilon \tag{5.8}$$

and

$$\ln y = \alpha + \beta x + \gamma \ln x + \delta x \ln x + \epsilon \tag{5.9}$$

---

[11] Banks, Blundell and Lewbel (1992, p. 21).

where y denotes household expenditure on (a particular category of) non durables, x denotes household income and ϵ is an error term. Remember that in Section 5.1, as in Leser (1963) and subsequent literature, income was denoted by M and expenditure by v. A disadvantage of specification (5.9) is that it is unable to cope with zero observations on expenditure.

Special cases of (5.8) are the linear specification

$$y = \alpha + \beta x + \epsilon \qquad (5.10)$$

the semi-logarithmic specification

$$y = \alpha + \gamma \ln x + \epsilon$$

and the Working specification

$$y = \beta x + \delta x \ln x + \epsilon \qquad (5.11)$$

which is usually written as

$$s = \beta + \delta \ln x + u \qquad (5.12)$$

where $s = y/x$ represents the share of expenditure on (the category of) non-durables in income and $u = \epsilon/x$ is a scaled error term. Although formulation (5.12) is consistent with the error specification adopted by Leser (1963), a disadvantage is that the dependent variable is restricted to the interval $(0,1)$ and the regressor variable is always positive (supposing income greater than 1), which most likely gives a skewed residual distribution. When the Working specification is formulated as (5.11), this problem can be avoided. Apart from the error specification, adding an intercept to (5.11) is equivalent to adding a regressor $1/x$ to (5.12), which gives the general specification (5.6) proposed by Leser (1963) and also considered by Muellbauer (1980, p. 169). This is not regarded as a separate case here, because a zero intercept is not imposed in any estimated Engel curve in this thesis.

Special cases of (5.9) are the semi-logarithmic specification

$$\ln y = \alpha + \beta x + \epsilon \qquad (5.13)$$

the logarithmic specification

$$\ln y = \alpha + \gamma \ln x + \epsilon$$

and what could be called a 'logarithmic Working' specification

$$\ln y = \beta x + \delta x \ln x + \epsilon \qquad (5.14)$$

The semi-logarithmic specification (5.13) is incompatible with Engel's Law, except for very large positive values of α and very small positive values of β, so it should only be used for luxury goods. The 'logarithmic Working' specification (5.14) has never, as far as is known, been used in practical applications. So, (5.8) comprises more commonly used powerful specifications than (5.9).

Of course, more special cases can be constructed by imposing other restrictions. For example, imposing $\alpha = \beta = 0$ in (5.8) or (5.9) leads to even more specifications of the Working type.

Estimating the general specifications (5.8) and (5.9) has some obvious advantages. Estimation of a general model and testing whether restrictions are allowed reduce the chances of misspecification. Furthermore, the commonly used functional specifications can easily be compared and tested. Therefore, Chapter 6 describes the trials (and errors) of estimating static Engel curves for food for the 1987 Continuous Budget Survey, starting with the general functional form specifications (5.8) and (5.9).

5.2.2 The role of household characteristics other than income

Taking account of the information given in Section 4.1.3, other household characteristics for which data are available and which may influence household expenditure can be classified as follows.

Household size: Available variables are household size as such (the number of persons), the number of children younger than 16 and the number of non-working unmarried children older than 16. To avoid multicollinearity problems among these three variables, household size as such should be replaced by a variable measuring the number of adults, constructed as household size minus number of children. However, the number of non-working unmarried children older than 16 is categorised inconveniently for this purpose. Therefore, the number of adults has been computed as household size minus number of children younger than 16, so it includes children older than 16. Next, dummy variables for number of adults and number of children younger than 16 have been constructed. To avoid a dummy representing too few households (leading to perfect multicollinearity when including interaction terms in the model specification), households with 3 or more adults are treated as a single class, as well as households with 2 or more children. The loss of explanatory power suffered by treating adults and older children as equivalents is presumably minor.

Age: Age is supposed to influence expenditure through changing needs, for quantity as well as quality. Therefore, dummy variables measuring the age of the head of the household in five-year intervals (see Section 4.1.3) have been constructed.

Socio-economic background: People with a different background may make different buying decisions and may have different needs. Dummy variables for the education of the head of the household as well as of the partner (if applicable) and for the profession of the head of the household are supposed to capture this effect. Analogous to the available information on the education of partners, household head's education levels 3.1 and 3.2 are represented by a single dummy.

Area: Dummy variables for the geographical region and the degree of urbanisation are supposed to capture differences in prices as well as in habits across the country.

Correction of measurement errors: Dummy variables for the month during which all expenses in the household were recorded may capture any imperfections in the correction scheme designed by the Central Bureau of Statistics (see Section 4.1.1). These dummies are expected to be less important for commodities with a relatively high price per piece, because expenditures above a certain threshold are recorded during the whole year. A variable measuring the number of days household members were on holiday (and therefore not recording anything on categories other than holiday expenses) may be useful too.

In Table 5.1, the dummy variables are listed, with the number of households in the sample for which a dummy equals 1 in the last column. (See Section 4.1.1 for the construction of the sample of 699 households.) From this table it is seen that the base group, where all dummy variables are zero, consists of households comprising a single non-working adult younger than 30, with first level education and no children, situated in one of the major cities Amsterdam, Rotterdam, the Hague or Utrecht and recording all expenses in December 1987.

Table 5.2 provides some insight into the distribution of annual disposable household income in the different subsamples that can be constructed according to the dummy variables: mean (in $f1000$), standard deviation (in $f1000$) and coefficient of variation ($\times 100\%$) of income are listed for each subsample. It is seen that household income increases strongly with the number of adults, which is not surprising: more adults means more people to earn money. Households with different numbers of children show only minor differences in income. Income first increases with age, reaches a top level in the age group from 45

Table 5.1: Dummy variables in the general specifications

variable name	description of variable	#
base group	1 adult in the household	116
ADULTS2	2 adults in the household	468
ADULTS3	3 or more adults in the household	115
base group	no children younger than 16	377
CHILDREN1	1 child younger than 16	97
CHILDREN2	2 or more children younger than 16	225
base group	age of household head < 30	59
AGE30	$30 \leq$ age of household head < 35	120
AGE35	$35 \leq$ age of household head < 40	123
AGE40	$40 \leq$ age of household head < 45	86
AGE45	$45 \leq$ age of household head < 50	52
AGE50	$50 \leq$ age of household head < 55	38
AGE55	$55 \leq$ age of household head < 60	42
AGE60	$60 \leq$ age of household head < 65	55
AGE65	age of household head ≥ 65	124
base group	education of household head level 1	93
EDUCATIONH21	education of household head level 2.1	135
EDUCATIONH22	education of household head level 2.2	290
EDUCATIONH3	education of household head level 3	181
base group	no partner in the household	135
EDUCATIONP1	education of partner level 1	80
EDUCATIONP21	education of partner level 2.1	174
EDUCATIONP22	education of partner level 2.2	221
EDUCATIONP3	education of partner level 3	89
PROFSCIENCE	science and arts	157
PROFMANAGEMENT	politics and top management	27
PROFADMIN	administration	80
PROFCOMMERCE	commerce	30
PROFSERVICE	service	19
PROFAGRICULTURE	agriculture and fishing	23
PROFMANUFACT	manufacturing and transport	132
base group	non-working	231
REGIONNORTH	household is situated in the north	67
REGIONEAST	household is situated in the east	140
REGIONSOUTH	household is situated in the south	181
REGIONWEST	household is situated in the west	200
base group	situated in one of the four major cities	111

Table 5.1: Continued

variable name	description of variable	#
URBCOUNTRY	situated in the countryside	76
URBVILLAGE	situated in a village	119
URBCOMMUTERTOWN	situated in a commuter town	71
URBSMALLCITY	situated in a small city	61
URBMIDDLECITY	situated in a middle-sized city	144
base group	situated in a big city	228
MONTHJAN	recording month is January	60
MONTHFEB	recording month is February	61
MONTHMAR	recording month is March	60
MONTHAPR	recording month is April	57
MONTHMAY	recording month is May	61
MONTHJUN	recording month is June	60
MONTHJUL	recording month is July	46
MONTHAUG	recording month is August	47
MONTHSEP	recording month is September	70
MONTHOCT	recording month is October	56
MONTHNOV	recording month is November	69
base group	recording month is December	52

Number of households in the sample for which a dummy equals 1 in the last column

to 50 years and decreases thereafter. The top income age group also shows
the highest variation in income (54% of the mean). As was to be expected,
higher education generally leads to higher incomes. Note that the education
of partner base group consists of households without a partner, which explains
the low level of average income of this group. As far as profession is concerned,
the highest incomes are earned by top managers, politicians and — believe it
or not! — academics, whereas, not surprisingly, the non-working base group
receives the lowest incomes. Nevertheless, this non-working group has the
highest relative variation in income among its members, which is no surprise
either when it is realised that they range from unemployed school leavers to
pensioned top managers. Income is more or less evenly distributed across geographical regions and degrees of urbanisation, but in the major and other
big cities average household income is slightly lower than in the rest of the
country. As it should be, no clear relationship can be seen between recording
month and income.

Table 5.3 gives means and standard deviations of the continuous explanatory variables in the general specifications (5.8) and (5.9), including the variable measuring the length of holidays. From this table, it is seen that the
average number of days household members were on holiday in 1987 was just
over 15.

Apart from the dummies listed in Table 5.1 and the continuous variables
listed in Table 5.3, a number of interaction terms have been included in the
general specifications. Interaction dummies between the number of adults
and age, between the number of children and age and between geographical
region and degree of urbanisation were constructed, because these variables are
thought to influence household expenditure simultaneously and interactively.
Where inclusion would have led to perfect multicollinearity, interaction terms
were omitted. Interaction dummies between education and profession were not
constructed in the first place, because these variables are too closely related.
Also, interaction terms of the holiday length variable and all dummies listed
in Table 5.1 with income were included. A summary of the interaction terms
is given in Table 5.4.

The income interactions can either be with income untransformed, or with
the natural logarithm of income. In this way four different general specifications, each with 135 explanatory variables, result: specification (5.8) with
linear income interactions, specification (5.8) with logarithmic income interactions, specification (5.9) with linear income interactions and specification (5.9)
with logarithmic income interactions.

Table 5.2: Distribution of 1987 household income in different subsamples

subsample	#	mean	standard deviation	variation
full sample	699	45.3	19.1	42.1%
base group	116	27.2	13.0	47.9%
ADULTS2	468	47.6	17.1	36.0%
ADULTS3	115	54.5	20.6	37.7%
base group	377	43.0	20.5	47.6%
CHILDREN1	97	49.4	20.3	41.2%
CHILDREN2	225	47.5	15.4	32.3%
base group	59	41.0	13.3	32.4%
AGE30	120	46.1	15.6	33.8%
AGE35	123	49.1	15.2	30.9%
AGE40	86	53.1	19.7	37.1%
AGE45	52	56.3	30.4	54.0%
AGE50	38	47.4	19.1	40.3%
AGE55	42	45.9	19.8	43.2%
AGE60	55	39.2	18.2	46.5%
AGE65	124	34.8	15.5	44.4%
base group	93	33.5	14.9	44.5%
EDUCATIONH21	135	39.4	16.2	41.0%
EDUCATIONH22	290	43.7	16.3	37.3%
EDUCATIONH3	181	58.5	20.0	34.3%
base group	135	28.6	13.3	46.5%
EDUCATIONP1	80	41.0	14.1	34.5%
EDUCATIONP21	174	46.1	13.3	28.9%
EDUCATIONP22	221	49.4	19.0	38.5%
EDUCATIONP3	89	63.1	19.6	31.0%
PROFSCIENCE	157	56.7	20.9	36.8%
PROFMANAGEMENT	27	66.1	25.3	38.3%
PROFADMIN	80	51.3	16.6	32.4%
PROFCOMMERCE	30	45.0	18.1	40.2%
PROFSERVICE	19	47.6	15.5	32.5%
PROFAGRICULTURE	23	42.8	15.7	36.7%
PROFMANUFACT	132	43.3	10.9	25.2%
base group	231	34.3	14.7	42.8%
REGIONNORTH	67	42.6	17.9	42.0%
REGIONEAST	140	44.5	15.7	35.3%
REGIONSOUTH	181	47.3	19.8	41.7%
REGIONWEST	200	46.7	20.7	44.4%
base group	111	42.2	19.1	45.3%

Table 5.2: Continued

subsample	#	mean	standard deviation	variation
URBCOUNTRY	76	45.1	16.5	36.6%
URBVILLAGE	119	48.7	21.6	44.4%
URBCOMMUTERTOWN	71	48.5	21.4	44.2%
URBSMALLCITY	61	46.9	22.9	48.8%
URBMIDDLECITY	144	45.8	17.2	37.6%
base group	228	42.0	17.3	41.3%
MONTHJAN	60	46.1	18.1	39.3%
MONTHFEB	61	43.3	20.3	46.8%
MONTHMAR	60	44.3	19.7	44.5%
MONTHAPR	57	44.4	16.4	36.9%
MONTHMAY	61	47.8	18.0	37.6%
MONTHJUN	60	46.7	19.5	41.8%
MONTHJUL	46	46.7	19.9	42.7%
MONTHAUG	47	42.6	14.7	34.4%
MONTHSEP	70	47.5	21.1	44.4%
MONTHOCT	56	44.5	17.6	39.7%
MONTHNOV	69	45.2	24.7	54.7%
base group	52	44.0	15.2	34.6%

Number of households, mean and standard deviation in $f1000$ and coefficient of variation $\times$ 100%

Table 5.3: Continuous explanatory variables in the general specifications

continuous explanatory variables	mean	standard deviation
INCOME (annual disposable income in $f1000$)	45.3	19.1
ln(INCOME)	3.7	0.4
INCOME $\times$ ln(INCOME)	176.7	94.7
HOL: total length of holidays	15.1	15.7

Table 5.4: Interaction terms in the general specifications

group of interactions	# continuous terms	# dummy terms
holiday length × income	1	
number of adults × age		14
number of adults × income	2	
number of children × age		11
number of children × income	2	
age × income	8	
education of head × income	3	
education of partner × income	4	
profession of head × income	7	
region × degree of urbanisation		13
region × income	4	
degree of urbanisation × income	5	
recording month × income	11	

5.2.3 The role of prices

The goal of this thesis is not to study price effects. However, it is considered important to eliminate possible biases caused by ignoring them.

As set out in Section 4.2, price indices for categories of commodities are available for each month. In the estimation of Engel curves, these indices can be used in two different ways. Firstly, expenditure and income may be deflated by the appropriate price indices. Secondly, the relative price may be included as a regressor.

In a world with rapidly increasing prices over time, a time-series regression of expenditure on income will tend to go through the origin, if based on nominal rather than real data. Therefore, income effects and elasticities estimated in a nominal time-series regression will be biased towards 1. However, for several reasons, the Engel curves estimated in Chapters 6 and 7 are unlikely to suffer much from this potential bias. Firstly, they are estimated on the basis of cross-section and panel data rather than time series. Secondly, as shown in Section 4.2, the prices of most categories of commodities do *not* increase rapidly over the years 1985 to 1987; in fact, for total expenditure and some categories they hardly change at all. Therefore, income and total food expenditure are not deflated. If Engel curves for other categories of commodities were estimated, then expenditures of a household on a particular category of commodities should be deflated with the price index of that category in the recording month of that household. This is especially important for both fruit and vegetables and clothing and shoes.

To capture price effects, the price index of the category of consumer goods under review divided by the price index of total expenditure should be included as a regressor. However, several problems arise in this respect.

First of all, the available price indices for seasonal products such as fruit and vegetables are corrected for seasonality. Therefore, the relative price regressor will be unable to explain an increase in demand for strawberries in the summer, caused by low prices.

Secondly, when estimating static Engel curves based on cross-section data, a price variable cannot be included. An annual price variable would be perfectly multicollinear with the constant term. And, since dummy variables for the recording month are included in the regressions (see Section 5.2.2), inclusion of a price variable which is equal for households with the same recording month would also lead to perfect multicollinearity. To see this, assume the values of the price index are given by P_t, with $t = 1, \ldots, 12$ denoting months. For household i the regressor variable PRICE will equal P_t if the recording month for household i is t. Now, the regressor variable PRICE can be written as a linear combination of the eleven recording month dummies and the intercept:

$$\text{PRICE} = P_1 \text{ MONTHJAN} + \ldots + P_{11} \text{ MONTHNOV}$$

$$+P_{12}(\text{ INTERCEPT} - \text{MONTHJAN} - \ldots - \text{MONTHNOV})$$

In theory, it might be worth trying to see whether one monthly price variable is able to replace eleven recording month dummies. Since there are many more possible reasons for seasonal patterns in expenditure than price only, this option is not considered fruitful here. When panel data are used, the price indices $P_1 \ldots P_{12}$ are different for each year, so perfect multicollinearity problems do not arise.

Summing up, a price regressor could be included in Engel curves based on panel data (static as well as dynamic). For reasons mentioned before, this will not be done in Engel curves for total expenditure on food. However, a monthly price variable should be included in Engel curves for categories such as fruit and vegetables.

5.2.4   Model selection procedure

Broadly speaking, the model selection methodology followed in Chapter 6 will be as follows. First, each of the four different general specifications with 135 explanatory variables is estimated. These four models are compared and one of them is chosen. The comparison involves measurement of explanatory power and testing for nonnormality and heteroscedasticity. Next, the chosen model is subjected to a sequential procedure of testing and imposing restrictions. In the general model, each continuous variable, each group of dummies representing a certain household characteristic and each group of interaction terms is tested separately. The continuous variable or group of variables with the lowest significance (measured as the highest p-value) is restricted to have zero coefficient(s), if common sense agrees (for instance, a group of dummies stays in the specification at least as long as any interaction term involving the dummies). In the resulting smaller model, each remaining variable or group is tested again. This procedure is repeated, until the coefficient of each remaining continuous variable and the collective effect of each remaining group of variables are significantly different from zero at the 10% level.

Chapter 6

Estimation of static Engel curves for food

6.1 Static cross-section Engel curves

This section describes the trials (and errors) of estimating static Engel curves for total expenditure on food for the 1987 Continuous Budget Survey, on the sample of 699 households constructed in Section 4.1. As described in Section 5.2, four general specifications are estimated, with 135 explanatory variables each (the continuous variables in Table 5.3, the dummy variables in Table 5.1 and the interaction terms in Table 5.4). These four specifications differ only with respect to the functional form of the dependent variable and of the interaction terms with income, and are given by specification (5.8) with linear income interactions, specification (5.8) with logarithmic income interactions, specification (5.9) with linear income interactions and specification (5.9) with logarithmic income interactions, where y in (5.8) and (5.9) is total expenditure on food and x annual disposable household income.

Comparison of explanatory power of models with linear and logarithmic dependent variables is possible in the following way. Since

$$\text{Variance } (\ln y) = \left(\frac{\partial \ln y}{\partial y} \right)^2 \text{Variance } (y) = \left(\frac{1}{y} \right)^2 \text{Variance } (y)$$

it is the case that:

$$\text{StandardDeviation } (\ln y) = \frac{1}{y} \text{StandardDeviation } (y)$$

This holds for the standard deviation conditional on the regressors as well. Therefore, if the standard error of the linear model is divided by the mean of the dependent variable, comparison with the standard error of the logarithmic model is justified. This procedure was first suggested by Sargan (1964).

Apart from comparison of explanatory power, testing for non-normality and heteroscedasticity is important. An approximately normal disturbance distribution is required for an accurate interpretation of the test statistics and associated p-values calculated in the sequential simplification procedure that follows. However, the estimator distribution is asymptotically normal anyway, so non-normality is not too disturbing. On the other hand, heteroscedastic disturbances lead to incorrect OLS estimation of the standard errors of the coefficients, in small as well as large samples. Thus, if heteroscedasticity is detected, then either the estimated standard errors need to be corrected, to make right decisions in the sequential simplification procedure possible, or Feasible GLS has to be applied. For Feasible GLS, assumptions about the functional form of the heteroscedasticity are necessary. This makes calculating heteroscedasticity-corrected standard errors according to White (1980) a more attractive option.

For detection of non-normality, it is convenient to use the Lagrange Multiplier statistic, proposed by Jarque and Bera (1980). This statistic is given by

$$LM_N = n \left(\frac{(\text{skewness})^2}{6} + \frac{(\text{excess kurtosis})^2}{24} \right) \sim \chi_2^2 | H_0 \qquad (6.1)$$

where n is the number of observations in the sample. Skewness is divided by $\hat{\sigma}^3$ and kurtosis is divided by $\hat{\sigma}^4$ and reduced by 3, so both should be close to zero if the disturbance distribution is normal. Under the null hypothesis of normality, this test statistic is asymptotically distributed as χ^2 with two degrees of freedom. Heteroscedasticity can be detected by the Lagrange Multiplier test devised by Breusch and Pagan (1979), where the alternative hypothesis allows the disturbance variance to vary with a set of regressors. This test statistic is

$$LM_H = \frac{1}{2} (\text{Explained Sum of Squares}) \qquad (6.2)$$

in the regression of

$$\frac{e_i^2}{\frac{1}{n} \sum_{i=1}^{n} e_i^2}$$

on a constant and a set of regressors. Under the null hypothesis of homoscedasticity, LM_H is asymptotically distributed as χ^2 with degrees of freedom equal to the number of regressors allowed to influence disturbance variance.

For the four general models, Table 6.1 shows overall significance, standard errors (and coefficients of variation for models with a linear dependent variable), skewness of residuals, excess kurtosis of residuals, Jarque-Bera LM_N sta-

Table 6.1: Performance of the four general models based on (5.8) and (5.9)

characteristic	(5.8)lin	(5.8)log	(5.9)lin	(5.9)log
overall significance: p-value	0.0001	0.0001	0.0001	0.0001
standard error of the regression	2.256	2.266	0.315	0.312
mean of dependent variable	7.371	7.371		
coefficient of variation	0.306	0.307		
skewness of residuals	0.852	0.861	−0.118	−0.095
excess kurtosis of residuals	1.729	1.847	0.760	0.670
LM_N	171	186	18.5	14.1
$LM_H(1)$: income only	12.5	18.1	20.3	12.5
$LM_H(135)$: all regressors	227	239	193	176

5% critical values: LM_N 5.99; $LM_H(1)$ 3.84; $LM_H(135)$ 163
1% critical values: LM_N 9.21; $LM_H(1)$ 6.63; $LM_H(135)$ 176
The dependent variable is annual household expenditure on food in f1000

tistics for non-normality and Breusch-Pagan LM_H statistics for heteroscedasticity. The Breusch-Pagan test statistics are given for two different sets of regressors, the first consisting of income only, the second of all 135 regressors.

It is seen from Table 6.1 that the general model with total food expenditure untransformed as dependent variable and with linear income interactions — model (5.8)lin — has slightly more explanatory power than the other models (the residual variation is comparatively low). However, the model with the logarithm of total food expenditure as dependent variable and with logarithmic income interactions — model (5.9)log — performs best with regard to non-normality and heteroscedasticity. Also, model (5.8)lin performs in all respects better than model (5.8)log, while model (5.9)log performs in all respects better than model (5.9)lin. Normality and homoscedasticity are rejected in all models.

Because of the possible sensitivity of the statistics to a few outlying residuals, it may be useful to calculate the LM_N and LM_H statistics in a sample, where the biggest (or smallest) outliers are removed. When two outliers are removed in model (5.8)lin, LM_N reduces to 99.5 and LM_H (income only) to 6.60. When two outliers are removed in model (5.9)log (these outliers are different from those referred to in the preceding sentence), LM_N reduces to 1.84 and LM_H (income only) to 9.03. So, model (5.8)lin seems to give less heteroscedastic residuals, while model (5.9)log seems to give more normal residuals. Although the test statistics in both models improve considerably, non-normality and/or heteroscedasticity still seem to be present. Because of this, and because households with inconsistent or absurd variable values have been removed from the sample in the first place (see Section 4.1.1), no outliers will be removed from the sample of 699 households.

It would seem that no clear choice between (5.8)lin and (5.9)log can be made on the basis of the data. With respect to theory, model (5.8) comprises more commonly used powerful specifications than model (5.9) (see Section 5.2). Therefore, model (5.8) with linear income interactions is preferred. When estimating this model, the estimated standard errors of the coefficients are corrected for heteroscedasticity.

Next, this preferred model (5.8)lin is subjected to the sequential procedure of testing and imposing restrictions, described in Section 5.2.4. Let

$$\hat{V}(b) = (X'X)^{-1} \left(\sum_{i=1}^{n} e_i^2 x_{i\cdot} x_{i\cdot}' \right) (X'X)^{-1} \tag{6.3}$$

with e_i the i-th residual and $x_{i\cdot}$ the i-th row of the regressor matrix X, be the heteroscedasticity-corrected estimated variance matrix of the OLS estimator b of the coefficients in a specification (see White (1980)), then the test statistic used to test the linear restrictions

$$R\beta = r$$

on the coefficient vector β is:

$$F = \frac{n-k}{n} \frac{(Rb - r)' \left(R\hat{V}(b)R' \right)^{-1} (Rb - r)}{h} \sim F_{n-k}^h | H_0 \tag{6.4}$$

where n is the number of observations, $n - k$ is the number of degrees of freedom in the unrestricted specification and h is the number of restrictions tested. Under the null hypothesis that the restrictions are true, this test statistic is distributed approximately as F with h and $n - k$ degrees of freedom. Table 6.2 summarises the results of the sequential simplification procedure. In the first column, each variable or group restricted to have zero coefficient(s) is described. In the second column, the degrees of freedom associated with each deleted variable or group are displayed. The third column lists the 'marginal p-values' associated with the imposed restrictions, when tested in the model in which these last restrictions are not yet but all previous restrictions are imposed. Finally, the fourth column contains the 'cumulative p-values' associated with these last and all previous restrictions, when tested simultaneously in the most general model. A set of restrictions is imposed only if the marginal as well as the cumulative p-value is 0.10 or higher. (For the Working specification only $\gamma = 0$ was tested, since imposing a zero intercept coefficient is not too reasonable with all these dummies around. So, the Working specification considered here is in fact the general specification (5.6) proposed by Leser (1963).)

Table 6.2: Results of the sequential simplification procedure of (5.8)lin

omitted variable or variable group	degrees of freedom	marginal p-value	cumulative p-value
education of partner: 1 category	2	0.78	0.78
degree of urbanisation × income	5	0.75	0.86
region × income	4	0.68	0.88
ln(INCOME): Working	1	0.65	0.91
holiday length × income	1	0.52	0.93
holiday length	1	0.63	0.93
number of adults × age	14	0.24	0.62
number of adults × income	2	0.54	0.64
degree of urbanisation × region	13	0.20	0.39
degree of urbanisation	5	0.82	0.45
region	4	0.40	0.33
number of children × income	2	0.13	0.24
profession of head × income	7	0.21	0.16
profession of head	7	0.62	0.10

Starting off from a general model of the form (5.8) with 135 explanatory variables, the sequential simplification procedure summarised in Table 6.2 leads to a model with $135 - 68 = 67$ explanatory variables. From the last column of Table 6.2, it is seen that the cumulative p-value of all imposed restrictions is 10%. Fourteen different variables or variable groups have disappeared from the specification. The first (education of partner: 1 category) may require some additional explanation. The education of partner base group (no partner) and the number of adults base group (1 adult) cover almost the same set of households (single-parent-households with children older than 16 make up the difference). This leads to multicollinearity problems in the form of high Variance Inflation Factors. Therefore, the education of partner group with least significant coefficients (for dummy and income interaction term) is added to the base group. In the course of the simplification procedure, four factors disappear altogether from the specification; these are holiday length, degree of urbanisation, region and profession of the head of the household. A simplified model of the Working form (5.11) remains, with 67 explanatory variables, measuring income untransformed and income times the logarithm of income, the number of adults, the number of children, age, education of head, education of partner and recording month, and interaction terms between number of children and age, between age and income, between education of head and income, between education of partner and income and between recording month and income. In Table C.1 in Appendix C, some characteristics and the coefficient estimates (with standard errors and p-values) of this Working specification are listed.

As can be seen from Table C.1, the coefficients of the adults dummies are all positive and extremely significant and imply a larger amount of money spent on food in households with more adults: households with 2 adults spend $f2156$ per year more and households with 3 or more adults $f3297$ more than households with 1 adult. Combining these figures with the mean expenditure on food per household ($f7371$, see Table 4.1) and the mean number of adults per household (2, see Table 5.1), it is found that households with 2 adults spend 41% more and households with 3 or more adults 63% more on food than households with 1 adult (at the overall mean income and ceteris paribus).

The effect of education of head and partner and of recording month varies with the level of income. As far as education of head is concerned, the dummies and interactions of level 2.1 and 2.2 are not significantly different from zero. The Engel curve is steeper for third level education than for first level education: third level means less food expenditure than first level for households with annual incomes lower than $f61400$ (which is by far the majority) and more food expenditure for households with incomes higher than this amount. A possible explanation may be, that third level education (university or polytechnic) generally leads to a more sedentary life than first level, so less food is needed by the head of the household, which is counterbalanced by higher quality demands only for high incomes. As it seems, the higher the education of the partner, the flatter the Engel curve: first level means less food expenditure than third level for households with annual incomes lower than $f43723$ (which constitute approximately 50% of the sample) and more food expenditure for households with incomes higher than this amount.

The coefficients for the recording month are all positive, but the interactions with income have negative coefficients. The relative magnitudes of these coefficients are such, that households with reasonably large incomes recording expenses in December recorded more than those recording expenses in any other month, with the exception of October. The differences can be substantial: a household with an annual disposable household income of $f30000$ recording in January seems to spend $f386$ ($1.324 - 0.057 \times 30 = -0.386$) per year less on food (more than 5% of the sample mean $f7371$) than a household with the same income recording in December. This leads to the conclusion that the correction scheme designed by the Central Bureau of Statistics does not capture the full effect of differences in food expenditures in different months.

The coefficients of number of children and age are less easy to interpret, since interaction terms involving these variables are part of the specification too. The effect of the number of children and the age of the head of the household is illustrated in Table 6.3, which is a cross table of age by number

Table 6.3: Composite coefficients of age and number of children

subsample	base group		CHILDREN1		CHILDREN2		total #
base group	28	0.000	12	-0.067	19	-0.151	59
AGE30	33	0.731	22	-0.031	65	1.476	120
AGE35	22	-0.186	17	1.166	84	1.336	123
AGE40	14	-1.293	23	0.559	49	0.682	86
AGE45	30	-0.232	18	0.520	4	-0.324	52
AGE50	34	-0.120	3	-0.756	1		38
AGE55	39	0.199	2	-2.527	1		42
AGE60	53	-0.262	0		2	2.337	55
AGE65	124	-0.419	0		0		124
total #	377		97		225		699

Number of households in each subsample and composite coefficients in the preferred equation for households with f30000 income

of children. Each cell of this table contains the number of households in the corresponding subsample and the composite coefficient of the number of children and age, for households with an annual disposable household income of f30000. So, the second column contains the coefficients of the age dummies plus the coefficients of the age-income interactions times 30, and the second row lists the coefficients of the children dummies. From this table it follows, for example, that f30000 income households in the 30 to 35 age group with 2 or more children spend f1476 − f731 = f745 per year more (or approximately f60 each month) than households in the same age and income group with no children. For households with 1 child younger than 16, food expenditure turns out to be increasing with age as long as the head of the household is younger than 35 to 40 and decreasing thereafter. For households with 2 or more children, the pattern is similar, with the exception of AGE60/CHILDREN2 households, of which there are only two in the sample. This relationship between food expenditure and age of the household head is possibly caused by the relationship between the age of the head and that of the children (of which no data are available). If the head of the household is 35 or older but younger than 50, food expenditure increases with the number of children, except for AGE45/CHILDREN2 households, of which there are four in the sample. For the other age groups, the effect of the number of children is less clear.

To illustrate the effect of income, Figure 6.1 shows the estimated Engel curves for three more or less common types of household. Yuppies (Young Urban Professionals) are households with 1 adult younger than 30 and no children, educated on level 3 and recording expenses in September. Dinkies (Double Income No Kids) are defined as households with 2 adults and no chil-

Food expenditure in f 1000

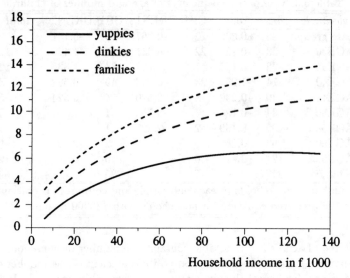

Household income in f 1000

Figure 6.1: Cross-section OLS Engel Curves

dren, with the head aged between 35 and 40, both head and partner educated on level 3 and recording expenses in September. Finally, Families consist of 2 adults and 2 or more children younger than 16, with the age of the family head between 40 and 45, both head and partner educated on level 2.1 and recording expenses in September too.

On the basis of the cross-section analysis carried out here, it can be concluded that Engel's Law seems to hold in this sample of 699 households.

6.2   Static panel data Engel curves

In Section 6.1, estimation results of static Engel curves for total food expenditure based on cross-section data for 1987 were presented. Before the estimation of dynamic Engel curves will be discussed in Chapter 7, in this section static Engel curves based on panel data for the years 1985 to 1987 are considered. Again, the sample of 699 households constructed in Section 4.1 is used.

The main difference between static models based on cross-section and panel data is that individual effects can be part of the specification in the latter. Inclusion of individual effects may result in lower significance of (other) explanatory variables and a more parsimonious specification with respect to these variables, but a more elaborate systematic specification is not very likely. Therefore, the model selection procedure of Section 6.1 will not be repeated completely here. Only specification (5.8) with linear income interactions will be considered. Those groups of interaction terms, groups of dummies and continuous variables that disappeared from the specification during the sequential simplification procedure, summarised in Table 6.2, are not part of any specification in this section (or the next chapter). So, the Working specification shown in Table C.1, with individual effects, is the most general specification considered. Since static panel data estimation is only regarded as an interlude between cross-section OLS and dynamic panel data estimation, the standard errors reported in this section are not corrected for heteroscedasticity.

In the next three tables in Appendix C, the estimation results of three different specifications are shown. Estimation results of the specification in Table C.1, without individual effects, but with time effects (i.e. a different intercept for each year), are shown in Table C.2. Time effects are included to ensure that the residuals of each wave sum to zero. This is desirable for the interpretation of the Lagrange Multiplier test statistics for non-normality and heteroscedasticity, which are calculated not only for all observations, but also for each wave separately.

Compared to the cross-section estimation results reported in Table C.1, the number of explanatory variables (excluding intercept) has increased from 67 to 69, because two interaction terms between number of children and age could be included, which had to be omitted in the cross-section case, due to perfect multicollinearity. Also, this specification allows for three intercepts instead of one. Nevertheless, the number of degrees of freedom has increased from 631 to 2025, because there are three times as many observations available. However, the pooled OLS estimation method assumes that (the error term of) any observation is independent of (the error term of) all other observations, among which are two observations of the same household in a different year. This assumption is most likely violated here, since the disturbances of the same household in three consecutive waves are presumably not independent. As a result, the standard errors of the coefficients are underestimated.[1] The results in Table C.2 suggest that a preferred specification for 1986 may be rather different from the preferred specification for 1987: in the second wave, non-normality and heteroscedasticity seem to be enormous. However, as mentioned before, this is only an interlude, so no attention will be paid to this problem.

To facilitate comparison of the pooled OLS results with the cross-section

---

[1]For instance, suppose $E\epsilon_i = 0$, $E\epsilon_i^2 = \sigma^2$ and $E\epsilon_i\epsilon_j = \rho\sigma^2$, then $E\hat{\sigma}^2 = \frac{1}{n-1}E\{\sum_i \epsilon_i^2 - \frac{1}{n}(\sum_i \epsilon_i)^2\} = \frac{1}{n-1}\{n\sigma^2 - \frac{1}{n}(n\sigma^2 + n(n-1)\rho\sigma^2)\} = (1-\rho)\sigma^2$. In other words, if $0 < \rho < 1$, the variance of the disturbances will be underestimated.

Food expenditure in f 1000

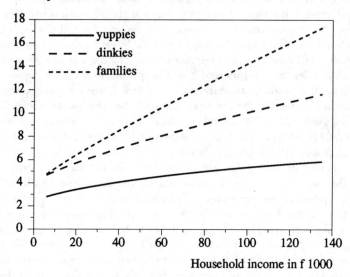

Household income in f 1000

Figure 6.2: Pooled OLS Engel Curves

OLS results reported in Section 6.1, Figure 6.2 shows the estimated Engel curves for Yuppies, Dinkies and Families (for a definition of these household types see Section 6.1). The estimated pooled OLS Engel curves are definitely more linear than the cross-section Engel curves. However, since the pooled OLS Engel curves all have a positive intercept, Engel's Law still seems to hold. (The intercept for a particular household type is calculated as the mean of the three time dummy coefficients plus the coefficients of the relevant categorical dummies.)

Estimation results of the same specification with fixed individual effects are shown in Table C.3. Compared to the pooled OLS estimation results, the number of explanatory variables has decreased from 69 to 68, because one interaction term between number of children and age had to be omitted, due to perfect multicollinearity. All other categorical dummies and interaction terms varied during the three years for at least one household, preventing the individual effect from being multicollinear with these variables. Generally speaking, the categorical dummies changed for many more than one household, ranging from 35 households for AGE65 (one can never get out of this age group) via 165 households for EDUCATIONH22 to even more for some recording month dummies.[2]

The inclusion of fixed individual effects leads to a drop in significance of many explanatory variables. To investigate the explanatory power of income in a fixed effects specification, the joint significance of the 27 income variables and interactions in the specification of Table C.3 is tested with an F-test. This leads to an F-value of 1.10 and an associated p-value of 0.332. The same procedure in the pooled OLS specification of Table C.2 leads to an F-value of 12.1 and an associated p-value smaller than 0.000005. It is tempting to conclude that income looses all explanatory power in a fixed effects specification. However, for two reasons, such a general conclusion cannot be drawn. Firstly, a single F-test is supposed to test the significance of many variables here, so the power of the test will presumably be low. However, a fixed effects specification with no regressors but income itself yields a coefficient of 0.009, a t-ratio of 1.34 and an associated p-value of 0.181, so income still doesn't seem to be important. Secondly, the preferred specification for 1987 is imposed on 1985 and 1986 here, so the alternative hypothesis may be incorrect as well. Anyway, fixed effects cannot be rejected: comparison of the specifications in Table C.2 and C.3 through an F-test of restrictions leads to an F-value of 3.72 and an associated p-value smaller than 0.000005. The apparent loss of explanatory power of the regressors might be partly caused by the fact that only three waves are available here: a small number of waves leaves little room for 'within-groups variation' and the 'between-groups variation' is completely accounted for by the fixed effects. The results of the simulation experiments, reported in Section 2.2.3, also showed a considerable variance of the FE estimator.

Again, the estimation results are illustrated in a figure: Figure 6.3 shows the estimated Engel curves for Yuppies, Dinkies and Families. The FE Engel curves look a bit weird for household incomes higher than ƒ100000: Families seem to spend less on food if their income is higher, and single-person Yuppies seem to spend more than four-person Families. However, two mitigating remarks can be made. Firstly, annual disposable incomes of this magnitude are extremely rare. Secondly, as noted earlier, the significance of the income variables in the FE specification is rather poor, so the Engel curves drawn in Figure 6.3 have wide confidence areas.

As an alternative to giving each household a different intercept, random individual effects may be employed. Maddala (1971) makes a plea for random effects specifications on several grounds. Firstly, the fixed effects method only considers the variation within households and ignores the so called between groups variation. Secondly, FE leads to a substantial loss of degrees of

---

[2]The recording months in two succeeding years are different for almost all households, but this does not mean that, for example, MONTHJAN changes for almost all households, since for most households it will be zero twice.

Food expenditure in f 1000

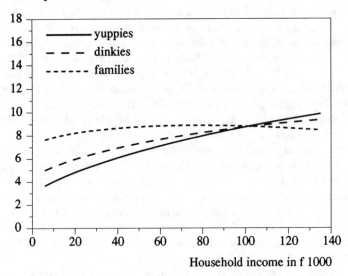

Household income in f 1000

Figure 6.3: FE Engel Curves

freedom. Thirdly, just like any disturbance term in regression models, individual effects represent the ignorance of the researcher. Fourthly, individual dummy variables rarely have a meaningful interpretation. However convincing this may be, an important caveat is that random effects specifications yield inconsistent estimates if the individual effects are correlated with (any of) the regressors. To find out whether this is the case, Hausman (1978) suggested comparing the coefficient vectors b_{FE} and b_{RE}. Under the null hypothesis of uncorrelated random individual effects, both are consistent and b_{RE} is asymptotically efficient. Under the alternative hypothesis, b_{FE} is still consistent but b_{RE} is not. Now, the Hausman test statistic is given by

$$H = q'[\text{var}(q)]^{-1}q \overset{a}{\sim} \chi_k^2 \text{ with } q = b_{FE} - b_{RE} \qquad (6.5)$$

where k denotes the dimension of the slope vector b. Mundlak (1978) has shown, that if the effects are correlated with all explanatory variables and this correlation is properly taken into account, the resulting estimator is equivalent to the FE estimator.

Estimation results of the specification with random individual effects are shown in Table C.4. The residual sum of squares reported in this table refers to the random disturbance part of the composite error term, so it excludes the

Food expenditure in f 1000

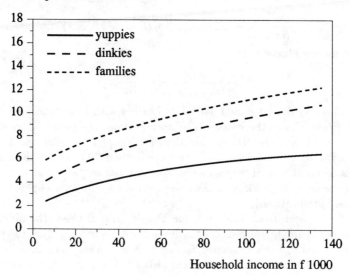

Figure 6.4: RE Engel Curves

individual effects. The same story applies to the R-squared and the standard error of the regression. Although the RE estimation results appear satisfactory, especially compared to the FE results, the Hausman test decisively rejects zero correlation between individual effects and regressors. Correlated effects imply that the estimated coefficients reported in Table C.4 are biased.

Figure 6.4 shows the estimated random effects Engel curves for Yuppies, Dinkies and Families. In contrast to the FE Engel curves, the RE Engel curves look quite nice.

The coefficient values in the cross-section specification in Table C.1, the pooled OLS specification in Table C.2, the FE specification in Table C.3 and the RE specification in Table C.4 differ considerably. However, the estimated income elasticities of total food expenditure are less divergent. Estimated partial derivatives with respect to income and income elasticities can be calculated in the following way. The estimated specifications considered here can be written as

$$y(x, D_1, \ldots, D_m) =$$
$$a_0 + a_1 D_1 + \ldots + a_m D_m + b_0 x + b_1 D_1 x + \ldots + b_k D_k x + c_0 x \ln x \quad (6.6)$$

where y is annual household expenditure on food, x is annual disposable household income and $D_1, \ldots, D_k, \ldots, D_m$ are dummy variables. The partial derivative with respect to income is

$$\frac{\partial y}{\partial x} = b_0 + b_1 D_1 + \ldots + b_k D_k + c_0(1 + \ln x) \qquad (6.7)$$

and the income elasticity is

$$\frac{x}{y(x, D_1, \ldots, D_m)} \frac{\partial y}{\partial x} \qquad (6.8)$$

Table 6.4 shows the estimated partial derivatives with respect to income and income elasticities in the cross-section specification, the pooled OLS specification, the FE and the RE specification, for Yuppies, Dinkies and Families (for a definition of these household types see Section 6.1). This is done at two different levels of annual disposable household income: $f30000$ and the mean level in the sample ($f45329$ for the cross-section specification and $f44152$ for the panel specifications).

As can be seen from Table 6.4, for Yuppies and Dinkies, the differences between the estimated income elasticities in the cross-section OLS, the pooled OLS, the Fixed and the Random Effects specifications are sometimes substantial, but small relative to the standard errors.[3] For Families, the estimated elasticities are close to zero in the Fixed Effects specification, while the estimated elasticities in both OLS specifications are again not really different from each other and in the Random Effects specification they are slightly lower. The same story applies to the estimated partial derivatives with respect to income.

On balance, compared to the cross-section estimation, the pooled OLS en FE estimation and testing results are rather disappointing. The preferred explanatory variables for the cross-section 1987 case have been imposed on the years 1985 and 1986 and the coefficients of these explanatory variables have been supposed to be the same in each year. Only the constant term is allowed to vary, over time in the pooled OLS specification and also over individuals in the FE specification. The poor results may be caused by the fact, that household behaviour does not obey these restrictions, which would stress the point that blind faith in cross-section analysis is dangerous. However, it may also be the case that a few atypical households disturb the estimation process.[4] Therefore, the fixed individual effects have been investigated. The

---

[3]A phrase like 'significantly different from each other' cannot be used here for the following reasons. The cross-section OLS specification is based on a subset of the data set on which the other three are based, and since this subset is of course not independent of the original data set, the cross-section specification cannot be compared to the other specifications in such a way. With respect to the three panel data specifications, only one of them can be correct. If, for instance, the FE specification is correct, then the pooled OLS estimates are biased and their standard errors unreliable.

[4]Households with inconsistent or absurd variable values have been removed from the sample before estimation: see Section 4.1.1.

Table 6.4: Partial derivatives with respect to income and income elasticities of total food expenditure

specification	partial derivative		elasticity	
	*f*30000	*sample mean*	*f*30000	*sample mean*
Yuppies:				
cross-section OLS	0.085	0.059	0.689	0.558
	(0.025)	(0.024)	(0.204)	(0.223)
pooled OLS	0.032	0.027	0.256	0.286
	(0.017)	(0.016)	(0.135)	(0.164)
Fixed Effects	0.063	0.054	0.344	0.378
	(0.024)	(0.023)	(0.134)	(0.161)
Random Effects	0.048	0.039	0.373	0.378
	(0.018)	(0.017)	(0.141)	(0.166)
Dinkies:				
cross-section OLS	0.111	0.085	0.585	0.535
	(0.025)	(0.023)	(0.132)	(0.143)
pooled OLS	0.063	0.058	0.295	0.353
	(0.015)	(0.012)	(0.071)	(0.075)
Fixed Effects	0.048	0.040	0.224	0.246
	(0.022)	(0.018)	(0.100)	(0.112)
Random Effects	0.068	0.058	0.335	0.368
	(0.016)	(0.013)	(0.078)	(0.082)
Families:				
cross-section OLS	0.124	0.098	0.520	0.502
	(0.026)	(0.024)	(0.107)	(0.125)
pooled OLS	0.106	0.101	0.425	0.498
	(0.017)	(0.015)	(0.066)	(0.076)
Fixed Effects	0.021	0.012	0.074	0.062
	(0.021)	(0.020)	(0.076)	(0.100)
Random Effects	0.066	0.056	0.252	0.284
	(0.017)	(0.016)	(0.064)	(0.079)

Derivatives and elasticities evaluated at *f*30000 and the sample mean
Estimated standard errors in parentheses

699 individual effects have mean 3.993 and standard deviation 2.389. Not one individual effect is smaller than the mean minus 2 times the standard deviation, but 33 effects are larger than the mean plus 2 times the standard deviation, and 7 of these are larger than the mean plus 3 times the standard deviation. In other words, there are no households which spend much less on food than they are expected to, given their income and other household characteristics. Since food is a necessity of life, this is not surprising. However, there are 33 households which spend more and 7 which spend much more on food than they are expected to. Tables C.5 and C.6 in Appendix C summarise the estimation results of the pooled OLS and FE specification respectively, when these 7 households are removed from the sample.

Comparing these tables with the corresponding tables based on the whole sample, one sees that several test statistics have improved strikingly, especially for 1986. Skewness and excess kurtosis of residuals are much lower: the residual distribution seems more like the normal. Also, heteroscedasticity is less apparent. It seems that households with extreme fixed effects have extreme residuals as well. So these households spend, ceteris paribus and averaged over time, not only more on food than other households, but their behaviour over time is also atypical. However, the coefficients have not changed a lot. This is also the case for the partial derivatives with respect to income and income elasticities: generally speaking, both are a little smaller here than in Table 6.4, but the differences are minor. Still, fixed effects cannot be rejected: comparison of the specifications in Table C.5 and C.6 with an F-test of restrictions leads to an F-value of 3.82 and an associated p-value smaller than 0.000005.

So, although the conclusions concerning income elasticities are not really affected, removal of some peculiar households from the sample leads to wonderful improvements of the estimation results. However, this magic formula is no fair play. In Chapter 7 it will be investigated, whether a dynamic specification can really *explain* the behaviour of typical *and* atypical households.

Chapter 7

Estimation of dynamic Engel curves for food

7.1 Adding lagged exogenous regressors to the static Engel curves

In Chapter 6, static Engel curves based on cross-section and panel data of the form (3.2) were estimated. Starting with a general static specification with many explanatory variables and interaction terms, a sequential simplification procedure has led to the preferred cross-section specification for 1987, given in Table C.1. In this chapter, lagged exogenous and lagged dependent variables are added to this preferred specification. After that, a new sequential simplification procedure will result in a preferred dynamic specification. This means that the final dynamic specification will have been achieved by first performing a general-to-specific procedure in 'static space', then generalising the result in the 'dynamics dimension', and finally performing a second general-to-specific procedure, which may seem a bit strange. However, following a fully genuine general-to-specific specification search procedure would have involved estimation of a dynamic panel data model with 140 explanatory variables. What is more, the 'best' static cross-section specification can now be compared with the preferred dynamic panel data specification.

The dynamic relationships considered in this chapter are (1.1) and its special cases (3.3), (3.4), (3.5) and (3.6). In this section, the static model (3.2) is generalised into the finite distributed lag model (3.3). In other words, lagged exogenous regressor variables are added to the preferred static specification. Only continuous variables are chosen for this exercise: the regressors INCOME and INCOME × ln(INCOME). To mitigate multicollinearity problems, first differences of these variables (instead of levels of lagged variables) are added

Table 7.1: Results of the sequential simplification procedure of lagged exogenous variables

omitted variable	degrees of freedom	marginal p-value	cumulative p-value
Δ (INCOME $\times$ ln(INCOME)) 1986	1	0.13	0.13
Δ (INCOME $\times$ ln(INCOME)) 1987	1	0.25	0.13
Δ (INCOME) 1986	1	0.33	0.17

to the specification.

To begin with, four first differences are included: INCOME 1987 minus INCOME 1986 and INCOME 1986 minus INCOME 1985, and the same for INCOME $\times$ ln(INCOME). This model is subjected to a sequential procedure of testing and imposing restrictions on these four new regressors. Table 7.1 summarises the results of this sequential simplification procedure. In the first column, the variable restricted to have a zero coefficient is listed. In the second column, the number of degrees of freedom associated with each deleted variable is displayed. The third column comprises the 'marginal p-values' associated with the imposed restriction, when tested in the model in which this last restriction is not yet but all previous restrictions are imposed. Finally, the fourth column contains the 'cumulative p-values' associated with this last and all previous restrictions, when tested simultaneously in the most general model. A restriction is imposed (i.e. a variable is deleted) only, if the marginal as well as the cumulative p-value are 0.10 or above.

Of the four first differences, only the difference between current and lagged values of income itself remains in the specification. The estimation results of the resulting dynamic specification are summarised in Table C.7 in Appendix C. Comparison of this table with Table C.1 learns that the inclusion of lagged exogenous information does not alter the estimation results considerably: roughly speaking, the coefficient values are similar. This holds even more for the long-run or equilibrium partial derivative with respect to income and for the income elasticity: they hardly differ from the figures for the cross-section OLS specification, given in Table 6.4. In other words, estimation of (3.3) leads to the same conclusions about long-run parameters than estimation of (3.2). However, the overall fit of the regression has improved slightly: the adjusted R-squared has increased from 0.477 to 0.484 and the standard error of the regression has decreased from 2.259 to 2.246.

7.2 Engel curves with lagged exogenous and endogenous regressors

In this section, the static model (3.2) is generalised into (1.1). In other words, besides lagged exogenous regressors, also a lagged dependent variable is added to the preferred static specification. In Section 3.1, some literature on panel data models with a lagged dependent variable was reviewed. For the empirical analysis in this thesis, only three time periods are available. This raises the question what can still be done when $T = 3$.

Equation (3.9), which is in first differences, can only be estimated for time period 3:

$$y_{i3} - y_{i2} = \sum_{j=1}^{J} \sum_{l=0}^{L(j)} \beta_{jl}(x_{ji,3-l} - x_{ji,2-l}) + \gamma(y_{i2} - y_{i1}) + (\epsilon_{i3} - \epsilon_{i2}) \qquad (7.1)$$

Of the orthogonality conditions in (3.10), only the first remains: E $y_{i1}(\epsilon_{i3} - \epsilon_{i2}) = 0$. Therefore, if lagged values of the exogenous variables are not being used as instruments for the lagged value of the dependent variable (for instance, because they appear as regressors), only one instrument is available and the parameters are just identified. In fact, in this special case the GMM estimator reduces to the estimator proposed by Anderson and Hsiao (1981) and Anderson and Hsiao (1982), with y_{i1} as instrument for $(y_{i2} - y_{i1})$.

The instrument set could be extended by adding lagged values of exogenous variables. In the empirical application considered here, the dummy regressor variables exhibit insufficient variation over time to be able to generate more than one instrument each (and this is the dummy regressor itself). Of the continuous variables, lagged differences of INCOME and INCOME × ln(INCOME) appear as regressors, so no extra instruments can be constructed from them neither. As long as we restrict ourselves to linear orthogonality restrictions, the only extra instruments available consist of lagged differences of interaction terms of dummy regressors and income.

Of course, a specification in first differences allows the presence of fixed individual effects. When only three time periods are available, this may lead to large standard errors. (Compare the large standard errors in the fixed effects static specification in Table C.3 and of the FE estimator in the simulation experiments reported in Section 2.2.) Another reason for expecting large standard errors in specification (7.1) is that the covariance of variables in first differences is usually smaller than in levels, which may lead to large values in the inverted matrix of cross products and to a large variance matrix of the estimator (3.8). Also, if γ is high (close to 1) and β_{jl} small, then differencing the dependent variable means much of the systematic information embodied in the variable values will be lost, since a large amount of systematic information in y_{i3} consists of γy_{i2}. Therefore, lagged differences will be bad instruments, whether the equation is differenced or not. For the same reason, lagged levels will be bad instruments in the differenced equation.

Generally speaking, the disturbances $(\epsilon_{it} - \epsilon_{i,t-1})$ of an equation in differences can only be white noise in the time dimension, if the disturbances ϵ_{it} of the corresponding equation in levels are integrated of order 1. However, since in the case of $T = 3$ only one wave is used for estimation, serial correlation will have no disturbing effects on standard errors and p-values.

As an alternative to estimating a differenced equation, equation (1.1) in levels can be estimated for time period 3:

$$y_{i3} = \alpha_0 + \sum_{j=1}^{J} \sum_{l=0}^{L(j)} \beta_{jl} x_{ji,3-l} + \gamma y_{i2} + \alpha_i + \epsilon_{i3} \tag{7.2}$$

Note that the individual effect α_i is not identified when only three waves are available. Instruments for y_{i2} in this equation should be in first-differenced form, to ensure independence of the individual effects α_i. So again, if lagged values of the exogenous variables are not being used as instruments, only one instrument $(y_{i2} - y_{i1})$ is available and the parameters are just identified.

Again, lagged values of continuous exogenous variables that have not been included as regressors could be used as extra instruments. When levels of regressors are used as instruments in an equation in levels, these regressors are implicitly assumed to be doubly exogenous. If this assumption is undesirable, levels of regressors will be invalid instruments, and first differences or deviations from individual means will have to be used instead. In the light of recent research on cointegration, the use of differences as instruments for variables in levels seems not advisable. In the instrumental variables procedure, the regressors are 'fitted' using the instruments. If the regressors are $I(1)$ — integrated of order 1 — (which they will most likely be when they are in levels and represent variables like income) and the instruments are $I(0)$ (which they will most likely be when they are in differences), then for $T \to \infty$ a regression of the regressors on the instruments yields $R^2 = 0$. On the contrary, if the regressors in levels are $I(1)$, then instruments in deviations from individual means are $I(1)$ too. Therefore, instruments in deviations from individual means seem (asymptotically for large T) preferable to instruments in differences. Incidentally, the use of deviations from individual means as an instrument for a singly exogenous variable was first proposed by Hausman and Taylor (1981). For reasons explained above, the standard errors of the coefficients in the levels equation are expected to be smaller than in the differenced equation.

For the empirical analysis in this section, the DPD estimation programme by Arellano and Bond (1988) was used. In all tables, standard errors and

p-values are robust to heteroskedasticity. In the overidentified cases, two-step estimates have been calculated (see Section 3.1). This ensures that random individual effects are taken into account in specification (7.2). Of course, when specification (7.1) is estimated, fixed or random effects may be present.

In the next six tables in Appendix C, GMM estimation results of (7.1) and (7.2) are given, where x contains all regressor variables appearing in the preferred cross-section equation of Table C.1 and the lagged exogenous variables considered in Section 7.1. The results of the sequential simplification procedure of lagged exogenous variables, summarised in Table 7.1, are ignored: all four lagged income variables appear as regressors.[1] In other words, with respect to the dynamic structure, a genuine general-to-specific procedure is being followed.

Table C.8 shows the results of estimating the equation in first differences (7.1), with y_{i1} as instrument for $(y_{i2} - y_{i1})$. In Table C.9, the estimation results of the same equation are listed, where also lagged differences of interaction terms of dummies and income are used as instruments. The parameters are here overidentified.

As has been expected, these tables show large standard errors for almost all coefficients. In Table C.8, only 4 variables are significant at the 10% level. The addition of lagged differences of x as instruments in Table C.9 has improved efficiency slightly, but still only 10 out of 68 regressors are significant at the 10% level. Interestingly, the lagged dependent variable seems not at all significantly different from zero. Despite the low precision of the estimates, it is clear that the 'static' differenced data model (3.6), which is a special case of the dynamic differenced data model in Tables C.8 and C.9, has to be rejected: both lagged differenced income variables are amongst the most significant regressors.

Next, in Table C.10 the results of estimating (7.2) in levels are displayed, with $(y_{i2} - y_{i1})$ as instrument for y_{i2}. Table C.11 shows the estimation results of this levels equation with also lagged levels of continuous exogenous variables as instruments. As mentioned before, if the regressors x are singly exogenous, levels of these regressors will be invalid instruments. Therefore, Table C.12 displays the results with $(y_{i2} - y_{i1})$, current differences of all exogenous variables and lagged differences of all continuous exogenous variables as instruments. And finally, Table C.13 considers the levels equation with instruments $(y_{i2} - y_{i1})$, $(x_{ji3} - x_{ji.})$ for all j, and also $(x_{hi2} - x_{hi.})$ for the continuous regressors x_h, where a dot denotes averaging over the respective index.[2]

---

[1] In the equation in levels, each of the two different income variables provides one current and two lagged regressors. In the differenced equation, only two differences are available for each income variable: a 'current' difference (the level in 1987 minus that in 1986) and a lagged one (that in 1986 minus that in 1985).

[2] If three waves of the instrument are used, the three values for each individual sum to

The estimated standard error of the disturbance, reported in any of the Tables C.10 to C.13, is larger than the reported standard error in the Tables C.8 and C.9. However, in the levels equation, this figure is an estimate of $\sqrt{\sigma_\alpha^2 + \sigma_\epsilon^2}$, while in the equation in differences it is the estimated standard error of ϵ alone.[3] So, one ought not to be taken in by the apparently small estimated standard error in the differenced equations. Looking back at the estimated standard error of the regression in levels without a lagged dependent variable, one sees that the lagged dependent variable has considerable explanatory power. Although estimation with instrumental variables usually leads to high standard errors, the IV results of the levels equation with a lagged dependent variable show lower estimated standard errors of the disturbance than the OLS results of the levels equation without a lagged dependent variable, reported in Table C.7.

The ratio of residual sum of squares to total sum of squares and the general significance of the regressors are quite good in the equations in levels, compared to the differenced equations. Together with the theoretical considerations mentioned above, this provides support for the equations in levels. The next question to be answered is which of the three equations in levels is preferred, or, equivalently, which set of instruments is best: levels of x (Table C.11), differences of x (Table C.12) or deviations of individual means of x (Table C.13).

With levels of x as instruments, the regressors x are assumed to be doubly exogenous. The choice between singly and doubly exogenous regressors or, in other words, between correlated and uncorrelated individual effects or, in fact, between fixed and random individual effects can be made on at least four grounds. Firstly, one could rely on economic theory and intuition about the regressors involved, which would no doubt force one to the conclusion that the individual effects are presumably correlated with many of the regressors. Secondly, one could compute a Hausman test for the dynamic specification considered here; Breitung (1992) and Arellano (1993) give different ways of doing this. Thirdly, for simplicity, one could naïvely rely on the Hausman test computed for the static specification in Chapter 6, which decisively rejected uncorrelated individual effects. And finally, one could try to judge from the obtained estimation results and decide which one looks more plausible from an economic point of view. However, since many dummies and interaction terms are insignificantly different from zero in both tables, this last method is not of much help. Since the first and third method provide ample evidence in favour

---

zero. Therefore, only two waves with deviations from individual means can be used as instrument.

[3]In the equation in differences, the reported figure is the estimated standard error of the disturbances $(\epsilon_{it} - \epsilon_{i,t-1})$ divided by 2.

Table 7.2: Results of the sequential simplification procedure of the dynamic specification

omitted variable or variable group	degrees of freedom	marginal p-value	cumulative p-value
recording month × income	11	0.94	0.94
age × income	8	0.89	0.96
education of partner × income	3	0.54	0.95
education of partner	3	0.65	0.95
number of children × age	11	0.10	0.71
age	8	0.16	0.47
$\triangle$ income$_{-1}$	2	0.34	0.51

of single exogeneity, this is the choice to make.

When only single exogeneity is assumed, it seems that deviations of individual means of x provide better instruments than differences of x. This follows not only from the estimation results, but also from the theoretical remarks made before. As a result, the specification listed in Table C.13 is preferred.

Next, this specification has been subjected to a general-to-specific specification search procedure, which resembles those shown in Tables 6.2 and 7.1. In Table 7.2, the results of this procedure are displayed. In the first column, the group of interaction terms, group of dummies or continuous variable restricted to have zero coefficients is given. In the second column, the number of degrees of freedom associated with each deleted variable group is listed. The third and fourth columns show, as before, the 'marginal' and 'cumulative' p-values, based on two-step estimation results robust to heteroskedasticity.

Beginning with the specification in Table C.13 with 72 explanatory variables, the simplification procedure leads to a specification with $72 - 46 = 26$ explanatory variables. From the last column of Table 7.2, it is seen that the cumulative p-value of all imposed restrictions is 51%. Seven different variable groups have disappeared from the specification. In the course of the simplification procedure, two factors have disappeared altogether from the specification: education of partner and age. In addition, the two income variables embodying information of 1985 have been removed. A simplified model with 26 explanatory variables remains, of which estimation results are given in Table C.14.

From this table, it is seen that the simplified specification yields a *smaller* residual sum of squares than the original specification, shown in Table C.13. This is possible here, because both specifications have been estimated with an instrumental variables procedure. Generally speaking, IV estimation of the model $y = X\beta + \epsilon$ with instrument set W entails that the regressors are 'fitted' using the instruments, yielding $\hat{X} = (W'W)^{-1}W'X$. To obtain the estimator

$\hat{\beta}_{IV}$, the residual sum of squares of $y = \hat{X}\hat{\beta}_{IV} + \hat{\epsilon}$ is minimised, but the reported residual sum of squares and standard error of the disturbance are based on $y = X\hat{\beta}_{IV} + \hat{\epsilon}^*$. In the case considered here, the estimated standard error of the composite disturbance has fallen too, from 2.174 to 2.052. Because the instrument set used in the simplified case is equal to that used in the original specification, the degree of overidentification has increased considerably to 69.

Since the Sargan test of overidentifying restrictions yields a p-value of 0.841, the instrument set seems to be valid. However, if serial correlation is present in ϵ_{it}, then $(y_{i2} - y_{i1})$ will be an invalid instrument. Therefore, the simplified specification has been estimated a second time, with $(y_{i2} - y_{i1})$ removed from the instrument set. The results are displayed in Table C.15. And finally, in Table C.16, estimation results of the same specification with an even smaller instrument set are given, in the sense that no instruments are included of variables that are not included as regressor.

Choosing between these three instrument sets, one has to bear in mind that a smaller instrument set may lead to the minor disadvantage of inefficient estimates, but a larger instrument set could yield inconsistency. In particular, if the instrument set in Table C.14 is valid, then the estimates reported in any of the Tables C.14 to C.16 are consistent for large N, but those in Tables C.15 and C.16 are less efficient. On the other hand, if the instrument set in Table C.14 is invalid, but that in Table C.15 is valid, then the estimates reported in Table C.14 are inconsistent, but those in Table C.15 are consistent. Since the possibility of serial correlation provides an a priori reason why the instruments in Table C.14 could be invalid, it is probably safest to assume that they are, despite the fact that the Sargan test is not significant. Furthermore, dropping the instrument $(y_{i2} - y_{i1})$ seems not to involve any loss of efficiency; on the contrary, the residual sum of squares and standard error of the disturbance have become slightly smaller. Since there is no a priori reason for the instruments that are included in Table C.15 but excluded in Table C.16 (i.e. instruments of variables that are not included as regressor) being invalid, and since dropping them involves a considerable loss of efficiency, the instrument set in Table C.15 is preferred to the other two sets.

Table 7.3 shows some estimated partial derivatives with respect to income and income elasticities that follow from the specification in Table C.15. As in Table 6.4, this is done for Yuppies, Dinkies and Families at two different levels of annual disposable household income: $f30000$ and the mean level in the sample ($f45329$). Since the specification considered here involves lagged food expenditure and lagged income variables, things are more complicated than in the static case. The estimated specification can be written as

$$y_t = a_0 + a_1 D_1 + \ldots + a_m D_m + b_0 x_t + b_1 D_1 x_t + \ldots + b_k D_k x_t + b_{k+1}(x_t - x_{t-1})$$

$$+ c_0 x_t \ln x_t + c_1 (x_t \ln x_t - x_{t-1} \ln x_{t-1}) + d_0 y_{t-1}$$

where y is annual household expenditure on food, x is annual disposable household income and $D_1, \ldots, D_k, \ldots, D_m$ are dummy variables. Employing $|d_0| < 1$, substitution yields

$$y_t = \frac{a_0 + a_1 D_1 + \ldots + a_m D_m}{1 - d_0} + (b_0 + b_1 D_1 + \ldots + b_k D_k + b_{k+1}) \sum_{i=0}^{\infty} d_0^i x_{t-i}$$

$$- \frac{b_{k+1}}{d_0} \sum_{i=1}^{\infty} d_0^i x_{t-i} + (c_0 + c_1) \sum_{i=0}^{\infty} d_0^i x_{t-i} \ln x_{t-i} - \frac{c_1}{d_0} \sum_{i=1}^{\infty} d_0^i x_{t-i} \ln x_{t-i} \quad (7.3)$$

In such a dynamic specification, several partial derivatives and elasticities can be calculated, depending on the time span taken into account. In Table 7.3, three different sets of figures are given: the impact multiplier and corresponding short-run elasticity, the one-period interim multiplier and corresponding medium-run elasticity, and the total multiplier and corresponding long-run elasticity. From (7.3), it follows that the impact multiplier is equal to

$$\frac{\partial y_t}{\partial x_t} = b_0 + b_1 D_1 + \ldots + b_k D_k + b_{k+1} + (c_0 + c_1)(1 + \ln x_t) \quad (7.4)$$

To calculate the interim and total multipliers, some assumption about the values of lagged income has to be made. A natural way to proceed is to assume that — prior to and after the time period in which the shock occurred — either a stationary equilibrium or a steady-state at a plausible rate of growth prevailed. For simplicity of exposition, stationary equilibrium is examined first. In such a case, the interim multiplier ($x_t = x_{t-1}$) is given by

$$\frac{\partial y_t}{\partial x_t} + \frac{\partial y_t}{\partial x_{t-1}} = (b_0 + b_1 D_1 + \ldots + b_k D_k + b_{k+1})(1 + d_0) - b_{k+1}$$

$$+ (c_0 + c_1)(1 + d_0)(1 + \ln x_t) - c_1(1 + \ln x_t)$$

$$= (b_0 + b_1 D_1 + \ldots + b_k D_k)(1 + d_0) + b_{k+1} d_0$$

$$+ c_0(1 + d_0)(1 + \ln x_t) + c_1 d_0(1 + \ln x_t) \quad (7.5)$$

and the total multiplier ($x_t = x_{t-1} = x_{t-2} = \ldots$) is

$$\frac{\partial y_t}{\partial x_t} + \frac{\partial y_t}{\partial x_{t-1}} + \frac{\partial y_t}{\partial x_{t-2}} + \ldots = \frac{b_0 + b_1 D_1 + \ldots + b_k D_k + b_{k+1}}{1 - d_0}$$

$$- \frac{b_{k+1}}{d_0} \frac{d_0}{1 - d_0} + \frac{c_0 + c_1}{1 - d_0}(1 + \ln x_t) - \frac{c_1}{d_0} \frac{d_0}{1 - d_0}(1 + \ln x_t)$$

Table 7.3: Partial derivatives with respect to income and income elasticities of total food expenditure

time span	partial derivative		elasticity	
	f30000	sample mean	f30000	sample mean
Yuppies:				
short run	0.056	0.050	2.149	0.824
medium run	0.103	0.082	3.970	1.363
long run	0.145	0.111	5.627	1.853
Dinkies:				
short run	0.056	0.050	0.419	0.379
medium run	0.103	0.082	0.774	0.626
long run	0.145	0.111	1.096	0.852
Families:				
short run	−0.027	−0.032	−0.084	−0.163
medium run	−0.019	−0.039	−0.058	−0.196
long run	−0.011	−0.045	−0.036	−0.226

Derivatives and elasticities evaluated at $f30000$ and the sample mean

$$= \frac{b_0 + b_1 D_1 + \ldots + b_k D_k}{1 - d_0} + \frac{c_0}{1 - d_0}(1 + \ln x_t) \qquad (7.6)$$

For the calculation of income elasticities, a measure of food expenditure itself is needed. The stationary long-run equilibrium is given by

$$y(x, D_1, \ldots, D_m) =$$

$$\frac{a_0 + a_1 D_1 + \ldots + a_m D_m}{1 - d_0} + \frac{b_0 + b_1 D_1 + \ldots + b_k D_k}{1 - d_0} x + \frac{c_0}{1 - d_0} x \ln x \qquad (7.7)$$

and, using this, the income elasticities follow as in (6.8).

Since education of partner and age have disappeared from the specification, the definition of the household types has been relaxed accordingly, compared to the definitions given in Section 6.1. Yuppies are now households with 1 adult, educated on level 3, and no children, recording expenses in September. Dinkies are defined as households with 2 adults and no children, with the head of the household educated on level 3 and recording expenses in September. Finally, Families consist of 2 adults and 2 or more children younger than 16, with the head educated on level 2.1 and recording expenses in September too. The only household characteristic that is also included as interaction with income is education. Since Yuppies and Dinkies have the same level of education, their partial derivatives are equivalent, as can be seen in Table 7.3.

Food expenditure in f 1000

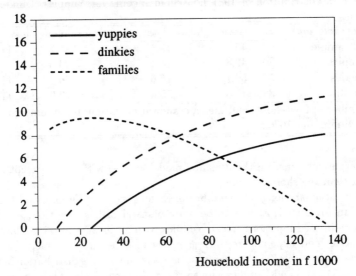

Figure 7.1: Dynamic Engel Curves: stationary long-run equilibrium

Since the interim and total multipliers involve products or quotients of coefficient estimates, their standard errors cannot be calculated straightforwardly. Therefore, no standard errors are reported in Table 7.3. Figure 7.1 shows the stationary long-run equilibrium Engel curves for Yuppies, Dinkies and Families, as in (7.7).

Unfortunately, both Table 7.3 and Figure 7.1 show some peculiar results. According to the estimated functional form, families have negative multipliers and elasticities, due to the low value of the coefficient of EDUCATIONH21 × INCOME (-0.054), compared with EDUCATIONH3 × INCOME (0.028) for Yuppies and Dinkies. Fortunately, these negative multipliers and elasticities are close to zero. Yuppies with an income of f30000 have a rather high income elasticity of food, caused by the low value of food expenditure at that income level (see Figure 7.1). Apart from these anomalies, the results for Yuppies and Dinkies are not implausible. The multipliers and elasticities increase when the time span is lengthened and the long-run income elasticities are close to or even greater than 1. In addition, each multiplier and income elasticity is lower at the sample mean of f45329 than at f30000. Comparing Table 7.3 with Table 6.4, one finds that — for Yuppies and Dinkies — the multipliers and elasticities obtained in static models are usually lower than their long-run

Table 7.4: Distribution of 1987 household income for Yuppies, Dinkies and Families

household type	#	mean	standard deviation	minimum	maximum
full sample	699	45.3	19.1	5.2	148.2
Yuppies	20	42.8	18.4	20.3	90.4
Dinkies	57	59.1	16.6	26.7	112.9
Families	38	43.0	13.4	23.9	111.9

Number of households and mean, standard deviation, minimum and maximum in $f1000$

counterpart obtained in the dynamic model and — with a few exceptions — higher than the short-run one.

The stationary long-run equilibrium Engel curves for Yuppies and Dinkies, shown in Figure 7.1, appear to be quite plausible. It is true that, according to the estimated functional form, Yuppies with an income below $f25000$ have a negative food expenditure, but such low incomes are extremely rare. To illustrate this, Table 7.4 gives some statistics of the income distribution of those Yuppies, Dinkies and Families who are found in the sample. The Yup with the lowest income earns as little as $f20300$ indeed, but the average income in the sample of Yuppies is $f42800$. The Engel curve for Dinkies is even better. On the other hand, the Engel curve for Families reaches its maximum at an income as disappointingly low as approximately $f25000$. As before, this behaviour is caused mainly by the coefficient value of the education and income interaction term.

In the calculations of the interim and total multipliers and the measure of food expenditure in (7.7) and Figure 7.1, a stationary equilibrium was assumed. Alternatively, a steady-state equilibrium could have been assumed. A plausible rate of growth in income would be 2% a year, since that is the average rate of growth in the sample (see Section 2.2.1 on the design of the simulation experiments). The calculations have been repeated using a rate of growth of 2%, but the results in both Table 7.3 and Figure 7.1 are hardly affected. They neither improve nor worsen and are therefore not reported here.

7.3   Using the exact similar tests for a lagged dependent variable

In this chapter, estimation results of dynamic Engel curves have been reported. Only lagged exogenous regressor variables were included in the specification in Section 7.1, allowing estimation with Ordinary Least Squares. In Section

Table 7.5: Exact similar inference on the significance of the lagged dependent variable

regressor	coefficient (critical value)	p-value	t-ratio (critical value)	p-value
y_{-1}	−0.466 (−0.444)	0.16	−13.34 (−12.85)	0.11

5% Critical values for testing $\gamma = 0$ versus $\gamma > 0$ in parentheses
The dependent variable is annual household expenditure on food in $f1000$

7.2, a lagged dependent variable was included in the specification and Generalised Method of Moments estimates were calculated. A specification search procedure resulted in the preferred specification shown in Table C.15, with one lagged dependent and two lagged exogenous regressor variables.

The Generalised Method of Moments provides estimates that are consistent for $N \to \infty$; it does not necessarily allow accurate inference in samples with finite T and N. The test statistics developed in Section 3.2, on the other hand, produce exact and similar — but probably less powerful — inference on the significance of the lagged dependent regressor variable. For the calculation of these test statistics in a specification with a lagged dependent variable and no lagged exogenous variables, three waves of data are needed, so the sample of 699 households over 3 time periods at issue here should suffice. However, if the specification involves lagged exogenous regressors too, then more waves are needed to construct the redundant regressors $(L \otimes I_N)X$ included in the augmented regression (3.21).

Since the preferred specification of Table C.15 involves lagged exogenous regressors and only three waves are available, the exact similar test statistics cannot be calculated for this specification. However, the statistics can be calculated for a specification equal to that in Table C.15 but excluding the lagged exogenous regressor variables Δ INCOME and Δ (INCOME $\times$ ln(INCOME)).

The augmented regression for this case has been estimated and the resulting test statistics $\hat{\gamma}_W$ and $t(\hat{\gamma}_W)$ are calculated, together with their exact p-values (assuming normality) and 5% critical values. The latter two have been obtained by generating 5000 replications of ϵ, statistic (3.28) and its studentised version. The results are given in Table 7.5.

A few general remarks about these exact test procedures are in order. Firstly, whether the regressor variables in the specification are correlated with the individual effects is of no consequence, since the test statistics allow for fixed effects. Secondly, the exact test statistics are based on a fixed effects estimator that is in itself inconsistent for finite T, which explains their rather odd location. If the estimated coefficient $\hat{\gamma}_W$ is larger than its critical value for testing $\gamma = 0$ against $\gamma > 0$, then the null hypothesis has to be rejected, even though the estimated coefficient is negative. For the estimated t-ratio $t(\hat{\gamma}_W)$, the same story applies. More information on the test procedures can be found in Chapter 3.

Table 7.5 shows that both exact test procedures in the preferred specification do not reject the null hypothesis that the coefficient of the lagged dependent variable is zero: the p-values are 0.16 and 0.11, respectively. Interpreting this result, one should bear in mind that, by excluding the lagged exogenous regressors, the specification has been violated. The 'redundant' regressors $(L \otimes I_N)X$ in the augmented regression are not really redundant here, since they should have been in the specification anyway. Another reason for the insignificance result may be lack of power, caused by the elaborate specification and the incidence of fixed effects where such a small number of time periods is available.

Chapter 8

Conclusions

Whereas in time-series econometrics an extensive literature exists on the effects of and tests against dynamic misspecification, in the context of cross-section or panel data it is a relative novelty. In Section 1.1 of the introduction to this thesis, some questions were formulated concerning dynamic processes in classical microeconomic relationships. The rest of the thesis is devoted to the pursuit of answers to those questions and also gives an empirical illustration. The empirical results bear upon Engel curves for food, based on data from the Continuous Budget Surveys 1985, 1986 and 1987 of the Dutch Central Bureau of Statistics.

The first question was whether the pure cross-section analysis of classical relationships, like Engel curves and age-earnings profiles, yields biased inference as a result of the neglect of processes in time. Or, to put it differently, whether anything goes wrong — and, if so, what — when dynamic processes are apparent in a microeconomic relationship, but are nevertheless neglected when the relationship is estimated.

The analytical results, obtained in Section 2.1, suggest that the answer to this question depends on whether the variables in the relationship are stationary or not. When microeconomic data are in reality generated by a dynamic relationship, involving both lagged dependent and current and lagged non-stationary exogenous variables, whereas a static cross-section or panel data model is estimated, then the estimators are found to be consistent (for $N \to \infty$) for the long-run effect. On the other hand, if the exogenous variables follow a stationary process, then the static estimators are found to underestimate the long-run effect. This inconsistency is less severe, the higher the autocorrelation of the exogenous variables.

From a Monte Carlo study in Section 2.2, where the exogenous variables are covariance stationary around a deterministic trend, it is concluded that most static estimators are only slightly biased in the presence of dynamic misspecification. As can be seen from Figures 2.4 and 2.8, the cross-section OLS and pooled OLS estimators are remarkably stable, while the Random Effects estimator is affected a bit more. However, the Fixed Effects or 'within' estimator seems to be extremely sensitive to dynamic misspecification, such that the downward bias could amount to as much as 50% of the long-run effect. Interpreting these results, one should keep in mind that the exogenous regressors in the simulation design are strongly autocorrelated. According to the analytical results mentioned above, high autocorrelation leads to a relatively minor underestimation of the long-run effect. At the same time, it induces a comparatively small within-groups variation (variation in x_i over time) compared to the between-groups variation (variation between x_i and x_j), which — according to Baltagi and Griffin (1984) — may explain the bad performance of the Fixed Effects estimator.

The empirical results confirm the above conclusions. In the static Engel curves, both OLS estimates are quite similar, the Random Effects estimate is almost 50% smaller, while the Fixed Effects estimate is even more so.

The next questions, formulated in the introduction in Section 1.1, were how a dynamic microeconomic relationship should be modelled and what techniques are available for its estimation, supposing dynamic processes are apparent in the relationship. In order to be able to estimate a dynamic microeconomic relationship, panel data must be available; a single cross section is not sufficient. Standard estimators for static panel data models are biased, and often inconsistent, in dynamic models with a lagged dependent variable. Dynamic panel data models can be estimated consistently with the Generalised Method of Moments. The standard Generalised Method of Moments estimator for dynamic panel data models consists basically of writing the model in first differences and employing instruments in levels. In the empirical results in Chapter 7, this estimator gives disappointingly large standard errors and unsatisfactory results that may have to do with the fact that only three waves are available in the data set. More satisfactory results are obtained with an alternative procedure, in which the model is specified in levels whereas instruments are employed in differenced form. Addition of lagged exogenous and lagged dependent variables in the preferred static Engel curve leads to the conclusion that both types of lagged variables are significant, especially the lagged expenditure variable.

Finally in Section 1.1, it was said that it would be desirable to know how possible dynamics in a microeconomic relationship can be detected. Existing tests for the presence of a lagged dependent variable among the regressors of a panel data model are valid only asymptotically, for either an infinite number of individuals or an infinite number of time periods. In Section 3.2, two tests for the presence of a lagged dependent variable in panel data models are developed, which are exact and similar — that is, independent of nuisance parameters — for finite T and N. Monte Carlo results, presented in Section 3.3, suggest a satisfactory power performance of these tests, compared to the asymptotic ones.

In the empirical application, both exact test statistics are unable to conclude that the lagged dependent variable is significant. However, since only three consecutive waves of the panel data set are available, this result must not be taken too seriously. With only three waves, neither the null nor the alternative hypothesis of these tests can include lagged exogenous variables. In other words, the tests can only compare a static specification to a specification involving a partial adjustment mechanism. Error correction mechanisms cannot be considered, since these require the availability of at least four waves. Yet, from the empirical results obtained with the Generalised Method of Moments, it was concluded that error correction mechanisms are apparent in the Engel curve for food.

Apart from being illustrative of the theoretical issues considered, the empirical results in the thesis are interesting in their own right. The empirical analysis starts with two general functional forms that include the most commonly used specifications as special cases. Apart from (several transformations of) household income, variables for household size, age, socio-economic background and residential area are included in these general forms, as well as two variables accounting for possible non-random measurement errors in the dependent variable (recording month and holiday length). Through statistical test procedures, the data are left to decide which of these general forms and which of its special cases is going to be the preferred static Engel curve for total food expenditure. In the preferred static specification, the income elasticity is estimated at approximately 0.5 to 0.7, depending on the level of income and several other household characteristics. These include number of adults and number of children in the household, age of the head of the household, education of the head of the household and of the partner and recording month. Of the variables included in the general forms, those measuring profession, geographical region, degree of urbanisation and holiday length are found to play an insignificant role in the determination of expenditure.

The general view is that the neglect of dynamics in Engel curves for everyday commodities such as food is justified. In Chapter 7, a thorough misspecification analysis is carried out to show whether this is indeed the case. Since only three consecutive waves of the panel data set are available, this analysis is unavoidably limited. Addition of lagged exogenous and lagged dependent variables in the preferred cross-section specification leads to the conclusion that both types of lagged variables are significant, especially the lagged expenditure variable. Although the estimated long-run income elasticities in the preferred dynamic specification do not differ considerably from their counterparts in the static cross-section Engel curve, the estimated short-run elasticities are typically lower.

In the static model, both OLS estimates are quite similar, the Random Effects estimate is almost 50% smaller, while the Fixed Effects estimate is even more so. From a cross-section analysis, one is inclined to infer that the income elasticity of food expenditure is about 0.6. However, a much lower elasticity estimate is produced by the Fixed Effects estimator, which allows for individual effects that may be correlated with the income variable. (Incidentally, the overwhelmingly significant Hausman test statistic shows that the individual effects are indeed correlated with the regressor.) In addition, the Generalised Method of Moments estimate, which allows for both singly exogenous regressors and dynamics, yields an even lower short-run income elasticity. Apparently, the permanent individual specific effects and the persistent influence of food consumption in the past capture the major part of individual consumer behaviour; any (in reality usually relatively minor) changes in income have no significant effect on food expenditure. It would seem that a change in income — ceteris paribus — does not change food consumption considerably. Presumably, the OLS estimates do not only suffer from a negative bias induced by dynamic misspecification, but also from a large positive heterogeneity bias of the form as illustrated by Hsiao (1986, Figure 1.1).

If household income follows a non-stationary process, just as its macroeconomic aggregate is generally found to do, then — in line with the results of Chapter 2 — it is not surprising that the income elasticity estimated in the cross-section regression approximates the long-run elasticity reasonably well. Judging from the high significance of the lagged variables and the estimated short-run elasticities, however, even in Engel curves for everyday commodities such as food, it is found that the neglect of dynamics is not justified.

The estimation of dynamic panel data models in this thesis has been hindered considerably by the fact that only three waves of the data set were available. If there had been more waves, the choice between several dynamic specifications and between several estimation methods would certainly have been much less ambiguous. In particular, with only three waves, neither the null nor the alternative hypothesis of the exact tests developed in Chapter 3 can include lagged exogenous variables. In other words, the exact tests can only compare a static specification to a specification involving a partial adjustment mechanism. Error correction mechanisms cannot be considered, since these require the availability of at least four waves.

Despite these limitations, an important conclusion about the relative costs of panel data can be drawn. Due to the individual effects, the preferred dynamic panel data specification involves only a few explanatory variables, while in the preferred cross-section specification no less than 67 regressors have to be included. Although for panel data more than one wave has to be collected, these waves need to include less variables each, so, as far as the analysis of Engel curves is concerned, it may be stated that the collection of panel data is not necessarily more expensive than cross sections. A further advantage is that shorter questionnaires would presumably lead to fewer drop-outs. Of course, where applications other than dynamic Engel curves are concerned, this thesis does not offer any guidance about what variables have to be included in the questionnaire.

In the thesis, only Engel curves for total food expenditure are estimated. It would be interesting to see how the conclusions are affected if separate categories of food (such as fruit and vegetables or dairy products) or semi-durable goods (such as clothing and shoes) were taken instead. In Chapter 4, it is explained for which categories of commodities data on both expenditure and prices are available. These categories of commodities were originally intended to be included in the empirical analysis of the thesis. Unfortunately, these original intentions turned out to be a shade too ambitious.

Appendix A

Asymptotic consequences of neglected dynamics

A.1 The long-run equilibrium in a steady-state

Upon omitting the error term, the data generating process (2.1) can be written as

$$\breve{y}_{it} = \gamma \breve{y}_{i,t-1} + (\beta_0 + \beta_1)\breve{x}_{it} + \alpha_i - \beta_1 \xi_i$$

When $\breve{x}_{i,t-s} = \breve{x}_{it} - s\xi_i$ is substituted, it is found that

$$\breve{y}_{it} = (\beta_0 + \beta_1) \sum_{s=0}^{\infty} \gamma^s (\breve{x}_{it} - s\xi_i) + \frac{1}{1-\gamma}(\alpha_i - \beta_1 \xi_i)$$

and (2.2) follows upon using $\sum_{s=0}^{\infty} s\gamma^s = \gamma/(1-\gamma)^2$.

A.2 The DGP in the non-stationary case

The data generating process (2.1) can be written as

$$y_{it} = \beta_0 \sum_{s=0}^{t-1} \gamma^s x_{i,t-s} + \beta_1 \sum_{s=0}^{t-1} \gamma^s x_{i,t-1-s} + \alpha_i \sum_{s=0}^{t-1} \gamma^s + \sum_{s=0}^{t-1} \gamma^s \epsilon_{i,t-s} + \gamma^t y_{i0}$$

and, after substitution of (2.6) and (2.7), this leads to:

$$y_{it} = \beta_0 \sum_{s=0}^{t-1} \gamma^s \left(x_{i0} + (t-s)\xi_i + \sum_{r=1}^{t-s} \omega_{ir} \right)$$

115

$$+\beta_1 \sum_{s=0}^{t-1} \gamma^s \left(x_{i0} + (t-1-s)\xi_i + \sum_{r=1}^{t-s} \omega_{ir} \right)$$

$$-\beta_1 \sum_{s=0}^{t-1} \gamma^s \omega_{i,t-s} + \frac{1-\gamma^t}{1-\gamma}\alpha_i + \sum_{s=0}^{t-1} \gamma^s \epsilon_{i,t-s}$$

$$+\gamma^t \left(\frac{\beta_0+\beta_1}{1-\gamma}x_{i0} + \frac{1}{1-\gamma}\alpha_i - \frac{\gamma\beta_0+\beta_1}{(1-\gamma)^2}\xi_i \right)$$

$$= \beta_0 \frac{1-\gamma^t}{1-\gamma}x_{i0} + \beta_1 \frac{1-\gamma^t}{1-\gamma}x_{i0} + \gamma^t \frac{\beta_0+\beta_1}{1-\gamma}x_{i0} + \frac{1-\gamma^t}{1-\gamma}\alpha_i + \frac{\gamma^t}{1-\gamma}\alpha_i$$

$$+\beta_0 \xi_i \sum_{s=0}^{t-1}(t-s)\gamma^s + \beta_1 \xi_i \sum_{s=0}^{t-1}(t-1-s)\gamma^s - \frac{\gamma\beta_0+\beta_1}{1-\gamma} \frac{\gamma^t}{1-\gamma}\xi_i$$

$$+(\beta_0+\beta_1)\sum_{s=0}^{t-1}\gamma^s \left(\sum_{r=1}^{t-s} \omega_{ir} \right) - \beta_1 \sum_{s=0}^{t-1} \gamma^s \omega_{i,t-s} + \sum_{s=0}^{t-1}\gamma^s \epsilon_{i,t-s}$$

Making use of:

$$\sum_{s=0}^{t-1}(t-1-s)\gamma^s = \frac{t}{1-\gamma} - \frac{1-\gamma^t}{(1-\gamma)^2}$$

$$\sum_{s=0}^{t-1}(t-s)\gamma^s = \frac{t}{1-\gamma} - \frac{1-\gamma^t}{(1-\gamma)^2} + \frac{1-\gamma^t}{1-\gamma}$$

$$\sum_{s=0}^{t-1}\gamma^s \left(\sum_{r=1}^{t-s} \omega_{ir} \right) = \sum_{s=1}^{t} \omega_{is}\frac{1-\gamma^{t-s+1}}{1-\gamma}$$

it follows that:

$$y_{it} = \frac{\beta_0+\beta_1}{1-\gamma}x_{i0} + \frac{1}{1-\gamma}\alpha_i + \beta_0 \left(\frac{t}{1-\gamma} - \frac{1-\gamma^t}{(1-\gamma)^2} + \frac{1-\gamma^t}{1-\gamma} \right)\xi_i$$

$$+\beta_1 \left(\frac{t}{1-\gamma} - \frac{1-\gamma^t}{(1-\gamma)^2} \right)\xi_i - \frac{\gamma\beta_0+\beta_1}{1-\gamma} \frac{\gamma^t}{1-\gamma}\xi_i$$

$$+(\beta_0+\beta_1)\sum_{s=1}^{t}\frac{1-\gamma^{t-s+1}}{1-\gamma}\omega_{is} - \beta_1 \sum_{s=1}^{t} \gamma^{t-s}\omega_{is} + \sum_{s=1}^{t} \gamma^{t-s}\epsilon_{is}$$

$$= \frac{\beta_0+\beta_1}{1-\gamma}x_{i0} + \frac{1}{1-\gamma}\alpha_i + \beta_0 \frac{1-\gamma^t}{1-\gamma}\xi_i$$

$$+\frac{\beta_0+\beta_1}{1-\gamma} \left(t - \frac{1-\gamma^t}{1-\gamma} \right)\xi_i - \frac{\gamma\beta_0+\beta_1}{1-\gamma} \frac{\gamma^t}{1-\gamma}\xi_i$$

$$+\frac{\beta_0+\beta_1}{1-\gamma}\sum_{s=1}^{t}(1-\gamma^{t-s+1})\omega_{is} - \beta_1 \sum_{s=1}^{t} \gamma^{t-s}\omega_{is} + \sum_{s=1}^{t} \gamma^{t-s}\epsilon_{is}$$

which is equivalent to (2.8).

A.3 Probability limits in the non-stationary case

The probability limit of the numerator of cross-section OLS estimator (2.11) can be derived as follows:

$$
\operatorname*{plim}_{N\to\infty} \tfrac{1}{N}\tilde{x}_t'\tilde{y}_t = \operatorname*{plim}_{N\to\infty} \tfrac{1}{N}\left(\tilde{x}_0' + t\tilde{\xi}' + \sum_{s=1}^{t}\tilde{\omega}_s' \right)
$$

$$
\left(\frac{\beta_0+\beta_1}{1-\gamma}\tilde{x}_0 + \frac{1}{1-\gamma}\tilde{\alpha} + \frac{\beta_0+\beta_1}{1-\gamma}t\tilde{\xi} - \frac{\gamma\beta_0+\beta_1}{(1-\gamma)^2}\tilde{\xi} \right.
$$

$$
\left. + \frac{\beta_0+\beta_1}{1-\gamma}\sum_{s=1}^{t}\tilde{\omega}_s - \frac{\gamma\beta_0+\beta_1}{1-\gamma}\sum_{s=1}^{t}\gamma^{t-s}\tilde{\omega}_s + \sum_{s=1}^{t}\gamma^{t-s}\tilde{\epsilon}_s \right)
$$

$$
= \frac{\beta_0+\beta_1}{1-\gamma}\sigma_{x_0}^2 + \frac{\beta_0+\beta_1}{1-\gamma}t\sigma_{x_0\xi} - \frac{\gamma\beta_0+\beta_1}{(1-\gamma)^2}\sigma_{x_0\xi} + \frac{\beta_0+\beta_1}{1-\gamma}t\sigma_{x_0\xi}
$$

$$
+ \frac{\beta_0+\beta_1}{1-\gamma}t^2\sigma_\xi^2 - \frac{\gamma\beta_0+\beta_1}{(1-\gamma)^2}t\sigma_\xi^2 + \frac{\beta_0+\beta_1}{1-\gamma}\sum_{s=1}^{t}\sigma_\omega^2 - \frac{\gamma\beta_0+\beta_1}{1-\gamma}\sum_{s=1}^{t}\gamma^{t-s}\sigma_\omega^2
$$

which is equivalent to (2.19).

For the panel data case, the probability limit of the numerator of estimator (2.24) is:

$$
\operatorname*{plim}_{N\to\infty} \tfrac{1}{NT}x'(M_J + \mu P_J)y =
$$

$$
\operatorname*{plim}_{N\to\infty} \tfrac{1}{NT}\left(x_0'(\iota_3' \otimes I_N) + \xi'(\iota_T'Z' \otimes I_N) + \omega'(Z' \otimes I_N) \right)(M_J + \mu P_J)
$$

$$
\left(\frac{\beta_0+\beta_1}{1-\gamma}(\iota_3 \otimes I_N)x_0 + \frac{1}{1-\gamma}(\iota_3 \otimes I_N)\alpha \right.
$$

$$
+ \frac{\beta_0+\beta_1}{1-\gamma}(Z\iota_T \otimes I_N)\xi - \frac{\gamma\beta_0+\beta_1}{(1-\gamma)^2}(\iota_3 \otimes I_N)\xi
$$

$$
\left. + \frac{\beta_0+\beta_1}{1-\gamma}(Z \otimes I_N)\omega - \frac{\gamma\beta_0+\beta_1}{1-\gamma}(\Gamma \otimes I_N)\omega + (\Gamma \otimes I_N)\epsilon \right)
$$

$$
= \operatorname*{plim}_{N\to\infty} \tfrac{1}{NT}\left(\frac{\beta_0+\beta_1}{1-\gamma}x_0'(\iota_3' \otimes I_N)(M_J + \mu P_J)(\iota_3 \otimes I_N)x_0 \right.
$$

$$
+ \frac{\beta_0+\beta_1}{1-\gamma}x_0'(\iota_3' \otimes I_N)(M_J + \mu P_J)(Z\iota_T \otimes I_N)\xi
$$

$$
- \frac{\gamma\beta_0+\beta_1}{(1-\gamma)^2}x_0'(\iota_3' \otimes I_N)(M_J + \mu P_J)(\iota_3 \otimes I_N)\xi
$$

$$+\frac{\beta_0+\beta_1}{1-\gamma}\xi'(\iota_T'Z'\otimes I_N)(M_J+\mu P_J)(\iota_3\otimes I_N)x_0$$

$$+\frac{\beta_0+\beta_1}{1-\gamma}\xi'(\iota_T'Z'\otimes I_N)(M_J+\mu P_J)(Z\iota_T\otimes I_N)\xi$$

$$-\frac{\gamma\beta_0+\beta_1}{(1-\gamma)^2}\xi'(\iota_T'Z'\otimes I_N)(M_J+\mu P_J)(\iota_3\otimes I_N)\xi$$

$$+\frac{\beta_0+\beta_1}{1-\gamma}\omega'(Z'\otimes I_N)(M_J+\mu P_J)(Z\otimes I_N)\omega$$

$$\left.-\frac{\gamma\beta_0+\beta_1}{1-\gamma}\omega'(Z'\otimes I_N)(M_J+\mu P_J)(\Gamma\otimes I_N)\omega\right)$$

$$=\operatorname*{plim}_{N\to\infty}\frac{1}{NT}\left(\frac{\beta_0+\beta_1}{1-\gamma}x_0'(3\mu\otimes I_N)x_0+\frac{\beta_0+\beta_1}{1-\gamma}x_0'(\mu\iota_3'Z\iota_T\otimes I_N)\xi\right.$$

$$-\frac{\gamma\beta_0+\beta_1}{(1-\gamma)^2}x_0'(3\mu\otimes I_N)\xi+\frac{\beta_0+\beta_1}{1-\gamma}\xi'(\mu\iota_T'Z'\iota_3\otimes I_N)x_0$$

$$+\frac{\beta_0+\beta_1}{1-\gamma}\xi'\{([-1,0,1]+\mu(T-1)\iota_3')Z\iota_T\otimes I_N\}\xi$$

$$-\frac{\gamma\beta_0+\beta_1}{(1-\gamma)^2}\xi'(\mu\iota_T'Z'\iota_3\otimes I_N)\xi+\frac{\beta_0+\beta_1}{1-\gamma}\omega'\{Z'(M_\iota+\mu P_\iota)Z\otimes I_N\}\omega$$

$$\left.-\frac{\gamma\beta_0+\beta_1}{1-\gamma}\omega'\{Z'(M_\iota+\mu P_\iota)\Gamma\otimes I_N\}\omega\right)$$

$$=\frac{\beta_0+\beta_1}{1-\gamma}3\mu\sigma_{x_0}^2+\frac{\beta_0+\beta_1}{1-\gamma}\mu(3T-3)\sigma_{x_0\xi}$$

$$-\frac{\gamma\beta_0+\beta_1}{(1-\gamma)^2}3\mu\sigma_{x_0\xi}+\frac{\beta_0+\beta_1}{1-\gamma}\mu(3T-3)\sigma_{x_0\xi}$$

$$+\frac{\beta_0+\beta_1}{1-\gamma}\{-(T-2)+T+\mu(T-1)(3T-3)\}\sigma_\xi^2-\frac{\gamma\beta_0+\beta_1}{(1-\gamma)^2}\mu(3T-3)\sigma_\xi^2$$

$$+\frac{\beta_0+\beta_1}{1-\gamma}\operatorname{trace}\{Z'(M_\iota+\mu P_\iota)Z\}\sigma_\omega^2-\frac{\gamma\beta_0+\beta_1}{1-\gamma}\operatorname{trace}\{Z'(M_\iota+\mu P_\iota)\Gamma\}\sigma_\omega^2$$

$$=\frac{\beta_0+\beta_1}{1-\gamma}3\mu\sigma_{x_0}^2+\frac{\beta_0+\beta_1}{1-\gamma}6\mu(T-1)\sigma_{x_0\xi}-\frac{\gamma\beta_0+\beta_1}{(1-\gamma)^2}3\mu\sigma_{x_0\xi}$$

$$+\frac{\beta_0+\beta_1}{1-\gamma}\{2+3\mu(T-1)^2\}\sigma_\xi^2-\frac{\gamma\beta_0+\beta_1}{(1-\gamma)^2}3\mu(T-1)\sigma_\xi^2$$

$$+\frac{\beta_0+\beta_1}{1-\gamma}\{(T-2)3\mu+(\tfrac{2}{3}+\tfrac{4}{3}\mu)+(\tfrac{2}{3}+\tfrac{1}{3}\mu)\}\sigma_\omega^2$$

$$-\frac{\gamma\beta_0 + \beta_1}{1 - \gamma}\{\mu(\gamma^{T-1} + \gamma^{T-2} + \gamma^{T-3}) + \ldots + \mu(\gamma^2 + \gamma^1 + \gamma^0)$$
$$+ (\tfrac{1}{3} + \tfrac{2}{3}\mu)(\gamma^1 + \gamma^0) + (\tfrac{2}{3} + \tfrac{1}{3}\mu)\gamma^0\}\sigma_\omega^2$$

which is equivalent to (2.31).

Appendix B

Consistent estimation of the variance components

The variance components in the random effects model can be estimated in various ways. Here, a derivation is given of the way in which they have been calculated in the simulation experiments described in Section 2.2, as well as in the empirical application in Chapter 6. In the model

$$y = X\beta + \iota_T \otimes \alpha + \epsilon = X\beta + J\alpha + \epsilon = X\beta + u = Z\theta + \epsilon$$

with $Z = [X : J]$, $\theta' = [\beta', \alpha']$ and $u = J\alpha + \epsilon$ and where $E\alpha = \bar{\alpha}\iota_N$, $Eu = \bar{\alpha}\iota_{NT}$ and

$$Euu' = V(u) + \bar{\alpha}^2 \iota_{NT} \iota'_{NT} = \sigma_\epsilon^2 M_J + (T\sigma_\alpha^2 + \sigma_\epsilon^2) P_J + T\bar{\alpha}^2 P_{\iota_{NT}}$$

the results for the FE estimator can be used to obtain estimates of σ_ϵ^2 and σ_α^2. For $\hat{\theta} = (Z'Z)^{-1}Z'y$ and $\hat{\epsilon} = y - Z\hat{\theta} = M_Z y = M_Z \epsilon$ it is found that

$$E\hat{\epsilon}'\hat{\epsilon} = \sigma_\epsilon^2 \, \text{tr} \, (M_Z) = \sigma_\epsilon^2 (NT - K - N)$$

Hence

$$\hat{\sigma}_\epsilon^2 = \hat{\epsilon}'\hat{\epsilon}/[(T-1)N - K]$$

is an unbiased estimator of σ_ϵ^2 if X is fixed, and for $N \to \infty$ it is consistent under much weaker regularity assumptions.

Now consider

$$\hat{u} = y - X\hat{\beta}_{FE} = y - X(X'M_J X)^{-1} X'M_J y$$

$$= [I - X(X'M_J X)^{-1} X'M_J]u = Ru$$

with R implicitly defined, and examine

$$E(\hat{u}'M_{\iota_{NT}} P_J M_{\iota_{NT}} \hat{u}) = E(u'R'M_{\iota_{NT}} P_J M_{\iota_{NT}} Ru)$$

121

$$= \text{tr}\ (R'M_{\iota_{NT}}P_JM_{\iota_{NT}}R[\sigma_\epsilon^2 M_J + (T\sigma_\alpha^2 + \sigma_\epsilon^2)P_J + T\bar{\alpha}^2 P_{\iota_{NT}}])$$
$$= \sigma_\epsilon^2\ \text{tr}\ (R'M_{\iota_{NT}}P_JM_{\iota_{NT}}RM_J) + (T\sigma_\alpha^2 + \sigma_\epsilon^2)\ \text{tr}\ (R'M_{\iota_{NT}}P_JM_{\iota_{NT}}RP_J)$$
$$+T\bar{\alpha}^2\ \text{tr}\ (R'M_{\iota_{NT}}P_JM_{\iota_{NT}}RP_{\iota_{NT}})$$

Note that

$$P_{\iota_{NT}}P_J\ =\ P_{\iota_{NT}}$$
$$M_{\iota_{NT}}P_J\ =\ P_J - P_{\iota_{NT}}$$
$$P_{\iota_{NT}}M_J\ =\ 0$$
$$M_{\iota_{NT}}M_J\ =\ M_J$$

and hence

$$M_{\iota_{NT}}RM_J\ =\ M_J - M_{\iota_{NT}}X(X'M_JX)^{-1}X'M_J$$
$$M_{\iota_{NT}}RP_J\ =\ P_J - P_{\iota_{NT}}$$
$$M_{\iota_{NT}}RP_{\iota_{NT}}\ =\ 0$$

Upon using these expressions, it is found that

$$\text{E}(\hat{u}'M_{\iota_{NT}}P_JM_{\iota_{NT}}\hat{u}) =$$

$$\sigma_\epsilon^2\ \text{tr}\ R'M_{\iota_{NT}}P_J[M_J - M_{\iota_{NT}}X(X'M_JX)^{-1}X'M_J]$$
$$+(T\sigma_\alpha^2 + \sigma_\epsilon^2)\ \text{tr}\ R'M_{\iota_{NT}}P_J(P_J - P_{\iota_{NT}})$$
$$= \sigma_\epsilon^2\ \text{tr}\ R'(P_J - P_{\iota_{NT}})M_{\iota_{NT}}X(X'M_JX)^{-1}X'M_J$$
$$+(T\sigma_\alpha^2 + \sigma_\epsilon^2)\ \text{tr}\ R'(P_J - P_{\iota_{NT}})$$

Making use of

$$R'(P_J - P_{\iota_{NT}}) = P_J - P_{\iota_{NT}} + M_JX(X'M_JX)^{-1}X'(P_{\iota_{NT}} - P_J)$$

it follows that

$$\text{tr}\ R'(P_J - P_{\iota_{NT}}) = \text{rank}(P_J) - \text{rank}(P_{\iota_{NT}})$$

$$+\ \text{tr}\ (X'M_JX)^{-1}X'(P_{\iota_{NT}} - P_J)M_JX = N - 1$$

and

$$\text{tr}\ R'(P_J - P_{\iota_{NT}})M_{\iota_{NT}}X(X'M_JX)^{-1}X'M_J$$
$$= \text{tr}\ (X'M_JX)^{-1}X'M_JR'(P_J - P_{\iota_{NT}})X$$
$$= \text{tr}\ (X'M_JX)^{-1}X'(P_{\iota_{NT}} - P_J)X = K'$$

with K' implicitly defined. Hence,

$$\mathrm{E}(\hat{u}'M_{\iota_{NT}}P_J M_{\iota_{NT}}\hat{u}) = \sigma_\alpha^2 T(N-1) + \sigma_\epsilon^2(N-1+K')$$

and

$$\hat{\sigma}_\alpha^2 = \frac{1}{T(N-1)}\hat{u}'M_{\iota_{NT}}P_J M_{\iota_{NT}}\hat{u} - \frac{N-1+K'}{T(N-1)}\hat{\sigma}_\epsilon^2$$

$$\approx \frac{1}{T(N-1)}\hat{u}'M_{\iota_{NT}}P_J M_{\iota_{NT}}\hat{u} - \frac{1}{T}\hat{\sigma}_\epsilon^2$$

is an estimator of σ_α^2 which is consistent for $N \to \infty$ under mild regularity conditions; see for instance Hsiao (1986, p. 40).

Appendix C

Full estimation results

This appendix consists of tables comprising the full estimation results of static and dynamic Engel curves for food, as described in Chapters 6 and 7 respectively. Tables C.1 to C.6 show several static Engel curves, while Tables C.7 to C.16 are concerned with dynamic specifications.

Table C.1: Cross-section estimation results of the preferred equation

characteristic	value	
number of observations	699	
degrees of freedom	631	
residual sum of squares	3221	
total sum of squares	6820	
R-squared (adjusted R-squared)	0.528	(0.477)
standard error of the regression	2.259	
skewness of residuals	0.938	
excess kurtosis of residuals	2.569	
LM_N	295	
$LM_H(1)$: income only	19.2	
$LM_H(67)$: all regressors	199	

variable or variable group	degrees of freedom
intercept	1
income	2
number of adults	2
number of children	2
age	8
age × income	8
number of children × age	11
education of head	3
education of head × income	3
education of partner	3
education of partner × income	3
recording month	11
recording month × income	11

variable	coefficient	standard error	p-value
INTERCEPT	−0.173	1.372	0.900
INCOME	0.367	0.098	0.000
INCOME × ln(INCOME)	−0.063	0.020	0.002

Table C.1: Continued			
variable	coefficient	standard error	p-value
ADULTS2	2.156	0.428	0.000
ADULTS3	3.297	0.504	0.000
CHILDREN1	−0.067	0.507	0.895
CHILDREN2	−0.151	0.474	0.750
AGE30	1.023	0.989	0.301
AGE35	−0.949	1.228	0.440
AGE40	−2.963	1.044	0.005
AGE45	−1.922	1.031	0.063
AGE50	−1.376	1.201	0.252
AGE55	−1.277	0.949	0.179
AGE60	−1.053	0.904	0.244
AGE65	−1.407	0.833	0.092
AGE30 × INCOME	−0.010	0.021	0.641
AGE35 × INCOME	0.025	0.022	0.256
AGE40 × INCOME	0.056	0.021	0.009
AGE45 × INCOME	0.056	0.021	0.009
AGE50 × INCOME	0.042	0.027	0.121
AGE55 × INCOME	0.049	0.023	0.030
AGE60 × INCOME	0.026	0.023	0.247
AGE65 × INCOME	0.033	0.022	0.132
CHILDREN1 × AGE30	−0.695	0.751	0.355
CHILDREN2 × AGE30	0.896	0.668	0.180
CHILDREN1 × AGE35	1.419	1.047	0.175
CHILDREN2 × AGE35	1.673	0.791	0.035
CHILDREN1 × AGE40	1.919	0.789	0.015
CHILDREN2 × AGE40	2.125	0.703	0.003
CHILDREN1 × AGE45	0.819	0.995	0.411
CHILDREN2 × AGE45	0.059	1.021	0.954
CHILDREN1 × AGE50	−0.569	1.837	0.757
CHILDREN1 × AGE55	−2.658	1.046	0.011
CHILDREN2 × AGE60	2.750	1.326	0.039
EDUCATIONH21	0.133	0.736	0.857
EDUCATIONH22	0.708	0.712	0.320
EDUCATIONH3	−1.842	0.832	0.027
EDUCATIONP1	−2.055	0.977	0.036
EDUCATIONP21	−0.848	0.935	0.365
EDUCATIONP22	−0.521	0.743	0.483

Table C.1: Continued

variable	coefficient	standard error	p-value
EDUCATIONH21 × INCOME	−0.014	0.021	0.502
EDUCATIONH22 × INCOME	−0.022	0.021	0.300
EDUCATIONH3 × INCOME	0.030	0.021	0.156
EDUCATIONP1 × INCOME	0.047	0.023	0.042
EDUCATIONP21 × INCOME	0.027	0.019	0.161
EDUCATIONP22 × INCOME	0.014	0.013	0.290
MONTHJAN	1.324	0.992	0.182
MONTHFEB	1.023	0.965	0.290
MONTHMAR	1.405	0.975	0.150
MONTHAPR	2.093	1.184	0.078
MONTHMAY	2.595	1.042	0.013
MONTHJUN	1.794	1.125	0.111
MONTHJUL	0.982	1.079	0.363
MONTHAUG	0.972	1.310	0.458
MONTHSEP	1.266	1.038	0.223
MONTHOCT	0.476	1.086	0.661
MONTHNOV	1.221	0.932	0.191
MONTHJAN × INCOME	−0.057	0.024	0.016
MONTHFEB × INCOME	−0.042	0.024	0.081
MONTHMAR × INCOME	−0.063	0.024	0.009
MONTHAPR × INCOME	−0.055	0.027	0.039
MONTHMAY × INCOME	−0.059	0.026	0.020
MONTHJUN × INCOME	−0.048	0.028	0.089
MONTHJUL × INCOME	−0.038	0.026	0.140
MONTHAUG × INCOME	−0.022	0.031	0.479
MONTHSEP × INCOME	−0.032	0.025	0.198
MONTHOCT × INCOME	−0.003	0.026	0.895
MONTHNOV × INCOME	−0.054	0.023	0.020

The dependent variable is annual household expenditure on food in f1000
Standard errors and test statistics are corrected for heteroscedasticity

Table C.2: Pooled OLS estimation results of equation (5.8)lin with time effects

characteristic		value	
number of observations		2097	
degrees of freedom		2025	
residual sum of squares		10800	
total sum of squares		21225	
R-squared (adjusted R-squared)		0.491	(0.473)
standard error of the regression		2.309	
skewness of residuals		1.679	
excess kurtosis of residuals		11.903	
LM_N		13365	
LM_N for separate waves	268	22455	289
$LM_H(1)$		173	
$LM_H(1)$ for separate waves	31.4	130	29.5
$LM_H(69)$		871	
$LM_H(69)$ for separate waves	167	1674	203

variable or variable group	degrees of freedom
time effects	3
income	2
number of adults	2
number of children	2
age	8
age × income	8
number of children × age	13
education of head	3
education of head × income	3
education of partner	3
education of partner × income	3
recording month	11
recording month × income	11

variable	coefficient	standard error	p-value
DUMMY 1985	3.564	0.901	0.000
DUMMY 1986	3.496	0.904	0.000
DUMMY 1987	3.368	0.905	0.000
INCOME	0.074	0.065	0.250
INCOME × ln(INCOME)	−0.013	0.014	0.335

Table C.2: Continued

variable	coefficient	standard error	p-value
ADULTS2	2.387	0.268	0.000
ADULTS3	3.745	0.313	0.000
CHILDREN1	0.239	0.387	0.538
CHILDREN2	0.713	0.377	0.058
AGE30	0.193	0.703	0.784
AGE35	−0.706	0.745	0.344
AGE40	−2.326	0.763	0.002
AGE45	−1.678	0.736	0.023
AGE50	−1.079	0.808	0.182
AGE55	−1.183	0.729	0.105
AGE60	−1.453	0.660	0.028
AGE65	−1.604	0.613	0.009
AGE30 × INCOME	0.016	0.014	0.269
AGE35 × INCOME	0.031	0.014	0.031
AGE40 × INCOME	0.065	0.015	0.000
AGE45 × INCOME	0.056	0.015	0.000
AGE50 × INCOME	0.049	0.017	0.003
AGE55 × INCOME	0.055	0.016	0.000
AGE60 × INCOME	0.051	0.015	0.000
AGE65 × INCOME	0.044	0.014	0.002
CHILDREN1 × AGE30	−0.603	0.543	0.267
CHILDREN2 × AGE30	0.052	0.474	0.912
CHILDREN1 × AGE35	0.719	0.577	0.213
CHILDREN2 × AGE35	0.693	0.504	0.169
CHILDREN1 × AGE40	0.712	0.633	0.261
CHILDREN2 × AGE40	0.995	0.590	0.092
CHILDREN1 × AGE45	0.440	0.561	0.433
CHILDREN2 × AGE45	0.521	0.752	0.488
CHILDREN1 × AGE50	0.268	0.822	0.744
CHILDREN2 × AGE50	0.289	1.246	0.816
CHILDREN1 × AGE55	−2.119	0.868	0.015
CHILDREN2 × AGE55	0.943	1.138	0.407
CHILDREN2 × AGE60	1.936	1.247	0.121
EDUCATIONH21	−0.098	0.501	0.845
EDUCATIONH22	0.264	0.477	0.580
EDUCATIONH3	−0.437	0.580	0.450
EDUCATIONP1	−1.584	0.606	0.009
EDUCATIONP21	−0.608	0.500	0.224
EDUCATIONP22	−0.276	0.460	0.549

Table C.2: Continued

variable	coefficient	standard error	p-value
EDUCATIONH21 × INCOME	0.004	0.013	0.787
EDUCATIONH22 × INCOME	−0.005	0.012	0.709
EDUCATIONH3 × INCOME	0.015	0.013	0.270
EDUCATIONP1 × INCOME	0.040	0.013	0.002
EDUCATIONP21 × INCOME	0.020	0.010	0.033
EDUCATIONP22 × INCOME	0.007	0.008	0.411
MONTHJAN	−0.867	0.754	0.251
MONTHFEB	−0.941	0.708	0.184
MONTHMAR	−0.791	0.696	0.256
MONTHAPR	−0.184	0.728	0.801
MONTHMAY	0.250	0.749	0.738
MONTHJUN	−0.272	0.686	0.692
MONTHJUL	−0.565	0.763	0.459
MONTHAUG	0.202	0.746	0.787
MONTHSEP	−0.632	0.667	0.343
MONTHOCT	−0.485	0.693	0.484
MONTHNOV	−0.255	0.670	0.704
MONTHJAN × INCOME	−0.011	0.016	0.489
MONTHFEB × INCOME	0.000	0.016	0.960
MONTHMAR × INCOME	−0.006	0.015	0.705
MONTHAPR × INCOME	−0.014	0.016	0.371
MONTHMAY × INCOME	−0.009	0.016	0.559
MONTHJUN × INCOME	−0.006	0.015	0.697
MONTHJUL × INCOME	−0.010	0.017	0.568
MONTHAUG × INCOME	−0.013	0.016	0.419
MONTHSEP × INCOME	0.000	0.015	0.977
MONTHOCT × INCOME	−0.000	0.015	0.968
MONTHNOV × INCOME	−0.017	0.014	0.249

The dependent variable is annual household expenditure on food in $f1000$

Table C.3: FE estimation results of equation (5.8)lin

characteristic		value	
number of observations		2097	
degrees of freedom		1328	
residual sum of squares		3657	
total sum of squares		21225	
R-squared (adjusted R-squared)		0.828	(0.728)
standard error of the regression		1.659	
skewness of residuals		1.127	
excess kurtosis of residuals		17.151	
LM_N		26146	
LM_N for separate waves	470	54969	1525
$LM_H(1)$		251	
$LM_H(1)$ for separate waves	52.4	177	52.2
$LM_H(68)$		1111	
$LM_H(68)$ for separate waves	232	2461	323

variable or variable group	degrees of freedom
fixed individual effects	699
time effects	2
income	2
number of adults	2
number of children	2
age	8
age × income	8
number of children × age	12
education of head	3
education of head × income	3
education of partner	3
education of partner × income	3
recording month	11
recording month × income	11

variable	coefficient	standard error	p-value
mean of individual effects	3.993		
DUMMY 1986	−0.004	0.064	0.945
DUMMY 1987	−0.001	0.067	0.983
INCOME	0.155	0.087	0.075
INCOME × ln(INCOME)	−0.023	0.018	0.213

Table C.3: Continued

variable	coefficient	standard error	p-value
ADULTS2	0.671	0.566	0.236
ADULTS3	1.375	0.633	0.030
CHILDREN1	0.771	0.509	0.130
CHILDREN2	1.085	0.622	0.081
AGE30	1.690	0.939	0.072
AGE35	0.761	1.225	0.535
AGE40	0.653	1.305	0.617
AGE45	1.260	1.347	0.350
AGE50	1.700	1.465	0.246
AGE55	−1.246	1.457	0.393
AGE60	−0.670	1.365	0.624
AGE65	0.652	1.399	0.641
AGE30 × INCOME	−0.018	0.019	0.358
AGE35 × INCOME	−0.014	0.022	0.510
AGE40 × INCOME	−0.000	0.022	0.980
AGE45 × INCOME	−0.012	0.024	0.598
AGE50 × INCOME	−0.035	0.026	0.179
AGE55 × INCOME	−0.002	0.026	0.934
AGE60 × INCOME	−0.001	0.025	0.963
AGE65 × INCOME	−0.047	0.025	0.064
CHILDREN1 × AGE30	−0.719	0.622	0.247
CHILDREN2 × AGE30	−0.251	0.635	0.692
CHILDREN1 × AGE35	0.858	0.800	0.284
CHILDREN2 × AGE35	0.540	0.855	0.527
CHILDREN1 × AGE40	−0.456	0.801	0.570
CHILDREN2 × AGE40	−0.211	0.924	0.819
CHILDREN1 × AGE45	−0.552	0.740	0.456
CHILDREN2 × AGE45	0.813	1.213	0.503
CHILDREN1 × AGE50	−0.781	1.108	0.481
CHILDREN2 × AGE50	−2.232	2.301	0.332
CHILDREN1 × AGE55	0.989	1.192	0.407
CHILDREN2 × AGE55	1.271	2.253	0.573
EDUCATIONH21	−0.441	0.708	0.533
EDUCATIONH22	−0.441	0.712	0.536
EDUCATIONH3	−0.386	0.919	0.675
EDUCATIONP1	1.233	1.064	0.247
EDUCATIONP21	2.099	0.887	0.018
EDUCATIONP22	1.749	0.813	0.032

Table C.3: Continued

variable	coefficient	standard error	p-value
EDUCATIONH21 × INCOME	0.008	0.017	0.629
EDUCATIONH22 × INCOME	0.011	0.017	0.528
EDUCATIONH3 × INCOME	0.013	0.020	0.504
EDUCATIONP1 × INCOME	−0.025	0.021	0.249
EDUCATIONP21 × INCOME	−0.036	0.016	0.027
EDUCATIONP22 × INCOME	−0.039	0.014	0.007
MONTHJAN	−1.020	0.671	0.129
MONTHFEB	−1.133	0.649	0.081
MONTHMAR	−1.233	0.621	0.047
MONTHAPR	−0.810	0.672	0.229
MONTHMAY	0.295	0.666	0.658
MONTHJUN	−0.638	0.616	0.300
MONTHJUL	0.201	0.704	0.775
MONTHAUG	−0.106	0.675	0.875
MONTHSEP	−0.683	0.601	0.256
MONTHOCT	−0.354	0.616	0.565
MONTHNOV	−0.811	0.620	0.191
MONTHJAN × INCOME	−0.014	0.015	0.329
MONTHFEB × INCOME	0.000	0.014	0.997
MONTHMAR × INCOME	0.000	0.014	0.987
MONTHAPR × INCOME	−0.002	0.015	0.884
MONTHMAY × INCOME	−0.024	0.014	0.091
MONTHJUN × INCOME	0.002	0.013	0.899
MONTHJUL × INCOME	−0.019	0.015	0.225
MONTHAUG × INCOME	−0.013	0.015	0.382
MONTHSEP × INCOME	−0.005	0.013	0.677
MONTHOCT × INCOME	−0.010	0.013	0.471
MONTHNOV × INCOME	−0.007	0.014	0.620

The dependent variable is annual household expenditure on food in f1000

Table C.4: RE estimation results of equation (5.8)lin

characteristic	value	
number of observations	2097	
degrees of freedom	2025	
standard error of individual effects	2.19	
standard error of random disturbance	1.66	
residual sum of squares	5040	
total sum of squares	21225	
R-squared (adjusted R-squared)	0.763	(0.754)
standard error of the regression	1.578	
skewness of residuals	2.227	
excess kurtosis of residuals	20.261	
Hausman test χ^2_{70} (p-value)	109.4	(0.002)

variable or variable group	degrees of freedom
random individual effects	2
time effects	2
income	2
number of adults	2
number of children	2
age	8
age $\times$ income	8
number of children $\times$ age	12
education of head	3
education of head $\times$ income	3
education of partner	3
education of partner $\times$ income	3
recording month	11
recording month $\times$ income	11

variable	coefficient	standard error	p-value
mean of individual effects	2.845		
DUMMY 1986	0.010	0.060	0.873
DUMMY 1987	−0.067	0.061	0.275
INCOME	0.143	0.068	0.036
INCOME $\times$ ln(INCOME)	−0.026	0.014	0.074

variable	coefficient	standard error	p-value
ADULTS2	2.000	0.346	0.000
ADULTS3	3.092	0.392	0.000
CHILDREN1	0.497	0.392	0.205
CHILDREN2	0.962	0.419	0.022
AGE30	1.059	0.746	0.156
AGE35	−0.375	0.867	0.665
AGE40	−0.658	0.871	0.450
AGE45	−0.077	0.863	0.928
AGE50	0.654	0.936	0.485
AGE55	−0.766	0.869	0.378
AGE60	−0.883	0.785	0.261
AGE65	−0.454	0.753	0.547
AGE30 × INCOME	−0.002	0.015	0.899
AGE35 × INCOME	0.020	0.016	0.224
AGE40 × INCOME	0.038	0.017	0.022
AGE45 × INCOME	0.034	0.017	0.050
AGE50 × INCOME	0.017	0.019	0.381
AGE55 × INCOME	0.033	0.019	0.075
AGE60 × INCOME	0.041	0.018	0.022
AGE65 × INCOME	0.015	0.017	0.385
CHILDREN1 × AGE30	−0.601	0.516	0.244
CHILDREN2 × AGE30	−0.153	0.495	0.758
CHILDREN1 × AGE35	0.894	0.611	0.143
CHILDREN2 × AGE35	0.671	0.589	0.254
CHILDREN1 × AGE40	−0.021	0.634	0.974
CHILDREN2 × AGE40	0.165	0.650	0.800
CHILDREN1 × AGE45	−0.098	0.577	0.865
CHILDREN2 × AGE45	0.808	0.866	0.351
CHILDREN1 × AGE50	−0.144	0.866	0.868
CHILDREN2 × AGE50	−1.025	1.557	0.510
CHILDREN1 × AGE55	0.130	0.925	0.888
CHILDREN2 × AGE55	0.817	1.433	0.569
EDUCATIONH21	−0.369	0.550	0.502
EDUCATIONH22	−0.105	0.538	0.846
EDUCATIONH3	−0.459	0.669	0.493
EDUCATIONP1	−0.113	0.727	0.876
EDUCATIONP21	0.864	0.602	0.152
EDUCATIONP22	0.639	0.559	0.253

Table C.4: Continued

variable	coefficient	standard error	p-value
EDUCATIONH21 × INCOME	0.011	0.014	0.441
EDUCATIONH22 × INCOME	0.008	0.013	0.568
EDUCATIONH3 × INCOME	0.023	0.015	0.127
EDUCATIONP1 × INCOME	0.007	0.015	0.667
EDUCATIONP21 × INCOME	−0.009	0.011	0.436
EDUCATIONP22 × INCOME	−0.012	0.010	0.211
MONTHJAN	−0.987	0.610	0.106
MONTHFEB	−1.041	0.583	0.074
MONTHMAR	−0.965	0.562	0.086
MONTHAPR	−0.740	0.604	0.220
MONTHMAY	0.216	0.604	0.721
MONTHJUN	−0.629	0.556	0.257
MONTHJUL	−0.051	0.631	0.935
MONTHAUG	−0.042	0.609	0.946
MONTHSEP	−0.691	0.544	0.204
MONTHOCT	−0.491	0.559	0.380
MONTHNOV	−0.650	0.557	0.243
MONTHJAN × INCOME	−0.014	0.013	0.300
MONTHFEB × INCOME	−0.002	0.013	0.892
MONTHMAR × INCOME	−0.004	0.012	0.719
MONTHAPR × INCOME	−0.004	0.013	0.748
MONTHMAY × INCOME	−0.020	0.013	0.130
MONTHJUN × INCOME	0.000	0.012	0.982
MONTHJUL × INCOME	−0.016	0.014	0.252
MONTHAUG × INCOME	−0.013	0.013	0.311
MONTHSEP × INCOME	−0.005	0.012	0.702
MONTHOCT × INCOME	−0.007	0.012	0.583
MONTHNOV × INCOME	−0.010	0.012	0.389

Table C.4: Continued

The dependent variable is annual household expenditure on food in $f1000$
The residual sum of squares is based on the random disturbance part only

Table C.5: Pooled OLS estimation results of equation (5.8)lin with time effects
when 7 atypical households are removed from the sample

characteristic		value	
number of observations		2076	
degrees of freedom		2004	
residual sum of squares		9338	
total sum of squares		18864	
R-squared (adjusted R-squared)		0.505	(0.487)
standard error of the regression		2.159	
skewness of residuals		0.900	
excess kurtosis of residuals		2.078	
LM_N		653	
LM_N for separate waves	324	149	171
$LM_H(1)$		87.9	
$LM_H(1)$ for separate waves	32.4	46.4	16.2
$LM_H(69)$		298	
$LM_H(69)$ for separate waves	196	223	134

variable or variable group	degrees of freedom
time effects	3
income	2
number of adults	2
number of children	2
age	8
age × income	8
number of children × age	13
education of head	3
education of head × income	3
education of partner	3
education of partner × income	3
recording month	11
recording month × income	11

variable	coefficient	standard error	p-value
DUMMY 1985	3.259	0.845	0.000
DUMMY 1986	3.137	0.848	0.000
DUMMY 1987	3.076	0.848	0.000
INCOME	0.076	0.061	0.212
INCOME × ln(INCOME)	−0.011	0.013	0.406

Table C.5: Continued			
variable	*coefficient*	*standard error*	*p-value*
ADULTS2	2.304	0.251	0.000
ADULTS3	3.716	0.294	0.000
CHILDREN1	0.237	0.362	0.512
CHILDREN2	0.720	0.352	0.041
AGE30	0.244	0.658	0.711
AGE35	−0.774	0.698	0.268
AGE40	−2.214	0.722	0.002
AGE45	−1.323	0.700	0.059
AGE50	−1.072	0.756	0.156
AGE55	−0.888	0.684	0.195
AGE60	−0.905	0.619	0.144
AGE65	−1.547	0.574	0.007
AGE30 × INCOME	0.015	0.014	0.277
AGE35 × INCOME	0.032	0.013	0.016
AGE40 × INCOME	0.059	0.014	0.000
AGE45 × INCOME	0.044	0.014	0.002
AGE50 × INCOME	0.049	0.016	0.002
AGE55 × INCOME	0.044	0.015	0.004
AGE60 × INCOME	0.031	0.014	0.034
AGE65 × INCOME	0.041	0.014	0.002
CHILDREN1 × AGE30	−0.558	0.508	0.272
CHILDREN2 × AGE30	0.084	0.443	0.850
CHILDREN1 × AGE35	0.744	0.540	0.169
CHILDREN2 × AGE35	0.736	0.471	0.118
CHILDREN1 × AGE40	0.910	0.596	0.127
CHILDREN2 × AGE40	1.138	0.555	0.040
CHILDREN1 × AGE45	0.538	0.528	0.309
CHILDREN2 × AGE45	0.915	0.704	0.194
CHILDREN1 × AGE50	0.399	0.769	0.603
CHILDREN2 × AGE50	0.244	1.165	0.834
CHILDREN1 × AGE55	−2.005	0.813	0.014
CHILDREN2 × AGE55	0.989	1.064	0.353
CHILDREN2 × AGE60	2.521	1.167	0.031
EDUCATIONH21	−0.120	0.470	0.799
EDUCATIONH22	0.319	0.449	0.478
EDUCATIONH3	−0.018	0.546	0.974
EDUCATIONP1	−1.420	0.568	0.012
EDUCATIONP21	0.082	0.471	0.862
EDUCATIONP22	0.047	0.443	0.916

Table C.5: Continued

variable	coefficient	standard error	p-value
EDUCATIONH21 × INCOME	0.004	0.012	0.740
EDUCATIONH22 × INCOME	-0.006	0.012	0.605
EDUCATIONH3 × INCOME	0.005	0.013	0.703
EDUCATIONP1 × INCOME	0.036	0.012	0.004
EDUCATIONP21 × INCOME	0.002	0.009	0.861
EDUCATIONP22 × INCOME	-0.002	0.008	0.792
MONTHJAN	-0.377	0.707	0.593
MONTHFEB	-0.659	0.668	0.324
MONTHMAR	-0.636	0.658	0.334
MONTHAPR	-0.209	0.681	0.758
MONTHMAY	0.223	0.702	0.751
MONTHJUN	-0.051	0.643	0.937
MONTHJUL	-0.633	0.713	0.375
MONTHAUG	0.020	0.698	0.977
MONTHSEP	-0.401	0.628	0.523
MONTHOCT	-0.464	0.658	0.480
MONTHNOV	-0.185	0.634	0.770
MONTHJAN × INCOME	-0.026	0.015	0.093
MONTHFEB × INCOME	-0.006	0.015	0.689
MONTHMAR × INCOME	-0.009	0.014	0.539
MONTHAPR × INCOME	-0.013	0.015	0.392
MONTHMAY × INCOME	-0.009	0.015	0.567
MONTHJUN × INCOME	-0.012	0.014	0.396
MONTHJUL × INCOME	-0.007	0.016	0.679
MONTHAUG × INCOME	-0.009	0.015	0.544
MONTHSEP × INCOME	-0.006	0.014	0.667
MONTHOCT × INCOME	0.000	0.014	0.993
MONTHNOV × INCOME	-0.017	0.014	0.213

The dependent variable is annual household expenditure on food in $f1000$

Table C.6: FE estimation results of equation (5.8)lin when 7 atypical households are removed from the sample

characteristic	value		
number of observations	2076		
degrees of freedom	1314		
residual sum of squares	3104		
total sum of squares	18864		
R-squared (adjusted R-squared)	0.835	(0.740)	
standard error of the regression	1.537		
skewness of residuals	0.582		
excess kurtosis of residuals	3.442		
LM_N	1142		
LM_N for separate waves	607	441	136
$LM_H(1)$	167		
$LM_H(1)$ for separate waves	42.2	107	39.6
$LM_H(68)$	471		
$LM_H(68)$ for separate waves	209	429	209

variable or variable group	degrees of freedom
fixed (individual) effects	692
time effects	2
income	2
number of adults	2
number of children	2
age	8
age × income	8
number of children × age	12
education of head	3
education of head × income	3
education of partner	3
education of partner × income	3
recording month	11
recording month × income	11

variable	coefficient	standard error	p-value
mean of individual effects	3.825		
DUMMY 1986	−0.033	0.059	0.582
DUMMY 1987	0.005	0.062	0.942
INCOME	0.151	0.081	0.062
INCOME × ln(INCOME)	−0.020	0.017	0.241

Table C.6: Continued			
variable	coefficient	standard error	p-value
ADULTS2	0.764	0.525	0.146
ADULTS3	1.572	0.586	0.007
CHILDREN1	0.709	0.472	0.133
CHILDREN2	1.028	0.576	0.075
AGE30	1.804	0.870	0.038
AGE35	0.807	1.135	0.477
AGE40	0.791	1.213	0.514
AGE45	0.929	1.251	0.458
AGE50	1.501	1.359	0.270
AGE55	−1.002	1.355	0.460
AGE60	0.050	1.269	0.969
AGE65	0.262	1.298	0.840
AGE30 × INCOME	−0.021	0.018	0.242
AGE35 × INCOME	−0.014	0.020	0.488
AGE40 × INCOME	−0.002	0.021	0.928
AGE45 × INCOME	−0.013	0.022	0.560
AGE50 × INCOME	−0.039	0.024	0.107
AGE55 × INCOME	−0.015	0.025	0.553
AGE60 × INCOME	−0.026	0.023	0.258
AGE65 × INCOME	−0.025	0.024	0.286
CHILDREN1 × AGE30	−0.662	0.576	0.250
CHILDREN2 × AGE30	−0.228	0.588	0.699
CHILDREN1 × AGE35	0.793	0.741	0.285
CHILDREN2 × AGE35	0.478	0.792	0.546
CHILDREN1 × AGE40	−0.650	0.749	0.385
CHILDREN2 × AGE40	−0.378	0.861	0.661
CHILDREN1 × AGE45	−0.488	0.696	0.483
CHILDREN2 × AGE45	0.950	1.127	0.399
CHILDREN1 × AGE50	−0.655	1.026	0.523
CHILDREN2 × AGE50	−2.751	2.134	0.198
CHILDREN1 × AGE55	1.000	1.104	0.366
CHILDREN2 × AGE55	1.061	2.094	0.613
EDUCATIONH21	−0.400	0.657	0.543
EDUCATIONH22	−0.157	0.661	0.812
EDUCATIONH3	−0.097	0.858	0.910
EDUCATIONP1	0.988	0.988	0.317
EDUCATIONP21	2.472	0.825	0.003
EDUCATIONP22	1.372	0.756	0.070

Table C.6: Continued

variable	coefficient	standard error	p-value
EDUCATIONH21 × INCOME	0.007	0.016	0.673
EDUCATIONH22 × INCOME	0.003	0.016	0.871
EDUCATIONH3 × INCOME	0.005	0.019	0.790
EDUCATIONP1 × INCOME	-0.028	0.020	0.164
EDUCATIONP21 × INCOME	-0.054	0.015	0.000
EDUCATIONP22 × INCOME	-0.031	0.013	0.019
MONTHJAN	-0.535	0.623	0.390
MONTHFEB	-0.868	0.612	0.157
MONTHMAR	-1.172	0.581	0.044
MONTHAPR	-0.661	0.623	0.289
MONTHMAY	-0.037	0.617	0.953
MONTHJUN	-0.547	0.571	0.338
MONTHJUL	0.078	0.653	0.905
MONTHAUG	-0.135	0.626	0.830
MONTHSEP	-0.664	0.560	0.236
MONTHOCT	-0.576	0.579	0.320
MONTHNOV	-0.873	0.583	0.134
MONTHJAN × INCOME	-0.029	0.014	0.031
MONTHFEB × INCOME	-0.008	0.014	0.551
MONTHMAR × INCOME	-0.002	0.013	0.903
MONTHAPR × INCOME	-0.006	0.014	0.648
MONTHMAY × INCOME	-0.014	0.013	0.299
MONTHJUN × INCOME	-0.001	0.012	0.931
MONTHJUL × INCOME	-0.016	0.014	0.269
MONTHAUG × INCOME	-0.012	0.014	0.368
MONTHSEP × INCOME	-0.006	0.012	0.640
MONTHOCT × INCOME	-0.004	0.013	0.753
MONTHNOV × INCOME	-0.006	0.013	0.643

The dependent variable is annual household expenditure on food in $f1000$

Table C.7: OLS estimation results of equation (5.8)lin with lagged income

characteristic	value	
number of observations	699	
degrees of freedom	630	
residual sum of squares	3178	
total sum of squares	6820	
R-squared (adjusted R-squared)	0.534	(0.484)
standard error of the regression	2.246	
skewness of residuals	0.938	
excess kurtosis of residuals	2.656	
LM_N	308	
$LM_H(1)$: income only	19.4	
$LM_H(68)$: all regressors	207	

variable or variable group	degrees of freedom
intercept	1
current income	2
lagged income	1
number of adults	2
number of children	2
age	8
age × income	8
number of children × age	11
education of head	3
education of head × income	3
education of partner	3
education of partner × income	3
recording month	11
recording month × income	11

variable	coefficient	standard error	p-value
INTERCEPT	−0.049	1.384	0.972
INCOME	0.345	0.098	0.000
Δ (INCOME)	−0.030	0.010	0.004
INCOME × ln(INCOME)	−0.058	0.020	0.005

variable	coefficient	standard error	p-value
ADULTS2	2.045	0.430	0.000
ADULTS3	3.187	0.504	0.000
CHILDREN1	−0.132	0.516	0.798
CHILDREN2	−0.285	0.493	0.563
AGE30	0.684	0.989	0.489
AGE35	−1.199	1.255	0.340
AGE40	−3.193	1.030	0.002
AGE45	−2.360	1.042	0.024
AGE50	−1.621	1.183	0.171
AGE55	−1.344	0.941	0.154
AGE60	−1.257	0.910	0.168
AGE65	−1.687	0.842	0.045
AGE30 × INCOME	−0.000	0.021	0.969
AGE35 × INCOME	0.030	0.023	0.179
AGE40 × INCOME	0.059	0.021	0.005
AGE45 × INCOME	0.061	0.022	0.005
AGE50 × INCOME	0.044	0.027	0.099
AGE55 × INCOME	0.048	0.022	0.033
AGE60 × INCOME	0.029	0.023	0.206
AGE65 × INCOME	0.038	0.022	0.081
CHILDREN1 × AGE30	−0.740	0.763	0.332
CHILDREN2 × AGE30	0.953	0.682	0.163
CHILDREN1 × AGE35	1.386	1.044	0.185
CHILDREN2 × AGE35	1.827	0.806	0.024
CHILDREN1 × AGE40	1.970	0.796	0.014
CHILDREN2 × AGE40	2.303	0.717	0.001
CHILDREN1 × AGE45	1.026	1.009	0.310
CHILDREN2 × AGE45	0.311	1.034	0.764
CHILDREN1 × AGE50	−0.438	1.738	0.801
CHILDREN1 × AGE55	−2.574	1.145	0.025
CHILDREN2 × AGE60	2.884	1.363	0.035
EDUCATIONH21	0.344	0.733	0.639
EDUCATIONH22	0.771	0.710	0.278
EDUCATIONH3	−1.726	0.828	0.037
EDUCATIONP1	−1.960	0.958	0.041
EDUCATIONP21	−0.822	0.928	0.376
EDUCATIONP22	−0.523	0.735	0.477

Table C.7: Continued

Table C.7: Continued

variable	coefficient	standard error	p-value
EDUCATIONH21 × INCOME	−0.020	0.021	0.330
EDUCATIONH22 × INCOME	−0.024	0.021	0.250
EDUCATIONH3 × INCOME	0.026	0.021	0.228
EDUCATIONP1 × INCOME	0.047	0.022	0.037
EDUCATIONP21 × INCOME	0.028	0.019	0.146
EDUCATIONP22 × INCOME	0.016	0.013	0.229
MONTHJAN	1.477	1.023	0.149
MONTHFEB	1.107	0.985	0.261
MONTHMAR	1.407	0.982	0.152
MONTHAPR	2.049	1.206	0.090
MONTHMAY	2.789	1.060	0.009
MONTHJUN	2.117	1.179	0.073
MONTHJUL	1.099	1.090	0.314
MONTHAUG	1.163	1.315	0.377
MONTHSEP	1.427	1.050	0.175
MONTHOCT	0.649	1.133	0.567
MONTHNOV	1.240	0.953	0.194
MONTHJAN × INCOME	−0.059	0.025	0.016
MONTHFEB × INCOME	−0.043	0.025	0.080
MONTHMAR × INCOME	−0.065	0.025	0.009
MONTHAPR × INCOME	−0.054	0.027	0.047
MONTHMAY × INCOME	−0.065	0.026	0.013
MONTHJUN × INCOME	−0.055	0.029	0.062
MONTHJUL × INCOME	−0.041	0.026	0.117
MONTHAUG × INCOME	−0.026	0.031	0.407
MONTHSEP × INCOME	−0.036	0.025	0.153
MONTHOCT × INCOME	−0.007	0.027	0.786
MONTHNOV × INCOME	−0.053	0.023	0.023

The dependent variable is annual household expenditure on food in f1000
Standard errors and test statistics are corrected for heteroscedasticity

Table C.8: GMM estimation results of equation (7.1) in differences with y_{i1} and current differences of x as instruments

characteristic	value	
number of observations	699	
degrees of freedom	631	
residual sum of squares	3818	
total sum of squares	3941	
standard error of ϵ	1.739	
degree of overidentification	0	

variable or variable group	regressors	instruments
lagged expenditure	1	1
'current' income	2	2
lagged income	2	2
number of adults	2	2
number of children	2	2
age	8	8
age × income	8	8
number of children × age	9	9
education of head	3	3
education of head × income	3	3
education of partner	3	3
education of partner × income	3	3
recording month	11	11
recording month × income	11	11

variable	coefficient	standard error	p-value
Δy_{-1}	0.162	0.231	0.482
Δ INCOME	0.177	0.160	0.270
Δ INCOME$_{-1}$	0.326	0.138	0.018
Δ (INCOME × ln(INCOME))	−0.022	0.033	0.498
Δ (INCOME × ln(INCOME))$_{-1}$	−0.064	0.028	0.025

variable	coefficient	standard error	p-value
△ ADULTS2	1.011	0.925	0.274
△ ADULTS3	0.871	1.019	0.393
△ CHILDREN1	0.051	0.631	0.936
△ CHILDREN2	0.705	0.803	0.380
△ AGE30	2.505	1.205	0.038
△ AGE35	1.223	1.761	0.487
△ AGE40	0.332	1.785	0.853
△ AGE45	0.051	1.867	0.978
△ AGE50	−0.702	2.120	0.740
△ AGE55	−0.368	2.030	0.856
△ AGE60	−4.555	3.735	0.223
△ AGE65	0.138	1.875	0.941
△ AGE30 × INCOME	−0.042	0.028	0.140
△ AGE35 × INCOME	−0.021	0.031	0.489
△ AGE40 × INCOME	−0.005	0.033	0.887
△ AGE45 × INCOME	−0.010	0.032	0.752
△ AGE50 × INCOME	0.000	0.040	0.999
△ AGE55 × INCOME	−0.016	0.045	0.726
△ AGE60 × INCOME	0.099	0.106	0.349
△ AGE65 × INCOME	−0.075	0.053	0.161
△ CHILDREN1 × AGE30	−0.364	0.912	0.690
△ CHILDREN2 × AGE30	−0.361	0.973	0.711
△ CHILDREN1 × AGE35	1.698	1.239	0.171
△ CHILDREN2 × AGE35	0.139	1.344	0.917
△ CHILDREN1 × AGE40	0.182	0.978	0.852
△ CHILDREN2 × AGE40	0.145	1.283	0.910
△ CHILDREN1 × AGE45	0.300	0.978	0.759
△ CHILDREN1 × AGE50	−0.778	0.901	0.388
△ CHILDREN1 × AGE55	0.703	1.458	0.630
△ EDUCATIONH21	0.341	1.044	0.744
△ EDUCATIONH22	0.216	0.882	0.806
△ EDUCATIONH3	−0.958	1.317	0.467
△ EDUCATIONP1	1.824	1.751	0.298
△ EDUCATIONP21	1.464	1.606	0.362
△ EDUCATIONP22	1.711	1.259	0.174

Table C.8: Continued

Table C.8: Continued

variable	coefficient	standard error	p-value
$\triangle$ EDUCATIONH21 × INCOME	−0.011	0.030	0.705
$\triangle$ EDUCATIONH22 × INCOME	−0.008	0.025	0.741
$\triangle$ EDUCATIONH3 × INCOME	0.019	0.031	0.536
$\triangle$ EDUCATIONP1 × INCOME	−0.031	0.036	0.397
$\triangle$ EDUCATIONP21 × INCOME	−0.017	0.043	0.699
$\triangle$ EDUCATIONP22 × INCOME	−0.043	0.025	0.088
$\triangle$ MONTHJAN	−1.240	1.097	0.258
$\triangle$ MONTHFEB	−1.548	1.086	0.154
$\triangle$ MONTHMAR	−0.780	0.974	0.423
$\triangle$ MONTHAPR	−1.082	1.204	0.369
$\triangle$ MONTHMAY	−0.301	1.106	0.786
$\triangle$ MONTHJUN	−1.008	1.067	0.344
$\triangle$ MONTHJUL	0.343	0.999	0.731
$\triangle$ MONTHAUG	−1.059	0.964	0.272
$\triangle$ MONTHSEP	−0.652	0.919	0.478
$\triangle$ MONTHOCT	−0.625	1.027	0.543
$\triangle$ MONTHNOV	−0.677	0.900	0.452
$\triangle$ MONTHJAN × INCOME	0.002	0.029	0.950
$\triangle$ MONTHFEB × INCOME	0.015	0.029	0.620
$\triangle$ MONTHMAR × INCOME	−0.008	0.025	0.748
$\triangle$ MONTHAPR × INCOME	−0.001	0.029	0.972
$\triangle$ MONTHMAY × INCOME	−0.005	0.029	0.865
$\triangle$ MONTHJUN × INCOME	0.011	0.026	0.688
$\triangle$ MONTHJUL × INCOME	−0.022	0.025	0.379
$\triangle$ MONTHAUG × INCOME	0.005	0.024	0.842
$\triangle$ MONTHSEP × INCOME	−0.005	0.024	0.838
$\triangle$ MONTHOCT × INCOME	0.006	0.025	0.809
$\triangle$ MONTHNOV × INCOME	−0.011	0.023	0.623

The dependent variable is the difference of annual household expenditure on food in $f1000$

Standard errors and test statistics are corrected for heteroscedasticity

Table C.9: GMM two-step estimation results of equation (7.1) in differences with y_{i1} and current and lagged differences of x as instruments

characteristic	value	
number of observations	699	
degrees of freedom	631	
residual sum of squares	3173	
total sum of squares	3941	
standard error of ϵ	1.586	
degree of overidentification	25	
Sargan test (p-value)	24.767	(0.476)

variable or variable group	regressors	instruments
lagged expenditure	1	1
'current' income	2	2
lagged income	2	2
number of adults	2	2
number of children	2	2
age	8	8
age × income	8	16
number of children × age	9	9
education of head	3	3
education of head × income	3	6
education of partner	3	3
education of partner × income	3	6
recording month	11	11
recording month × income	11	22

variable	coefficient	standard error	p-value
Δy_{-1}	0.000	0.092	0.997
Δ INCOME	0.136	0.123	0.271
Δ INCOME$_{-1}$	0.264	0.115	0.022
Δ (INCOME × ln(INCOME))	−0.020	0.026	0.434
Δ (INCOME × ln(INCOME))$_{-1}$	−0.051	0.023	0.028

Table C.9: Continued

variable	coefficient	standard error	p-value
△ ADULTS2	1.344	0.792	0.090
△ ADULTS3	1.232	0.856	0.150
△ CHILDREN1	0.166	0.525	0.752
△ CHILDREN2	1.058	0.684	0.122
△ AGE30	2.094	1.077	0.052
△ AGE35	1.529	1.587	0.335
△ AGE40	0.993	1.496	0.507
△ AGE45	0.368	1.446	0.799
△ AGE50	−0.653	1.845	0.724
△ AGE55	−0.171	1.732	0.921
△ AGE60	−3.300	1.849	0.074
△ AGE65	0.204	1.677	0.903
△ AGE30 × INCOME	−0.024	0.024	0.304
△ AGE35 × INCOME	−0.023	0.028	0.410
△ AGE40 × INCOME	−0.010	0.028	0.731
△ AGE45 × INCOME	−0.015	0.027	0.588
△ AGE50 × INCOME	−0.003	0.034	0.936
△ AGE55 × INCOME	−0.016	0.036	0.651
△ AGE60 × INCOME	0.072	0.051	0.157
△ AGE65 × INCOME	−0.055	0.037	0.132
△ CHILDREN1 × AGE30	−0.694	0.790	0.379
△ CHILDREN2 × AGE30	−0.838	0.834	0.315
△ CHILDREN1 × AGE35	1.484	1.091	0.174
△ CHILDREN2 × AGE35	−0.425	1.174	0.717
△ CHILDREN1 × AGE40	−0.099	0.878	0.911
△ CHILDREN2 × AGE40	−0.706	1.102	0.522
△ CHILDREN1 × AGE45	0.333	0.739	0.652
△ CHILDREN1 × AGE50	−0.407	0.761	0.592
△ CHILDREN1 × AGE55	0.229	1.097	0.835
△ EDUCATIONH21	−0.447	0.758	0.555
△ EDUCATIONH22	−0.201	0.721	0.780
△ EDUCATIONH3	−1.332	1.056	0.207
△ EDUCATIONP1	2.492	1.448	0.085
△ EDUCATIONP21	1.970	1.200	0.101
△ EDUCATIONP22	1.607	1.078	0.136

variable	coefficient	standard error	p-value
$\triangle$ EDUCATIONH21 $\times$ INCOME	0.012	0.023	0.595
$\triangle$ EDUCATIONH22 $\times$ INCOME	0.007	0.020	0.747
$\triangle$ EDUCATIONH3 $\times$ INCOME	0.032	0.024	0.194
$\triangle$ EDUCATIONP1 $\times$ INCOME	−0.047	0.030	0.113
$\triangle$ EDUCATIONP21 $\times$ INCOME	−0.028	0.025	0.267
$\triangle$ EDUCATIONP22 $\times$ INCOME	−0.041	0.021	0.053
$\triangle$ MONTHJAN	−1.103	0.838	0.188
$\triangle$ MONTHFEB	−1.682	0.834	0.044
$\triangle$ MONTHMAR	−1.431	0.785	0.068
$\triangle$ MONTHAPR	−1.357	0.948	0.152
$\triangle$ MONTHMAY	−0.619	0.824	0.452
$\triangle$ MONTHJUN	−1.252	0.860	0.145
$\triangle$ MONTHJUL	−0.183	0.810	0.822
$\triangle$ MONTHAUG	−1.370	0.788	0.082
$\triangle$ MONTHSEP	−1.069	0.740	0.149
$\triangle$ MONTHOCT	−0.667	0.858	0.437
$\triangle$ MONTHNOV	−1.183	0.730	0.105
$\triangle$ MONTHJAN $\times$ INCOME	−0.000	0.020	0.978
$\triangle$ MONTHFEB $\times$ INCOME	0.023	0.021	0.268
$\triangle$ MONTHMAR $\times$ INCOME	0.008	0.019	0.681
$\triangle$ MONTHAPR $\times$ INCOME	0.011	0.022	0.611
$\triangle$ MONTHMAY $\times$ INCOME	0.003	0.021	0.901
$\triangle$ MONTHJUN $\times$ INCOME	0.022	0.020	0.288
$\triangle$ MONTHJUL $\times$ INCOME	−0.006	0.020	0.770
$\triangle$ MONTHAUG $\times$ INCOME	0.014	0.019	0.439
$\triangle$ MONTHSEP $\times$ INCOME	0.006	0.018	0.741
$\triangle$ MONTHOCT $\times$ INCOME	0.009	0.021	0.675
$\triangle$ MONTHNOV $\times$ INCOME	0.003	0.018	0.859

Table C.9: Continued

The dependent variable is the difference of annual household expenditure on food in $f1000$

Standard errors and test statistics are corrected for heteroscedasticity

The Sargan test of overidentifying restrictions is given

Table C.10: GMM estimation results of equation (7.2) in levels with $(y_{i2} - y_{i1})$ and current levels of x as instruments

characteristic	value	
number of observations	699	
degrees of freedom	626	
residual sum of squares	2616	
total sum of squares	6820	
standard error of composite disturbance	2.044	
degree of overidentification	0	

variable or variable group	regressors	instruments
intercept	1	1
lagged expenditure	1	1
current income	2	2
lagged income	4	4
number of adults	2	2
number of children	2	2
age	8	8
age × income	8	8
number of children × age	11	11
education of head	3	3
education of head × income	3	3
education of partner	3	3
education of partner × income	3	3
recording month	11	11
recording month × income	11	11

variable	coefficient	standard error	p-value
INTERCEPT	−0.795	1.317	0.546
y_{-1}	0.196	0.093	0.035
INCOME	0.321	0.102	0.002
△ INCOME	−0.013	0.133	0.920
△ INCOME$_{-1}$	0.210	0.122	0.085
INCOME × ln(INCOME)	−0.051	0.021	0.016
△ (INCOME × ln(INCOME))	−0.002	0.027	0.939
△ (INCOME × ln(INCOME))$_{-1}$	−0.044	0.025	0.074

variable	coefficient	standard error	p-value
ADULTS2	1.520	0.446	0.000
ADULTS3	2.362	0.568	0.000
CHILDREN1	-0.203	0.470	0.665
CHILDREN2	-0.413	0.465	0.374
AGE30	0.599	0.894	0.503
AGE35	-0.837	1.217	0.492
AGE40	-2.744	0.965	0.004
AGE45	-1.911	0.943	0.043
AGE50	-1.202	1.065	0.259
AGE55	-0.952	0.845	0.260
AGE60	-1.225	0.834	0.142
AGE65	-0.986	0.785	0.209
AGE30 × INCOME	-0.003	0.019	0.884
AGE35 × INCOME	0.020	0.021	0.346
AGE40 × INCOME	0.046	0.020	0.018
AGE45 × INCOME	0.045	0.020	0.027
AGE50 × INCOME	0.030	0.024	0.207
AGE55 × INCOME	0.032	0.021	0.137
AGE60 × INCOME	0.025	0.021	0.228
AGE65 × INCOME	0.016	0.020	0.436
CHILDREN1 × AGE30	-0.616	0.688	0.371
CHILDREN2 × AGE30	1.004	0.628	0.109
CHILDREN1 × AGE35	1.400	0.988	0.156
CHILDREN2 × AGE35	1.627	0.774	0.035
CHILDREN1 × AGE40	1.774	0.777	0.022
CHILDREN2 × AGE40	2.161	0.690	0.002
CHILDREN1 × AGE45	1.012	0.881	0.251
CHILDREN2 × AGE45	0.741	0.830	0.372
CHILDREN1 × AGE50	-0.408	1.724	0.813
CHILDREN1 × AGE55	-1.777	1.052	0.091
CHILDREN2 × AGE60	1.793	1.188	0.131
EDUCATIONH21	0.614	0.647	0.343
EDUCATIONH22	0.852	0.643	0.185
EDUCATIONH3	-1.352	0.751	0.072
EDUCATIONP1	-1.402	0.899	0.119
EDUCATIONP21	-0.620	0.821	0.450
EDUCATIONP22	-0.229	0.688	0.739

Table C.10: Continued

Table C.10: Continued

variable	coefficient	standard error	p-value
EDUCATIONH21 × INCOME	−0.027	0.018	0.137
EDUCATIONH22 × INCOME	−0.025	0.019	0.196
EDUCATIONH3 × INCOME	0.018	0.019	0.352
EDUCATIONP1 × INCOME	0.035	0.021	0.096
EDUCATIONP21 × INCOME	0.025	0.017	0.151
EDUCATIONP22 × INCOME	0.010	0.013	0.464
MONTHJAN	1.485	0.932	0.111
MONTHFEB	1.325	0.901	0.141
MONTHMAR	1.172	0.876	0.181
MONTHAPR	2.296	1.174	0.050
MONTHMAY	2.572	0.999	0.010
MONTHJUN	1.789	1.076	0.096
MONTHJUL	1.259	1.026	0.220
MONTHAUG	1.300	1.186	0.273
MONTHSEP	1.521	0.953	0.111
MONTHOCT	0.552	1.025	0.590
MONTHNOV	1.297	0.857	0.130
MONTHJAN × INCOME	−0.059	0.023	0.010
MONTHFEB × INCOME	−0.049	0.023	0.033
MONTHMAR × INCOME	−0.059	0.022	0.008
MONTHAPR × INCOME	−0.063	0.027	0.019
MONTHMAY × INCOME	−0.064	0.025	0.011
MONTHJUN × INCOME	−0.047	0.027	0.078
MONTHJUL × INCOME	−0.042	0.025	0.091
MONTHAUG × INCOME	−0.031	0.028	0.264
MONTHSEP × INCOME	−0.040	0.023	0.084
MONTHOCT × INCOME	−0.006	0.024	0.813
MONTHNOV × INCOME	−0.055	0.021	0.009

The dependent variable is annual household expenditure on food in f1000
Standard errors and test statistics are corrected for heteroscedasticity

Table C.11: GMM two-step estimation results of equation (7.2) in levels with $(y_{i2} - y_{i1})$ and current and lagged levels of x as instruments

characteristic	value	
number of observations	699	
degrees of freedom	626	
residual sum of squares	2420	
total sum of squares	6820	
standard error of composite disturbance	1.966	
degree of overidentification	50	
Sargan test (p-value)	58.784	(0.185)

variable or variable group	regressors	instruments
intercept	1	1
lagged expenditure	1	1
current income	2	2
lagged income	4	4
number of adults	2	2
number of children	2	2
age	8	8
age × income	8	24
number of children × age	11	11
education of head	3	3
education of head × income	3	9
education of partner	3	3
education of partner × income	3	9
recording month	11	11
recording month × income	11	33

variable	coefficient	standard error	p-value
INTERCEPT	−1.438	1.148	0.210
y_{-1}	0.308	0.065	0.000
INCOME	0.279	0.089	0.002
Δ INCOME	−0.123	0.112	0.274
Δ INCOME$_{-1}$	0.076	0.103	0.460
INCOME × ln(INCOME)	−0.039	0.018	0.032
Δ (INCOME × ln(INCOME))	0.020	0.023	0.382
Δ (INCOME × ln(INCOME))$_{-1}$	−0.017	0.021	0.402

Table C.11: Continued

variable	coefficient	standard error	p-value
ADULTS2	1.289	0.369	0.000
ADULTS3	1.857	0.449	0.000
CHILDREN1	−0.080	0.411	0.846
CHILDREN2	−0.268	0.408	0.511
AGE30	0.888	0.816	0.277
AGE35	−0.148	1.135	0.896
AGE40	−1.965	0.891	0.027
AGE45	−1.226	0.827	0.138
AGE50	−0.736	0.966	0.446
AGE55	−0.539	0.760	0.478
AGE60	−0.789	0.722	0.275
AGE65	−0.271	0.683	0.692
AGE30 × INCOME	−0.011	0.017	0.526
AGE35 × INCOME	0.006	0.019	0.765
AGE40 × INCOME	0.038	0.018	0.032
AGE45 × INCOME	0.027	0.018	0.133
AGE50 × INCOME	0.015	0.021	0.480
AGE55 × INCOME	0.021	0.019	0.272
AGE60 × INCOME	0.017	0.017	0.332
AGE65 × INCOME	0.002	0.017	0.918
CHILDREN1 × AGE30	−0.460	0.582	0.429
CHILDREN2 × AGE30	0.884	0.534	0.098
CHILDREN1 × AGE35	1.313	0.886	0.138
CHILDREN2 × AGE35	1.465	0.722	0.042
CHILDREN1 × AGE40	0.773	0.684	0.258
CHILDREN2 × AGE40	1.435	0.638	0.025
CHILDREN1 × AGE45	0.952	0.709	0.179
CHILDREN2 × AGE45	1.026	0.638	0.108
CHILDREN1 × AGE50	−1.283	1.593	0.421
CHILDREN1 × AGE55	−1.643	0.957	0.086
CHILDREN2 × AGE60	0.994	0.919	0.279
EDUCATIONH21	0.679	0.548	0.215
EDUCATIONH22	0.958	0.516	0.063
EDUCATIONH3	−0.741	0.619	0.231
EDUCATIONP1	−0.878	0.770	0.254
EDUCATIONP21	−0.009	0.648	0.989
EDUCATIONP22	0.197	0.586	0.737

Table C.11: Continued

variable	coefficient	standard error	p-value
EDUCATIONH21 × INCOME	−0.030	0.015	0.047
EDUCATIONH22 × INCOME	−0.027	0.015	0.066
EDUCATIONH3 × INCOME	0.006	0.015	0.714
EDUCATIONP1 × INCOME	0.021	0.018	0.241
EDUCATIONP21 × INCOME	0.008	0.013	0.563
EDUCATIONP22 × INCOME	−0.004	0.011	0.685
MONTHJAN	1.493	0.837	0.075
MONTHFEB	1.409	0.789	0.074
MONTHMAR	1.076	0.775	0.165
MONTHAPR	1.915	0.999	0.055
MONTHMAY	2.719	0.843	0.001
MONTHJUN	1.619	0.904	0.073
MONTHJUL	1.228	0.924	0.184
MONTHAUG	1.609	1.061	0.129
MONTHSEP	1.417	0.844	0.093
MONTHOCT	0.842	0.919	0.360
MONTHNOV	1.223	0.765	0.110
MONTHJAN × INCOME	−0.058	0.020	0.004
MONTHFEB × INCOME	−0.051	0.020	0.010
MONTHMAR × INCOME	−0.055	0.019	0.004
MONTHAPR × INCOME	−0.055	0.023	0.017
MONTHMAY × INCOME	−0.069	0.021	0.000
MONTHJUN × INCOME	−0.043	0.021	0.046
MONTHJUL × INCOME	−0.040	0.022	0.075
MONTHAUG × INCOME	−0.045	0.025	0.074
MONTHSEP × INCOME	−0.044	0.020	0.031
MONTHOCT × INCOME	−0.013	0.022	0.534
MONTHNOV × INCOME	−0.052	0.019	0.005

The dependent variable is annual household expenditure on food in $f1000$
Standard errors and test statistics are corrected for heteroscedasticity
The Sargan test of overidentifying restrictions is given

Table C.12: GMM two-step estimation results of equation (7.2) in levels with $(y_{i2} - y_{i1})$ and current and lagged differences of x as instruments

characteristic	value	
number of observations	699	
degrees of freedom	626	
residual sum of squares	3361	
total sum of squares	6820	
standard error of composite disturbance	2.317	
degree of overidentification	23	
Sargan test (p-value)	20.529	(0.610)

variable or variable group	regressors	instruments
intercept	1	1
lagged expenditure	1	1
current income	2	0
lagged income	4	4
number of adults	2	2
number of children	2	2
age	8	8
age $\times$ income	8	16
number of children $\times$ age	11	11
education of head	3	3
education of head $\times$ income	3	6
education of partner	3	3
education of partner $\times$ income	3	6
recording month	11	11
recording month $\times$ income	11	22

variable	coefficient	standard error	p-value
INTERCEPT	0.842	8.708	0.923
y_{-1}	0.409	0.081	0.000
INCOME	0.220	0.722	0.760
$\triangle$ INCOME	-0.133	0.476	0.780
$\triangle$ INCOME$_{-1}$	0.155	0.302	0.609
INCOME $\times$ ln(INCOME)	-0.034	0.137	0.804
$\triangle$ (INCOME $\times$ ln(INCOME))	0.022	0.098	0.820
$\triangle$ (INCOME $\times$ ln(INCOME))$_{-1}$	-0.032	0.061	0.596

Table C.12: Continued

variable	coefficient	standard error	p-value
ADULTS2	1.764	1.663	0.289
ADULTS3	2.919	1.996	0.144
CHILDREN1	−2.740	2.082	0.188
CHILDREN2	−1.804	1.950	0.355
AGE30	−2.329	5.492	0.671
AGE35	−3.917	6.207	0.528
AGE40	−6.202	5.579	0.266
AGE45	−4.000	4.824	0.407
AGE50	−3.711	5.317	0.485
AGE55	−0.512	5.639	0.928
AGE60	−3.127	5.185	0.547
AGE65	−3.993	4.894	0.415
AGE30 × INCOME	0.066	0.120	0.583
AGE35 × INCOME	0.067	0.121	0.583
AGE40 × INCOME	0.090	0.115	0.432
AGE45 × INCOME	0.054	0.106	0.614
AGE50 × INCOME	0.040	0.116	0.727
AGE55 × INCOME	−0.001	0.114	0.993
AGE60 × INCOME	0.036	0.111	0.747
AGE65 × INCOME	0.060	0.107	0.575
CHILDREN1 × AGE30	0.691	2.495	0.782
CHILDREN2 × AGE30	0.766	1.988	0.700
CHILDREN1 × AGE35	4.795	2.738	0.080
CHILDREN2 × AGE35	2.124	2.437	0.383
CHILDREN1 × AGE40	2.945	2.518	0.242
CHILDREN2 × AGE40	3.035	2.374	0.201
CHILDREN1 × AGE45	3.272	2.428	0.178
CHILDREN2 × AGE45	6.499	6.077	0.285
CHILDREN1 × AGE50	1.483	3.285	0.652
CHILDREN1 × AGE55	−3.414	7.932	0.667
CHILDREN2 × AGE60	3.942	2.274	0.083
EDUCATIONH21	1.449	1.802	0.421
EDUCATIONH22	0.140	1.859	0.940
EDUCATIONH3	−1.846	3.500	0.598
EDUCATIONP1	1.885	2.982	0.527
EDUCATIONP21	3.680	3.089	0.233
EDUCATIONP22	1.708	2.671	0.523

Table C.12: Continued

variable	coefficient	standard error	p-value
EDUCATIONH21 × INCOME	−0.049	0.040	0.217
EDUCATIONH22 × INCOME	−0.020	0.041	0.634
EDUCATIONH3 × INCOME	0.012	0.063	0.855
EDUCATIONP1 × INCOME	−0.026	0.062	0.671
EDUCATIONP21 × INCOME	−0.057	0.061	0.356
EDUCATIONP22 × INCOME	−0.027	0.048	0.577
MONTHJAN	1.037	2.553	0.685
MONTHFEB	0.610	2.548	0.811
MONTHMAR	0.847	2.252	0.707
MONTHAPR	1.488	2.662	0.576
MONTHMAY	0.731	2.630	0.781
MONTHJUN	0.389	2.557	0.879
MONTHJUL	0.886	2.236	0.692
MONTHAUG	−0.935	2.845	0.742
MONTHSEP	1.621	2.461	0.510
MONTHOCT	0.434	2.492	0.862
MONTHNOV	0.357	2.204	0.871
MONTHJAN × INCOME	−0.056	0.055	0.303
MONTHFEB × INCOME	−0.042	0.057	0.465
MONTHMAR × INCOME	−0.058	0.049	0.235
MONTHAPR × INCOME	−0.058	0.057	0.310
MONTHMAY × INCOME	−0.041	0.058	0.482
MONTHJUN × INCOME	−0.021	0.057	0.714
MONTHJUL × INCOME	−0.034	0.048	0.473
MONTHAUG × INCOME	−0.000	0.065	0.998
MONTHSEP × INCOME	−0.050	0.051	0.332
MONTHOCT × INCOME	−0.021	0.051	0.686
MONTHNOV × INCOME	−0.043	0.049	0.379

The dependent variable is annual household expenditure on food in f1000
Standard errors and test statistics are corrected for heteroscedasticity
The Sargan test of overidentifying restrictions is given

Table C.13: GMM two-step estimation results of equation (7.2) in levels with $(y_{i2} - y_{i1})$ and current and lagged deviations of individual means of x as instruments

characteristic	value	
number of observations	699	
degrees of freedom	626	
residual sum of squares	2958	
total sum of squares	6820	
standard error of composite disturbance	2.174	
degree of overidentification	23	
Sargan test (p-value)	22.867	(0.469)

variable or variable group	regressors	instruments
intercept	1	1
lagged expenditure	1	1
current income	2	2
lagged income	4	2
number of adults	2	2
number of children	2	2
age	8	8
age × income	8	16
number of children × age	11	11
education of head	3	3
education of head × income	3	6
education of partner	3	3
education of partner × income	3	6
recording month	11	11
recording month × income	11	22

variable	coefficient	standard error	p-value
INTERCEPT	−1.535	7.421	0.836
y_{-1}	0.355	0.079	0.000
INCOME	0.504	0.599	0.400
Δ INCOME	−0.276	0.418	0.509
Δ INCOME$_{-1}$	−0.022	0.273	0.936
INCOME × ln(INCOME)	−0.089	0.114	0.436
Δ (INCOME × ln(INCOME))	0.052	0.086	0.549
Δ (INCOME × ln(INCOME))$_{-1}$	0.005	0.056	0.935

Table C.13: Continued			
variable	coefficient	standard error	p-value
ADULTS2	2.118	1.140	0.063
ADULTS3	2.762	1.327	0.037
CHILDREN1	-3.095	2.060	0.133
CHILDREN2	-1.998	1.873	0.286
AGE30	0.257	4.378	0.953
AGE35	-2.862	4.728	0.545
AGE40	-4.089	4.616	0.376
AGE45	-3.670	4.217	0.384
AGE50	-4.332	4.813	0.368
AGE55	-2.024	4.692	0.666
AGE60	-1.876	4.479	0.675
AGE65	-1.786	4.057	0.660
AGE30 × INCOME	-0.002	0.091	0.981
AGE35 × INCOME	0.038	0.090	0.673
AGE40 × INCOME	0.052	0.091	0.566
AGE45 × INCOME	0.050	0.087	0.569
AGE50 × INCOME	0.051	0.100	0.611
AGE55 × INCOME	0.016	0.092	0.862
AGE60 × INCOME	0.013	0.092	0.890
AGE65 × INCOME	0.011	0.087	0.896
CHILDREN1 × AGE30	1.214	2.068	0.557
CHILDREN2 × AGE30	1.219	1.752	0.487
CHILDREN1 × AGE35	4.634	2.535	0.068
CHILDREN2 × AGE35	2.358	2.266	0.298
CHILDREN1 × AGE40	3.232	2.542	0.204
CHILDREN2 × AGE40	2.517	2.362	0.287
CHILDREN1 × AGE45	3.844	2.367	0.104
CHILDREN2 × AGE45	1.946	4.670	0.677
CHILDREN1 × AGE50	0.820	2.853	0.774
CHILDREN1 × AGE55	-6.734	7.289	0.356
CHILDREN2 × AGE60	2.817	2.024	0.164
EDUCATIONH21	1.222	1.405	0.384
EDUCATIONH22	-0.523	1.632	0.748
EDUCATIONH3	-2.790	2.574	0.278
EDUCATIONP1	0.177	2.066	0.932
EDUCATIONP21	4.174	2.297	0.069
EDUCATIONP22	1.263	1.863	0.498

Table C.13: Continued

variable	coefficient	standard error	p-value
EDUCATIONH21 × INCOME	−0.046	0.030	0.131
EDUCATIONH22 × INCOME	−0.011	0.034	0.750
EDUCATIONH3 × INCOME	0.030	0.045	0.501
EDUCATIONP1 × INCOME	0.006	0.041	0.891
EDUCATIONP21 × INCOME	−0.076	0.044	0.088
EDUCATIONP22 × INCOME	−0.024	0.035	0.486
MONTHJAN	0.118	1.890	0.950
MONTHFEB	0.935	1.873	0.618
MONTHMAR	−0.160	1.881	0.932
MONTHAPR	0.199	2.005	0.921
MONTHMAY	0.283	2.108	0.893
MONTHJUN	−0.069	1.777	0.969
MONTHJUL	0.767	1.928	0.691
MONTHAUG	0.336	2.319	0.885
MONTHSEP	0.778	1.785	0.663
MONTHOCT	−0.717	1.641	0.662
MONTHNOV	0.128	1.664	0.939
MONTHJAN × INCOME	−0.042	0.041	0.299
MONTHFEB × INCOME	−0.050	0.042	0.237
MONTHMAR × INCOME	−0.043	0.041	0.298
MONTHAPR × INCOME	−0.031	0.045	0.493
MONTHMAY × INCOME	−0.029	0.046	0.531
MONTHJUN × INCOME	−0.017	0.042	0.689
MONTHJUL × INCOME	−0.034	0.040	0.392
MONTHAUG × INCOME	−0.032	0.054	0.553
MONTHSEP × INCOME	−0.035	0.038	0.349
MONTHOCT × INCOME	0.008	0.035	0.809
MONTHNOV × INCOME	−0.042	0.036	0.239

The dependent variable is annual household expenditure on food in f1000
Standard errors and test statistics are corrected for heteroscedasticity
The Sargan test of overidentifying restrictions is given

Table C.14: GMM two-step estimation results of the preferred dynamic specification in levels with $(y_{i2} - y_{i1})$ and current and lagged deviations of individual means of x as instruments

characteristic	value	
number of observations	699	
degrees of freedom	672	
residual sum of squares	2831	
total sum of squares	6820	
standard error of composite disturbance	2.052	
degree of overidentification	69	
Sargan test (p-value)	57.321	(0.841)

variable or variable group	regressors	instruments
intercept	1	1
lagged expenditure	1	1
current income	2	2
lagged income	2	2
number of adults	2	2
number of children	2	2
age	0	8
age × income	0	16
number of children × age	0	11
education of head	3	3
education of head × income	3	6
education of partner	0	3
education of partner × income	0	6
recording month	11	11
recording month × income	0	22

variable	coefficient	standard error	p-value
INTERCEPT	0.361	1.251	0.773
y_{-1}	0.365	0.053	0.000
INCOME	0.254	0.123	0.039
Δ INCOME	−0.141	0.082	0.085
INCOME × ln(INCOME)	−0.043	0.025	0.083
Δ (INCOME × ln(INCOME))	0.026	0.017	0.123

Table C.14: Continued

variable	coefficient	standard error	p-value
ADULTS2	2.067	0.532	0.000
ADULTS3	3.305	0.628	0.000
CHILDREN1	0.039	0.273	0.886
CHILDREN2	1.109	0.257	0.000
EDUCATIONH21	2.025	0.981	0.039
EDUCATIONH22	−0.075	0.958	0.938
EDUCATIONH3	−2.687	1.342	0.045
EDUCATIONH21 × INCOME	−0.067	0.024	0.005
EDUCATIONH22 × INCOME	−0.019	0.023	0.404
EDUCATIONH3 × INCOME	0.025	0.027	0.351
MONTHJAN	−1.801	0.382	0.000
MONTHFEB	−1.141	0.406	0.005
MONTHMAR	−1.944	0.405	0.000
MONTHAPR	−1.034	0.472	0.028
MONTHMAY	−0.865	0.411	0.035
MONTHJUN	−0.838	0.422	0.047
MONTHJUL	−1.032	0.450	0.022
MONTHAUG	−1.083	0.426	0.011
MONTHSEP	−0.924	0.433	0.033
MONTHOCT	−0.576	0.441	0.192
MONTHNOV	−1.773	0.381	0.000

The dependent variable is annual household expenditure on food in $f1000$
Standard errors and test statistics are corrected for heteroscedasticity
The Sargan test of overidentifying restrictions is given

Table C.15: GMM two-step estimation results of the preferred dynamic specification in levels with current and lagged deviations of individual means of x as instruments

characteristic	value	
number of observations	699	
degrees of freedom	672	
residual sum of squares	2708	
total sum of squares	6820	
standard error of composite disturbance	2.007	
degree of overidentification	68	
Sargan test (p-value)	55.377	(0.864)

variable or variable group	regressors	instruments
intercept	1	1
lagged expenditure	1	0
current income	2	2
lagged income	2	2
number of adults	2	2
number of children	2	2
age	0	8
age × income	0	16
number of children × age	0	11
education of head	3	3
education of head × income	3	6
education of partner	0	3
education of partner × income	0	6
recording month	11	11
recording month × income	0	22

variable	coefficient	standard error	p-value
INTERCEPT	0.417	1.208	0.730
y_{-1}	0.476	0.061	0.000
INCOME	0.238	0.119	0.046
Δ INCOME	−0.147	0.081	0.069
INCOME × ln(INCOME)	−0.043	0.024	0.075
Δ (INCOME × ln(INCOME))	0.029	0.017	0.088

Table C.15: Continued

variable	coefficient	standard error	p-value
ADULTS2	1.679	0.527	0.001
ADULTS3	2.731	0.628	0.000
CHILDREN1	0.158	0.258	0.541
CHILDREN2	1.110	0.247	0.000
EDUCATIONH21	1.584	0.935	0.091
EDUCATIONH22	−0.219	0.917	0.811
EDUCATIONH3	−2.667	1.288	0.038
EDUCATIONH21 × INCOME	−0.054	0.023	0.018
EDUCATIONH22 × INCOME	−0.013	0.022	0.563
EDUCATIONH3 × INCOME	0.028	0.025	0.272
MONTHJAN	−1.751	0.374	0.000
MONTHFEB	−1.107	0.395	0.005
MONTHMAR	−1.912	0.389	0.000
MONTHAPR	−1.025	0.458	0.025
MONTHMAY	−0.884	0.405	0.029
MONTHJUN	−0.851	0.407	0.036
MONTHJUL	−0.944	0.433	0.029
MONTHAUG	−1.086	0.408	0.008
MONTHSEP	−0.924	0.417	0.027
MONTHOCT	−0.520	0.427	0.224
MONTHNOV	−1.803	0.371	0.000

The dependent variable is annual household expenditure on food in $f1000$
Standard errors and test statistics are corrected for heteroscedasticity
The Sargan test of overidentifying restrictions is given

Table C.16: GMM two-step estimation results of the preferred dynamic specification in levels with current and lagged deviations of individual means of x as instruments

characteristic	value	
number of observations	699	
degrees of freedom	672	
residual sum of squares	4263	
total sum of squares	6820	
standard error of composite disturbance	2.519	
degree of overidentification	2	
Sargan test (p-value)	2.779	(0.249)

variable or variable group	regressors	instruments
intercept	1	1
lagged expenditure	1	0
current income	2	2
lagged income	2	2
number of adults	2	2
number of children	2	2
education of head	3	3
education of head × income	3	6
recording month	11	11

variable	coefficient	standard error	p-value
INTERCEPT	−4.369	5.562	0.432
y_{-1}	0.620	0.635	0.329
INCOME	0.699	0.315	0.027
Δ INCOME	−0.321	0.201	0.111
INCOME × ln(INCOME)	−0.143	0.068	0.037
Δ (INCOME × ln(INCOME))	0.065	0.043	0.130

Table C.16: Continued

variable	coefficient	standard error	p-value
ADULTS2	2.422	1.335	0.070
ADULTS3	2.884	1.150	0.012
CHILDREN1	0.419	1.047	0.689
CHILDREN2	0.770	1.862	0.679
EDUCATIONH21	−0.396	1.522	0.795
EDUCATIONH22	−1.380	1.663	0.407
EDUCATIONH3	−5.620	4.097	0.170
EDUCATIONH21 × INCOME	−0.005	0.036	0.889
EDUCATIONH22 × INCOME	0.018	0.043	0.681
EDUCATIONH3 × INCOME	0.093	0.078	0.234
MONTHJAN	−1.760	0.624	0.005
MONTHFEB	−1.454	0.739	0.049
MONTHMAR	−2.167	0.688	0.002
MONTHAPR	−1.503	0.883	0.089
MONTHMAY	−1.307	0.931	0.160
MONTHJUN	−1.089	0.693	0.116
MONTHJUL	−0.985	0.918	0.283
MONTHAUG	−1.051	0.683	0.124
MONTHSEP	−1.042	1.195	0.383
MONTHOCT	−0.522	0.685	0.446
MONTHNOV	−1.783	0.673	0.008

The dependent variable is annual household expenditure on food in $f1000$
Standard errors and test statistics are corrected for heteroscedasticity
The Sargan test of overidentifying restrictions is given

Stellingen bij het proefschrift van Inge T. van den Doel

1 Niet-stationariteit van de verklarende variabele in een datagenererend proces met daarnaast ook vertragingen van deze en van de afhankelijke variabele als regressoren heeft tot gevolg dat schatting van een eenvoudige statische specificatie op basis van dwarsdoorsnede- of paneldata het langetermijneffect geeft.

2 Tijdreeks- en micro-econometristen kunnen nog veel van elkaar leren.

3 Sommige econometristen geven iets wat zij niet begrijpen liever het predikaat *random* dan dat zij nadenken.

4 Economen realiseren zich onvoldoende dat de waarheid van vandaag morgen als een dwaling beschouwd kan worden.

5 Economen realiseren zich onvoldoende dat de waarheid van gisteren vandaag nog steeds waar kan zijn.

6 De op zondag 22 november 1857 wereldkundig gemaakte *Wet van Engel* geldt nog steeds.

7 Het individualisme van de jaren negentig maakt internalisering van externe effecten meer dan ooit noodzakelijk.

8 Paaltjes, balken en driehoeken leiden tot het onder automobilisten wijdverbreide misverstand dat zij overal mogen parkeren waar dergelijke fysieke versperringen niet zijn aangebracht.

9 De monumentale schoonheid van Amsterdam berust niet alleen op de afzonderlijke gebouwen, maar op de eenheid van verhoudingen in het stadsbeeld.

10 De staat van onderhoud van de Westertoren in vergelijking tot die van de particuliere Westerkerk illustreert hoe de gemeente Amsterdam met haar *eigen* monumenten omgaat.

11 Het enthousiasme bij vakantiegangers in exotische landen wordt vaak door onwetendheid en een gebrek aan referentiekader veroorzaakt.

12 Het begrip *reizen* is aan sterke inflatie onderhevig door de grote vlucht die het vliegverkeer heeft genomen.

Bibliography

Ahn, S. C. and P. Schmidt (1992a). Efficient estimation of models for dynamic panel data. Working paper, Michigan State University. First version: 1989.

Ahn, S. C. and P. Schmidt (1992b). Efficient estimation of panel data models with exogenous and lagged dependent regressors. Working paper, Michigan State University.

Aitchison, J. and J. A. C. Brown (1954). A synthesis of Engel curve theory. *Review of Economic Studies 22*, 35–46.

Allen, R. G. D. and A. L. Bowley (1935). *Family Expenditure.* London: P.S. King and Son.

Amemiya, T. and T. E. MaCurdy (1986). Instrumental-variable estimation of an error-components model. *Econometrica 54*, 869–880.

Anderson, T. W. and C. Hsiao (1981). Estimation of dynamic models with error components. *Journal of the American Statistical Association 76*, 598–606.

Anderson, T. W. and C. Hsiao (1982). Formulation and estimation of dynamic models using panel data. *Journal of Econometrics 18*, 47–82.

Arellano, M. (1989). A note on the Anderson-Hsiao estimator for panel data. *Economics Letters 31*, 337–341.

Arellano, M. (1993). On the testing of correlated effects with panel data. *Journal of Econometrics 59*, 87–97.

Arellano, M. and S. R. Bond (1988). Dynamic panel data estimation using DPD: A guide for users. Working Paper 88/15, Institute for Fiscal Studies.

Arellano, M. and S. R. Bond (1991). Some tests of specification for panel data: Monte Carlo evidence and an application to employment equations. *Review of Economic Studies 58*, 277–297.

Arellano, M. and O. Bover (1990). Another look at the instrumental-variable estimation of error-components models. Discussion Paper 7, Centre for Economic Performance. Forthcoming in *Journal of Econometrics*.

Balestra, P. and M. Nerlove (1966). Pooling cross section and time series data in the estimation of a dynamic model: The demand for natural gas. *Econometrica 34*, 585–612.

Baltagi, B. H. and J. M. Griffin (1984). Short and long run effects in pooled models. *International Economic Review 25*, 631–645.

Baltagi, B. H. and S. Khanti-Akom (1990). On efficient estimation with panel data: An empirical comparison of instrumental variables estimators. *Journal of Applied Econometrics 5*, 401–406.

Banks, J., R. W. Blundell and A. Lewbel (1992). Quadratic Engel curves, welfare measurement and consumer demand. Working Paper 92/14, Institute for Fiscal Studies.

Beggs, J. J. and M. Nerlove (1988). Biases in dynamic models with fixed effects. *Economics Letters 26*, 29–31.

Bhargava, A. and J. D. Sargan (1983). Estimating dynamic random effects models from panel data covering short time periods. *Econometrica 51*, 1635–1659.

Bierens, H. J. and H. A. Pott-Buter (1990). Specification of household Engel curves by nonparametric regression. *Econometric Reviews 9(2)*, 123–210. With comments and reply.

Blundell, R. W. (1988). Consumer behaviour: Theory and empirical evidence—A survey. *The Economic Journal 98*, 16–65.

Blundell, R. W., S. R. Bond, M. Devereux and F. Schiantarelli (1992). Investment and Tobin's Q: Evidence from company panel data. *Journal of Econometrics 51*, 233–257.

Blundell, R. W., P. Pashardes and G. Weber (1993). What do we learn about consumer demand patterns from micro data? *American Economic Review 83*, 570–597.

Breitung, J. (1992). A general test procedure to decide between random and fixed effects specifications. Working paper, Universität Hannover.

Breitung, J. and W. Meyer (1991). Testing for unit roots in panel data: Are wages on different bargaining levels cointegrated? Working paper, Universität Hannover.

Breusch, T. S., G. E. Mizon and P. Schmidt (1989). Efficient estimation using panel data. *Econometrica 57*, 695–700.

Breusch, T. S. and A. R. Pagan (1979). A simple test for heteroscedasticity and random coefficient variation. *Econometrica 47*, 1287–1294.

Brown, J. A. C. and A. S. Deaton (1972). Surveys in applied economics: Models of consumer behaviour. *The Economic Journal 82*, 1145–1236.

CBS (1978). *Budgetonderzoek 1978: Methode van Onderzoek; Enquête-documenten.* SDU-uitgeverij.

CBS (1985). Tabel 1.5: Gezinsconsumptie, reeks voor de totale bevolking, prijsindexcijfers 1980=100. *Maandstatistiek van de Prijzen July 1985 to February 1988.*

CBS (1988). *Budgetonderzoek 1984–1985: Kerncijfers.* SDU-uitgeverij.

CBS (1989). *Budgetonderzoek 1986: Kerncijfers.* SDU-uitgeverij.

CBS (1990a). *Budgetonderzoek 1987: Kerncijfers.* SDU-uitgeverij.

CBS (1990b). Consumentenprijsindexcijfers: Beschrijving van de methode. BPA 15614-90-E7, CBS, Hoofdafdeling Statistieken van de Prijzen.

Chamberlain, G. (1982). Multivariate regression models for panel data. *Journal of Econometrics 18*, 5–46.

Chamberlain, G. (1984). Panel data. In Z. Griliches and M. D. Intriligator (Eds.), *Handbook of Econometrics*, Volume II, pp. 1247–1318. Amsterdam: North-Holland.

Chamberlain, G. (1987). Asymptotic efficiency in estimation with conditional moment restrictions. *Journal of Econometrics 34*, 305–334.

Cornwell, C. and P. Rupert (1988). Efficient estimation with panel data: An empirical comparison of instrumental variables estimators. *Journal of Applied Econometrics 3*, 149–155.

Cornwell, C., P. Schmidt and D. Wyhowski (1992). Simultaneous equations and panel data. *Journal of Econometrics 51*, 151–181.

Cramer, J. S. (1969). *Empirical Econometrics.* Amsterdam: North-Holland.

Currie, D. (1981). Some long run features of dynamic time series models. *The Economic Journal 91*, 704–715.

Davies, R. B. (1980). Algorithm AS155: The distribution of a linear combination of χ^2 random variables. *Applied Statistics 29*, 323–333.

Deaton, A. S. (1986). Demand analysis. In Z. Griliches and M. D. Intriligator (Eds.), *Handbook of Econometrics*, Volume III, pp. 1767–1839. Amsterdam: North-Holland.

Deaton, A. S. and J. Muellbauer (1980). *Economics and Consumer Behavior.* Cambridge University Press.

Doel, I. T. van den (1991). Asymptotic consequences of neglected dynamics in cross-section models. *Tinbergen Institute Research Bulletin 3*, 231–241.

Doel, I. T. van den and J. F. Kiviet (1991a). Asymptotic consequences of neglected dynamics in individual effects models. Report AE 23/91, Institute of Actuarial Science & Econometrics, University of Amsterdam.

Doel, I. T. van den and J. F. Kiviet (1991b). Neglected dynamics in individual effects models: Consequences and detection. Report AE 17/91, Institute of Actuarial Science & Econometrics, University of Amsterdam.

Doel, I. T. van den and J. F. Kiviet (1993). Neglected dynamics in panel data models; Consequences and detection in finite samples. Discussion Paper TI 93–142, Tinbergen Institute.

Doel, I. T. van den and J. F. Kiviet (1994). Asymptotic consequences of neglected dynamics in individual effects models. *Statistica Neerlandica 48*, 71–85.

Donkers, H. W. J. (1981). Methodologie van de prijsanalyse, met een toepassing op het prijsverloop van de finale bestedingen 1970–1978. CBS, Statistische Onderzoekingen M12, SDU-uitgeverij.

Engel, E. (1895). Die Lebenskosten Belgischer Arbeiter-Familien Früher und Jetzt. *Bulletin de l'Institut International de Statistique 9*, 1–124 and appendix 1–54.

Engle, R. F., D. F. Hendry and J.-F. Richard (1983). Exogeneity. *Econometrica 51*, 277–304.

Gorman, W. M. (1981). Some Engel curves. In A. S. Deaton (Ed.), *Essays in the Theory and Measurement of Consumer Behaviour in honour of Sir Richard Stone*, pp. 7–29. Cambridge University Press.

Greene, W. H. (1990). *Econometric Analysis*. New York: MacMillan.

Grunfeld, Y. (1961). The interpretation of cross section estimates in a dynamic model. *Econometrica 29*, 397–404.

Haavelmo, T. (1947). Family expenditures and the marginal propensity to consume. *Econometrica 15*, 335–341.

Hansen, L. P. (1982). Large sample properties of generalized method of moments estimators. *Econometrica 50*, 1029–1054.

Harberger, A. C. (1955). Book review of "The measurement of consumers' expenditure and behaviour in the United Kingdom, 1920–1938" by Richard Stone. *Econometrica 23*, 217–218.

Hausman, J. A. (1978). Specification tests in econometrics. *Econometrica 46*, 1251–1271.

Hausman, J. A. and W. E. Taylor (1981). Panel data and unobservable individual effects. *Econometrica 49*, 1377–1398.

Hendry, D. F., A. R. Pagan and J. D. Sargan (1984). Dynamic specification. In Z. Griliches and M. D. Intriligator (Eds.), *Handbook of Econometrics*, Volume II, pp. 1023–1100. Amsterdam: North-Holland.

Holtz-Eakin, D. (1988). Testing for individual effects in autoregressive models. *Journal of Econometrics 39*, 297–307.

Holtz-Eakin, D., W. Newey and H. S. Rosen (1988). Estimating vector autoregressions with panel data. *Econometrica 56*, 1371–1395.

Hsiao, C. (1986). *Analysis of Panel Data*. Cambridge University Press.

Jarque, C. M. and A. K. Bera (1980). Efficient tests for normality, homoscedasticity and serial independence of regression residuals. *Economics Letters 6*, 255–259.

Kiviet, J. F. (1992). On bias, inconsistency and efficiency of some estimators in dynamic panel data models. Working paper, Tinbergen Institute, Amsterdam. Presented at the Far Eastern Meeting of the Econometric Society, Taipei, Taiwan 1993.

Kiviet, J. F. and G. D. A. Phillips (1990). Exact similar tests for the root of a first-order autoregressive regression model. Report AE 12/90, Institute of Actuarial Science & Econometrics, University of Amsterdam.

Kiviet, J. F. and G. D. A. Phillips (1992). Exact similar tests for unit roots and cointegration. *Oxford Bulletin of Economics and Statistics 54*, 349–367.

Leser, C. E. V. (1963). Forms of Engel functions. *Econometrica 31*, 694–703.

Levin, A. and C.-F. Lin (1992). Unit root tests in panel data: Asymptotic and finite-sample properties. Working paper, University of California, San Diego.

Maddala, G. S. (1971). The use of variance components models in pooling cross section and time series data. *Econometrica 39*, 341–358.

Muellbauer, J. (1980). The estimation of the Prais-Houthakker model of equivalence scales. *Econometrica 48*, 153–176.

Mundlak, Y. (1978). On the pooling of time series and cross section data. *Econometrica 46*, 69–85.

Nerlove, M. (1967). Experimental evidence on the estimation of dynamic economic relations from a time series of cross sections. *Economic Studies Quarterly 18*, 42–74.

Nerlove, M. (1971). Further evidence on the estimation of dynamic economic relations from a time series of cross sections. *Econometrica 39*, 359–382.

Nickell, S. J. (1981). Biases in dynamic models with fixed effects. *Econometrica 49*, 1417–1426.

Pol, F. J. R. van de (1989). Panel effects in the CBS budget survey. *CBS Select, Statistical Essays 5*, 101–110.

Prais, S. J. (1952). Non-linear estimates of the Engel curve. *Review of Economic Studies 20*, 87–104.

Prais, S. J. and H. S. Houthakker (1955). *The Analysis of Family Budgets.* Cambridge University Press.

Revankar, N. S. (1992). Exact equivalence of instrumental variable estimators in an error component structural system. *Empirical Economics 17*, 77–84.

Ridder, G. and T. J. Wansbeek (1990). Dynamic models for panel data. In F. van der Ploeg (Ed.), *Advanced Lectures in Quantitative Economics*, pp. 557–582. London: Academic Press.

Sargan, J. D. (1958). The estimation of economic relationships using instrumental variables. *Econometrica 26*, 393–415.

Sargan, J. D. (1964). Wages and prices in the United Kingdom: A study in econometric methodology. In P. E. Hart, G. Mills and J. K. Whitaker (Eds.), *Econometric Analysis for National Economic Planning*, pp. 25–54. London: Butterworth.

Simon, J. L. and D. J. Aigner (1970). Cross-section and time-series tests of the permanent-income hypothesis. *American Economic Review 60*, 341–351.

Stock, J. H. (1987). Asymptotic properties of least squares estimators of cointegrating vectors. *Econometrica 55*, 1035–1056.

Stone, R. (1954). *The Measurement of Consumers' Expenditure and Behaviour in the United Kingdom, 1920–1938*, Volume I. Cambridge University Press.

Trognon, A. (1978). Miscellaneous asymptotic properties of ordinary least squares and maximum likelihood estimators in dynamic error components models. *Annales de l'Insee 30/31*, 631–657.

Verbeek, M. (1990). On the estimation of a fixed effects model with selectivity bias. *Economics Letters 34*, 267–270.

Verbeek, M. (1991). *The Design of Panel Surveys and the Treatment of Missing Observations.* Ph. D. thesis, Tilburg University.

Verbeek, M. and T. E. Nijman (1992). Testing for selectivity bias in panel data models. *International Economic Review 33*, 681–703.

White, H. (1980). A heteroskedasticity-consistent covariance matrix estimator and a direct test for heteroskedasticity. *Econometrica 48*, 817–838.

White, H. (1982). Instrumental variables regression with independent observations. *Econometrica 50*, 483–499.

Witte, M. A. C. de and J. S. Cramer (1986). Functional form of Engel curves for foodstuffs. *European Economic Review 30*, 909–913.

Working, H. (1943). Statistical laws of family expenditure. *Journal of the American Statistical Association 38*, 43–56.

Author Index

Samenvatting

Nog niet zo lang geleden bestonden er in de econometrie twee soorten mensen: de tijdreekseconometristen, die zich bezig hielden met de analyse van macroeconomische relaties op basis van geaggregeerde tijdreeksen, en de microeconometristen, die micro-economisch gedrag van individuen, huishoudens of bedrijven bestudeerden aan de hand van dwarsdoorsnede-gegevens. Deze twee groepen wetenschappers bestonden naast elkaar, zonder elkaars problemen en verworvenheden te begrijpen en dus ook zonder iets van elkaar op te steken.

Haavelmo (1947) was de eerste die opmerkte dat beide takken van wetenschap verschillende resultaten opleverden. Later werden verschillende pogingen ondernomen om deze verschillen te verklaren. Hiermee was het kruisbestuivingsproces begonnen. Er verschenen empirische studies waarin dwarsdoorsnede- en tijdreeksgegevens werden samengevoegd, waarvan Balestra en Nerlove (1966) wel de bekendste is. De econometrische analyse van paneldata, zoals dergelijke gegevens worden genoemd, nam een grote vlucht. Er groeide zo niet alleen een derde tak aan de boom der econometrische kennis, maar ook een nieuwe wortel, zodat de reeds bestaande takken konden floreren.

Toch zijn er binnen de beide oude takken nog veel resultaten geboekt, die niet of nauwelijks zijn doorgedrongen in de andere. Zo is er binnen de tijdreekseconometrie veel aandacht besteed aan de specificatie van dynamische processen, de misspecificatie-analyse van dergelijke processen en de gevolgen van niet-stationariteiten in economische reeksen voor de modellering van economische relaties. Als dynamische processen in de micro-economie net zo belangrijk zijn als in de macro-economie, dan zou veel van de algemeen aanvaarde empirische kennis — afgeleid uit dwarsdoorsnede-onderzoek — vertekend kunnen zijn. Het lijkt daarom interessant om de dwarsdoorsnede-analyse van klassieke micro-economische relaties, zoals Engelcurven, in dit licht te beschouwen. De vraag is dan of deze statische analyse tot vertekende resultaten leidt wanneer dynamische processen een rol spelen in de relatie. Ook kan het relevant zijn te weten of bepaalde eigenschappen van de relatie, zoals eventuele niet-stationariteiten, het antwoord op deze vraag beïnvloeden. Als blijkt dat een puur statische analyse inderdaad tot onjuiste uitspraken kan leiden, dan is een logische volgende vraag hoe mogelijke dynamiek kan worden opgespoord.

Dit proefschrift beoogt een antwoord te formuleren op de hierboven gestelde vragen door diverse statische en dynamische specificaties voor dwarsdoorsneden en paneldata te bestuderen. Hierbij worden zowel een theoretische als een empirische weg gevolgd. Over het theoretische deel van het onderzoek wordt in de Hoofdstukken 2 en 3 gerapporteerd, terwijl de empirische toepassing op Engelcurven voor voedsel zijn beslag krijgt in de Hoofdstukken 4 tot en met 7. Hoofdstukken 1 en 8 bevatten respectievelijk een inleiding en conclusies.

In Hoofdstuk 2 wordt allereerst analytisch bepaald of standaardschatters voor statische dwarsdoorsnede- en paneldatamodellen al dan niet raak zijn, wanneer de onderliggende economische relatie door dynamische aanpassingsmechanismen wordt gekenmerkt. Als de exogene regressoren in de relatie een stationair proces volgen, dan blijken de statische schatters het langetermijneffect te onderschatten. Zijn de regressoren echter niet-stationair, dan blijken deze schatters raak te zijn voor het lange-termijneffect. Vervolgens wordt bestudeerd in hoeverre deze uitspraken gelden in kleine steekproeven. De veel gebruikte schatter voor paneldatamodellen met vaste individuele effecten blijkt bijzonder gevoelig te zijn voor dynamische misspecificatie.

Hoofdstuk 3 vervolgt met de vraag hoe mogelijke dynamiek kan worden opgespoord. De bestaande schattingsmethoden en toetsen voor dynamische paneldatamodellen zijn raak voor hetzij een oneindig groot aantal individuen, hetzij een oneindig groot aantal tijdsperioden. Twee nieuwe toetsen op de aanwezigheid van een vertraagde afhankelijke variabele in paneldatamodellen worden gepresenteerd. Deze toetsen zijn exact in kleine steekproeven en lijken veelbelovende statistische eigenschappen te bezitten. Een nadeel van deze toetsen is wel, dat zij minder eenvoudig toepasbaar zijn dan de reeds bestaande.

In Hoofdstuk 4 wordt de gegevensverzameling beschreven, die gebruikt is in het empirische deel van het proefschrift. Het betreft de golven 1985 tot en met 1987 van het Doorlopend Budgetonderzoek van het Centraal Bureau voor de Statistiek. Hoofdstuk 5 doet verslag van een literatuuronderzoek naar de functionele vorm van Engelcurven en beziet dit mede in het licht van de beschikbare gegevens.

In Hoofdstuk 6 worden statische Engelcurven voor voedsel geschat. Een uitgebreide zoektocht naar de beste statische specificatie leidt tot een niet-lineaire relatie waarin naast het inkomen ook het aantal volwassenen en het aantal kinderen in een huishouden een rol spelen, alsmede leeftijd en opleiding van het gezinshoofd en opleiding van de partner. Volgens deze statische specificatie geldt de Wet van Engel nog steeds en varieert de inkomenselasticiteit van voedsel van ongeveer 0,5 tot 0,7.

Hoofdstuk 7 beschrijft de schattingsresultaten van dynamische Engelcurven voor voedsel. Aangezien slechts drie golven beschikbaar zijn, is deze dynamische analyse noodzakelijkerwijs beperkt. De standaardschattingsmethode voor dynamische paneldatamodellen, waarbij het model in eerste verschillen geschreven wordt en instrumenten in niveaus gebruikt worden, geeft teleurstellend grote standaardfouten en onbevredigende resultaten, die waarschijnlijk veroorzaakt zijn door het kleine aantal tijdsperioden waarvoor gegevens beschikbaar zijn. Daarom wordt een alternatieve procedure voorgesteld, waarin het model in niveaus wordt geschreven. Geconcludeerd wordt, dat de coëfficiënten van zowel vertraagde afhankelijke als vertraagde onafhankelijke variabelen significant verschillen van nul. Ook worden de twee in Hoofdstuk 3 gepresenteerde toetsen gebruikt. Deze kunnen niet concluderen dat de coëfficiënt van de vertraagde afhankelijke variabele significant is.

The Tinbergen Institute is the Netherlands Research Institute and Graduate School for General and Business Economics founded by the Faculties of Economics (and Econometrics) of the Erasmus University in Rotterdam, the University of Amsterdam and the Free University in Amsterdam. The Tinbergen Institute, named after the Nobel prize laureate professor Jan Tinbergen, is responsible for the PhD-program of the three faculties mentioned. Since January 1991 also the Economic Institute of the University of Leiden participates in the Tinbergen Institute.

Copies of the books which are published in the Tinbergen Institute Research Series can be ordered through Thesis Publishers, P.O. Box 14791, 1001 LG Amsterdam, The Netherlands, phone: +3120 6255429; fax: +3120 6203395.

The following books already appeared in this series:

Subseries A. General Economics

no. 1 Otto H. Swank, "Policy Makers, Voters and Optimal Control, Estimation of the Preferences behind Monetary and Fiscal Policy in the United States".

no. 2 Jan van der Borg, "Tourism and Urban Development. The impact of tourism on urban development: towards a theory of urban tourism, and its application to the case of Venice, Italy".

no. 3 Albert Jolink, "Liberté, Egalité, Rareté. The Evolutionary Economics of Léon Walras".

no. 5 Rudi M. Verburg, "The Two Faces of Interest. The problem of order and the origins of political economy and sociology as distinctive fields of inquiry in the Scottish Enlightenment".

no. 6 Harry P. van Dalen, "Economic Policy in a Demographically Divided World".

no. 8 Marjan Hofkes, "Modelling and Computation of General Equilibrium".

no. 12 Kwame Nimako, "Economic Change and Political Conflict in Ghana 1600–1990".

no. 13 Ans Vollering, "Care Services for the Elderly in the Netherlands. The PACKAGE model".

no. 35 G.E. Hebbink, "Human capital, labour demand and wages. Aspects of labour market heterogeneity".

no. 36 J.J.M. Potters, "Lobbying and pressure: theory and experiments".

no. 37 H. Peter Boswijk, "Cointegration, identification and exogeneity. Inference in structural error correction models".

no. 38 M. Boumans, "A case of limited physics transfer. Jan Tinbergen's resources for re-shaping economics".

no. 42 Jan Kees Martijn, "Exchange-rate variability and trade: Essays on the impact of exchange-rate variability on international trade flows".

no. 43 Jos Verbeek, "Studies on Economic Growth Theory. The role of imperfections and externalities".

no. 45 F. Kalshoven, "Over Marxistische Economie in Nederland, 1883–1939".

no. 46 W. Swaan, "Behaviour and Institutions under Economic Reform. Price Regulation and Market Behaviour in Hungary".

no. 47 J.J. Capel, "Exchange Rates and Strategic Decisions of Firms".

no. 48 M.F.M. Canoy, "Bertrand meets the Fox and the Owl — Essays in the Theory of Price Competition".

no. 50 Elles A.M. Bulder, "The social economics of old age: strategies to maintain income in later life in the Netherlands 1880–1940".

no. 51 Jaap Barendregt, "The Dutch Money Purge. The monetary consequences of German occupation and their redress after liberation, 1940–1952."

no. 55 Emiel F.M. Wubben, "Markets, Uncertainty and Decision-Making. A History of the Introduction of Uncertainty into Economics".

no. 57 R.M. de Jong, "Asymptotic Theory of Expanding Parameter Space Methods and Data Dependence in Econometrics".

no. 59 A. Lagendijk, "The internationalisation of the Spanish automobile industry and its regional impact. The emergence of a growth-periphery".

no. 60 B.M. Kling, "Life insurance, a non-life approach".

no. 64 Ralf Peeters, "System Identification Based on Riemannian Geometry: Theory and Algorithms".

no. 65 Olga Memedovic, "On the theory and measurement of comparative advantage. An empirical analysis of Yugoslav trade in manufactures with the OECD countries, 1970–1986".

no. 68 René A. Belderbos, "Strategic Trade Policy and Multinational Enterprises: Essays on Trade and Investment by Japanese Electronics Firms".

no. 69 Inge T. van den Doel, "Dynamics in Cross-Section and Panel Data Models".

Subseries B. Business Economics

no. 4 Rob Buitendijk, "Towards an Effective Use of Relational Database Management Systems".

no. 7 P.J. Verbeek, "Two Case Studies on Manpower Planning in an Airline".

no. 9 T.C.R. van Someren, "Innovatie, emulatie en tijd. De rol van de organisatorische vernieuwingen in het economische proces".

no. 10 M. van Vliet, "Optimization of manufacturing system design".

no. 11 R.M.C. van Waes, "Architectures for Information Management. A pragmatic approach on architectural concepts and their application in dynamic environments".

no. 14 Shuzhong Zhang, "Stochastic Queue Location Problems".

no. 17 Paul Th. van de Laar, "Financieringsgedrag in de Rotterdamse maritieme sector, 1945–1960".

no. 25 E. Smeitink, "Stochastic Models for Repairable Systems".

no. 32 H.E. Romeijn, "Global Optimization by Random Walk Sampling Methods".

no. 39 J.B.J.M. de Kort, "Edge-disjointness in combinatorial optimization: problems and algorithms".